Key Concepts in
Operations
Management

MICHEL LESEURE

Key Concepts in
Operations
Management

Los Angeles | London | New Delhi
Singapore | Washington DC

First published 2010

SAGE Publications Ltd
1 Oliver's Yard
55 City Road
London EC1Y 1SP

SAGE Publications Inc.
2455 Teller Road
Thousand Oaks, California 91320

SAGE Publications India Pvt Ltd
B 1/I 1 Mohan Cooperative Industrial Area
Mathura Road
New Delhi 110 044

SAGE Publications Asia-Pacific Pte Ltd
33 Pekin Street #02-01
Far East Square
Singapore 048763

Library of Congress Control Number: 2009937936

British Library Cataloguing in Publication data

A catalogue record for this book is available from the British Library

ISBN 978-1-84860-731-6
ISBN 978-1-84860-732-3 (pbk)

Typeset by C&M Digitals (P) Ltd, Chennai, India
Printed by CPI Antony Rowe, Chippenham, Wiltshire
Printed on paper from sustainable resources

To my parents, Jacques and Hélène Leseure, for their support and encouragement to study.

contents

key concepts in operations management

Introduction

Operations management is an odd member of the business studies family. Once the spearhead in the curriculum of American MBAs and a prestigious degree route in universities across the world, it is now more accurately described as a question mark in the strategic portfolio of subject groups within business schools. Top business schools still run operations management departments but today's popularity of the finance and marketing fields literally 'dwarfs' operations. As a result, operations degree routes are rare and whether or not to keep an operations management course within an MBA curriculum is often an ongoing debate.

Is operations management a discipline of the past? Although some may answer 'yes', it is important to keep in mind that operations management is an evolving discipline, and thus, a more productive question is 'What is the future of operations management?'

There are complex demographic changes that are ongoing at the time of writing this book. In particular, a serious question exists regarding society's ability to cope with the aging of populations in the developed world. The challenge is simple: rich economies will see an increasing proportion of old and retired individuals who have, somehow, to be supported by a smaller and decreasing active workforce. A potential solution to this demographic time bomb is to improve the productivity of future workers, so that this smaller workforce can continue to produce at adequate levels of output and, thus, address the needs of their societies. This challenge can be addressed by operations management, a discipline which has witnessed, from the dawn of the Industrial Revolution until today, incredible leaps in the efficiency of productive processes.

In parallel to the aging population challenge, most developing and emerging economies are experiencing extreme population growths, and demographic forecasts for these show the opposite – the advent of very young populations. In their introspective book, *The 86 Percent Solution* (2005), Vijay Mahajan and Kamini Banga highlighted that business companies currently serve the needs of 14 per cent of the world population, leaving open a market opportunity made up of 86 per cent (nearly 11 billion people) of the world's population. The World Bank has for a long time encouraged and sponsored training in marketing and finance in these economies: it may not be long before the need for training in management and operations management becomes more pressing.

It is within this context of an academic discipline with a potentially rich and important future that this book was written. Its purpose is to provide a concise and straight-to-the point presentation of key concepts and theories in operations management. This book covers the same scope as a traditional operations management textbook but focuses on presenting only the core concepts, the history of thought around these, and their practical applications, as well as the relevance of these concepts today. Due to its modularity, it can be used by a variety of audiences: practitioners or policy makers seeking a concise presentation, students undertaking an introduction to operations management, and a variety of readers seeking a compromise between a dictionary and a handbook.

REFERENCES

Mahajan, V. and Banga, K. (2005) *The 86 Percent Solution: How to Succeed in the Next Biggest Market Opportunity of the Next 50 Years*. Upper Saddle River, NJ: Wharton School Publishing.

key concepts in operations management

The Operations Function

> **Operations Management is the business function dealing with the management of all the processes directly involved with the provision of goods and services to customers.**

OPERATIONS MANAGEMENT AS A DISCIPLINE

Operations management is both an academic discipline and a professional occupation. It is generally classified as a subset of business studies but its intellectual heritage is divided. On the one hand, a lot of operations management concepts are inherited from management practice. On the other hand, other concepts in operations management are inherited from engineering, and more especially, industrial engineering.

Neither management nor industrial engineering is recognised as a 'pure science' and both are often viewed as pragmatic, hands-on fields of applied study. This often results in the image of operations management as a low-brow discipline and a technical subject. Meredith (2001: 397) recognises this when he writes that *'in spite of the somewhat-glorious history of operations, we are perceived as drab, mundane, hard, dirty, not respected, out of date, low-paid, something one's father does, and other such negative characteristics'*.

This is not a flattering statement, but it is worth moderating it quickly by the fact that economic development, economic success, and economic stability seem to go hand in hand with the mastery of operations management. Operations management is an Anglo-Saxon concept which has spread effectively throughout many cultures, but has often failed to diffuse into others. For example, there is no exact translation of the term 'operations management' in French, or at least, not one that is readily agreed upon. This is not to say that French organisations do not manage operations: the lack of a direct translation may be due to the fact that the operations function 'belongs' to engineers rather than managers in French culture. In other cultures, however, the very idea that one should manage operations may not be a concern. For example, it is not unusual in some countries to have to queues for two hours or more to deposit a cheque in a bank, whereas other countries will have stringent specifications requiring immediate management attention if a customer has to wait more than five minutes.

If indeed the mastery of operations management is associated with economic success, this means that despite its potential image problems operations management as a practice may play a fundamental role in society. As acknowledged by Schmenner and Swink (1998), operations management as a field has been too harsh on itself, as it both informs and complements economic theories (see **Theory**).

WHY OPERATIONS MANAGEMENT?

A theory of operations management

The purpose of a theory of operations is to explain:

- why operations management exists;
- the boundaries of operations management;
- what operations management consists of.

Note that the concept of operations predates the concept of operations management. Hunters and gatherers, soldiers, slaves and craftsmen have throughout human history engaged in 'operations', i.e. the harvest, transformation, or manipulation of objects, feelings and beliefs. Operations management, as we know it today, is an *organisational* function: it only exists and has meaning when considered in the context of the function that it serves within a firm or an institution. Thus, in order to propose a theory of operations management we first need to ask ourselves – 'Why do firms exist?'

In a Nobel-prize winning essay in 1937, Ronald Coase explained how firms are created and preferred as a form of economic organisation over specialist exchange economies. The key tenet of Coase's theory is that the firm prevails under conditions of marketing uncertainty. It is because of the fear of not finding a buyer, of not convincing the buyer to buy, or of failing to match the buyer's expectations that an individual economic actor is exposed to marketing risk. When uncertainty exists, individuals will prefer to specialise and to 'join forces', seeking synergistic effects in order to cope with uncertainty.

Figure 1 below builds on Coase's theory and proposes a theory of operations management. It shows that individuals seeking wealth are discouraged from working independently because of marketing risks. In order to reduce their exposure to uncertainty, they will prefer to enter into a collaborative agreement to pool risks in large organisational systems, there by capturing a broad range of complementary specialist skills. The rationale for this behaviour is that it pays to concentrate on what one is good at: a specialist will be more effective at executing a task than a non specialist. *Specialisation* was the major driver during the Industrial Revolution along with technological innovation. Specialisation patterns are commonly described through the theory of the *division of labour*.

The division of labour

The division of labour is a concept which can be analysed at several levels. When you wonder about whether to become a doctor, an engineer or a farmer, this choice of a specialist profession represents the *social division of labour* at work. The emergence of firms has resulted in the further specialisation of individuals with the *technical division of labour*.

To understand what the technical division of labour implies, consider the example of a craftsman assembling a car before 1900. Without the assistance of modern power tools, of automation, and of technological innovations such as interchangeable parts, building one car could require up to two years to complete. The craftsman was not only a manual worker but also an engineer: he knew perfectly the working principle of an internal combustion engine and what each part's function was. In a modern assembly factory today, it is not unusual for a car to be assembled from scratch in about nine hours by workers who know very little about automotive engineering. This incredible gain of efficiency is the result of the technical division of labour.

In 1776 Adam Smith published his treatise 'An Inquiry into the Nature and Causes of the Wealth of Nations', which is often regarded as one of the first business theory books ever written. Adam Smith was a pioneer in documenting how the division of labour would result in considerable productivity gains. Note that his contribution was only to *observe* that the division of labour was a major factor explaining why some firms and societies were wealthier than others. In other words, Adam Smith documented that such wealth seemed to stem from specialisation. The individuals who transformed the concept of division of labour into management principles were Charles Babbage and Frederick Taylor.

Babbage's intellectual contribution in 1835 was to build on Smith's observations and to highlight the benefits of the *horizontal division of labour*. The horizontal division of labour requires dividing tasks into

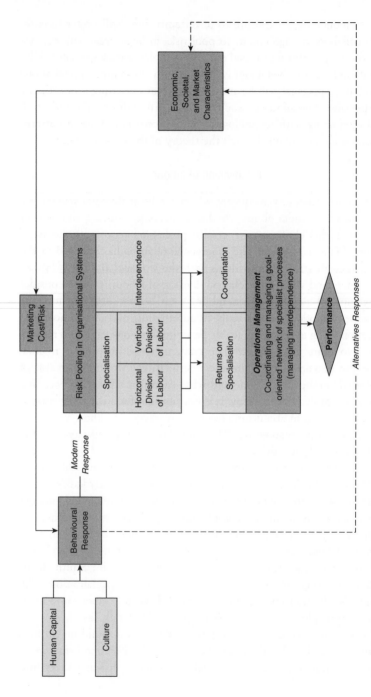

Figure 1   Theory of operations management

smaller and smaller sub-tasks. To be more productive, to generate more wealth, one should simplify jobs to their most simple expression.

Frederick Taylor, the author of *Scientific Management* (1911), went one step further. His theory was that effective operations in a business could only be achieved if work was studied scientifically. Taylor's contribution to management was the introduction of the *vertical division of labour*. This principle implies that the individual (or unit) who designs a job is usually not the individual (or unit) who implements it. This gave birth to a new field of business studies, called *work design* (see **Work**), which was the ancestor of modern **process management**.

Theory of the division of labour

Although the division of labour was for a long while not considered a theory, both the overwhelming evidence of its existence and recent economic research show that economists may one day finalise the formalisation of a theory of division of labour (Yang and Ng, 1993). Although this constitutes ongoing research, it is possible to speculate on what the fundamental laws of this theory are:

- *Law of specialisation*: In order to mitigate risk and to benefit from synergistic system effects, firms specialise tasks. It pays to concentrate on what one is good at. Increased specialisation tends to lead to increased performance levels.
- *Law of learning and experience curves*: The repetition of a task is associated with increasing efficiency at performing that task (see **Learning Curves**).
- *Law of technology*: Technology can be used to further increase the efficiency of specialised tasks (see **Technology**).
- *Law of waste reduction*: The refinement of an operations process results in the streaming of this process into a lean, non-wasteful production process (see **Lean**).
- *Law of improved quality*: Specialisation results in the ability to produce a better quality job (as the division of labour requires individuals to concentrate on what they are good at, it is easier to become better at a specialist task and to avoid performing poorly on peripheral tasks).

Interdependence

Specialisation, however, comes at a price. An individual economic actor will only depend on himself or herself for success. In a firm, though, specialist

operations

9

A relies on specialist B, and vice versa. In such a work context, the potential size of operations systems raises questions about feasibility. When assembling cars, how do you make sure that every single part and component needed is available in the inventory? How do you make sure that every worker knows what to do and how to do it? When running a restaurant, how do you ensure that you keep a fresh supply of all the ingredients required by your chef, given the fact that ordered items will only be known at the last minute? And how do you make sure that everybody is served quickly?

In other words, 'joining forces' in the pursuit of wealth is easier said than done. With the shift of work from individuals (craftsmen) to specialist networks, each process and task has been simplified or specialised, but their overall co-ordination has become more difficult. This trend is still taking place today, for example, with the distribution of manufacturing and service facilities across countries to take advantage of locational advantages (the *international division of labour*). Excellent co-ordination is a fundamental requirement of operations system, as individuals have – in exchange for reducing their exposure to risks – replaced independence with mutual dependence, or *interdependence*.

Interdependence is why we need operations management. Without operations management, inventory shortages, delays and a lack of communication between design and manufacturing would mean that a firm would never be able to convert risk pooling and specialisation into profits.

- *Law of managed interdependence*: The higher the interdependence of tasks, the higher the risk of organisational or system failure. This risk can be mitigated, hedged or eliminated altogether through co-ordination processes. Different types of interdependence require different types of co-ordination processes (see **Co-ordination**).

In a specialised firm, the application of the vertical division of labour means that a restricted set of employees, called the *technostructure* by Henry Mintzberg, is in charge of designing operations systems and supporting planning and control activities.

Return on specialisation

Today's economies, and therefore most of our daily lives, take place within the context of specialisation and the resulting need for trade and exchange. How specialisation works is the domain of many economic theories, such as the theory of absolute advantage and the theory of comparative advantage.

How specialisation, exchange and trade work together is the domain of much research on macro and international economics.

From an operations management perspective, it is important to appreciate fully the central role of specialisation. Operations management is nothing other than the 'art' or 'science' of making specialisation patterns work. The law of specialisation states that increased specialisation results in an increased performance level. Like most laws, this statement should be considered carefully: it is only under specific conditions that specialisation will lead to such performance benefits. To better appreciate these conditions, it is a good idea to consider the possible benefits and disadvantages of specialisation.

The benefits of specialisation

These are:

- Increased performance and efficiency.
- Increased quality.
- Learning curves.
- Waste reduction.
- Improvement opportunities: as a specialist focuses on one task only, it is easier for this specialist to discover and implement improvements to a process.
- Sense of professional pride.
- High job motivation.

The limits of specialisation

These are:

- *Low job motivation*: Intense specialisation may reduce a job to insignificant tasks. This results in low motivation, and potentially absenteeism and turnover. Practices such as job rotation and job enrichment are used to enrich jobs in order to diminish the negative impacts of specialisation in highly repetitive job environments.
- *Role ambiguity and conflicts*: Jobs can become so specialised that most people do not understand, and value, the job of a specialist. The exact nature of the job is misunderstood and conflicts of various types can then appear in the workplace because of misconceptions about 'what one does'.
- *Entrenchment*: The division of labour may create entrenched values in the workplace. For example, a quality manager will be overly committed to the quality mission whilst the production manager will be

overly committed to productivity targets. If each could better appreciate the task of the other specialist, co-ordination and collaboration between then would be easier.

- *Dependence*: Specialists depend on one another in terms of the quality of the final output. In the extreme case of organisational sabotage, specialists can purposefully reduce or modify their inputs in order to 'hurt' another specialist or the customer. There are complex responsibility patterns within specialist networks.
- *Co-ordination needs*: There is a need for synchronisation and co-ordination in the specialist firm. This does not come for free.
- *Traceability*: Given the number of individuals involved with production, it may be difficult to trace back the source of a problem. Poor traceability hampers the ability to improve processes and quality.

REFERENCES

Coase, R. (1937) 'The nature of the firm', *Economica*, 4(16): 386–405.
Meredith, J. (2001) 'Hopes for the future of operations management', *Journal of Operations Management*, 19: 397–402.
Schmenner, R. and Swink, M. (1998) 'On theory in operations management', *Journal of Operations Management*, 17: 97–113.
Yang, X. and Ng, Y. (1993) *Specialization and Economic Organization*. Amsterdam: North Holland Publishing Co.

System

> *An operations system is an objective-oriented network of specialist processes through which a collection of inputs are transformed into higher-value output. (Adapted from Hopp and Spearman, 2000)*

SYSTEM THEORY

In the 1940s, the biologist Ludwig von Bertalanffy was critical of the predominant use of reductionism in science. The reductionist approach means that to understand a phenomenon one should isolate and study individual characteristics of the elementary parts or components causing this phenomenon. For example, to understand medicine, one should study how the cells of the body function.

Von Bertalanffy stressed that real systems interact with an environment and that this open form of interaction induces consequences which cannot be modelled and understood within a reductionist approach. He also suggested that system theory – the idea of studying whole systems and how these interact with their environments – was a common task for a unified science, which he called *system science*. For example, biology, medicine, engineering, control, and economics researchers all use system theory nowadays. Further contributors to the development of system theory were Ross Ashby (cybernetics, in 1956) and Jay Forrester from MIT (system thinking, or system dynamics, also in 1956).

SYSTEMS AND THEIR CHARACTERISTICS

A *system* is a set of parts connected together for a specific end. Each part of the system is one of the necessary means to achieving that end. In the case of an operations systems, the parts are the different specialist processes which are networked together to provide a good or a service according to customers' specifications.

Systems have a number of important properties:

- *Parts synergy*: A system is more than a mere accumulation of parts. Most of the value of the system resides in the seamless integration of the different parts. In other words, the whole is greater than the sum of the parts.
- *Behaviour*: A system exhibits behaviours which are the result of the dynamic interactions of its parts. For example, a system can exhibit an adaptive behaviour. This is an extremely important behaviour for a firm faced with intense competition and fast-changing customer demands. A key mechanism in adaptation is learning through a *feedback loop*. Some systems behaviour may be less desirable, as for example resistance to change. Here an organisation might refuse to adapt to changing market conditions and impose aging products and technologies onto its customers. As a system's behaviour is not easily predictable, operation managers use planning activities to guide and direct future behaviour. In system theory, planning is the application of a *feedforward loop*.

- *Hierarchy*: Systems are structured in hierarchies. A market is an economic system. A firm producing goods in this market is a subsystem of the economic system, and a system itself. The finance, marketing, and operations departments are three subsystems of the organisational system.
- *Boundary*: Systems have boundaries delimiting where a system ends and where the external environment starts.
- *Openness*: Open systems interact to a great extent with their environment. Open systems need to 'read' signals from their external environment and adapt in order to keep themselves aligned with external requirements.

OPERATIONS SYSTEMS AS A TRANSFORMATION PROCESS

A widely used and popular way to model operations systems is as a transformation process as shown in Figure 2. In its most simple expression, it consists of stating that an operations system transforms inputs into outputs.

The transformation process model of operations was initially developed for manufacturing operations. In this context, it is easy to see that the inputs are raw materials and purchased components, the process is a collection of machining or assembly sub-processes, and the output is a tangible good.

The model, however, does not require that the inputs nor the outputs be tangible goods. In the most general case, both inputs and outputs will be bundles of goods and services. Some examples of the transformation process in a non-manufacturing context are:

- A transport company which does not transform the goods it carries but alters their locations.
- A surf check website which uses a variety of information inputs such as wave charts, weather forecasts, offshore buoy readings, and surf cams to provide as an output a clear, easy to read surf forecast.
- In the case of personal services, such as hairdressers, where the input and output are identical but their state has been modified.

The transformation process is what organisation theorists call the *technical core*. The technical core is the source of competitive advantage for firms, and it is the assemblage of a set of specialist processes. The notion of the technical core is also very close to the notion of *core competencies*

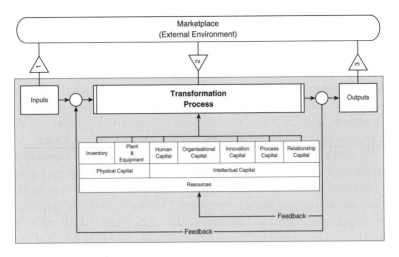

Figure 2   The transformation process model of operations systems

formulated by Hamel and Prahalad (1990), or to the notion of *strategic competencies* developed by Hall (2000). Strategic competencies are characterised by the following properties:

(i)   They are responsible for delivering a significant benefit to customers.
(ii) They are idiosyncratic to the firm.
(iii) They take time to acquire.
(iv) They are sustainable because they are difficult and time-consuming to imitate.
(v)   They comprise configuration of resources.
(vi) They have a strong tacit content and are socially complex – they are the product of experiential learning. (Hall, 2000: 101)

Resources

Developing and managing strategic competencies is only possible if managers can tap into a large pool of organisational resources. This is shown in the resources box below the transformation process in Figure 2.

The *resource-based view of the firm* is the strategic management school of thought which brought the importance of resources to the fore in the 1980s. The definition of what constitutes a resource is very broad. For example, Barney (1991), one of the pioneers of resource-based theory, described resources as '*all assets capabilities, organisational processes, firm attributes, information, knowledge, etc. controlled by a firm that enable the firm to conceive and implement strategies that improve its efficiency and effectiveness'.*

To some extent, this definition of resources is analogous to the accounting definition of an asset: a resource from which a firm can derive economic benefits in the future. The accounting definition highlights two fundamental properties of resources: (1) they require an investment and (2) there is some degree of uncertainty regarding the economic benefit which can be expected from them in the future.

Excellent business firms are those which invest in the development of resources that result in a competitive advantage. They take risky positions by investing in uncertain resources but receive high returns for the good management of these investments. The key challenge is to identify the required resources and to avoid under- or over-investing in them. In operations management, we are concerned with the following categories of resources: inventory, plant and equipment, and intellectual capital.

The job of an operations manager has traditionally been associated with the management of inventory and with the management of factories, or in the case of services, the management of the supporting facility. It was only in the 1990s, when managers started to exhibit maturity and excellence in their management of physical capital, that managerial attention turned to other resources such as intellectual capital.

In 1994, Skandia, a Swedish insurance company, was the first to point out that financial reporting was difficult when large differences existed between market value and book value (i.e. accounting value). In Sweden today, a ratio of 8:1 is common. In the United States, the market to book value ratio can be much higher. For example, Microsoft's market value in 1997 was 92 times its book value! This scale of difference is explained by the fact that most firms' resources are intangible (this is especially true in the service sector).

In order to fully inform its shareholders, Skandia included in its annual report a supplement describing its 'hidden' resources: those could explain a firm's competitive edge and its high market valuation, but are not captured, or are only captured partially, by standard accounting methods. This set of hidden resources was labelled *intellectual capital*. Figure 3 presents the different components of intellectual capital.

- *Human capital* refers to the distributed knowledge and sets of skills of the individual employees of a company.
- *Structural capital* refers to how individuals have organised themselves and how well co-ordinated they are.

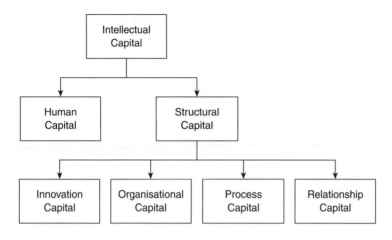

Figure 3   The components of intellectual capital

- *Organisational capital* refers to the organisational arrangements and structure which are in place and that form a framework for interaction and collaborative work.
- *Process capital* is of prime importance to operations managers. Process capital means possessing a full mastery of the inner working of the transformation process shown in Figure 2. It refers to whether or not all unnecessary delays, internal conflicts and non-value adding activities can be identified and eliminated. Operations management researchers have demonstrated through empirical research that proprietary processes and equipment are associated with higher levels of performance (Schroeder et al., 2002).
- *Innovation capital* refers to the extent to which the network of specialist processes within an operations system has been organised and structured in such a fashion that the system has high innovation capabilities. How often can new products be released? How expensive is it to bring a new generation of products onto the market? Are the core processes antiquated or state of the art?
- *Relationship capital* refers to how constructive the firm's relationships are with its suppliers and customers. Are these based on trust and collaboration and seek to maximise benefits for all parties, or do they suffer from adversarial practices which put a drain on profitability through penalties and legal settlements?

THE ENVIRONMENT OF OPERATIONS SYSTEMS

The transformation process model of operation systems (Figure 2) is generic enough to be applied to any type of organisation, but it does not display the fact that different operations systems positioned in different markets are subject to very different types of demand characteristics.

Firms subject to different types of demand will structure and organise their operations systems differently and will rely on a different set of resources. Therefore, being able to understand similarities and differences in operations systems' contexts is extremely important. Key dimensions to consider when studying the environment of an operations system are:

- *Volume*: The extent to which demand for the product offered for the firm is small or important. Low volume systems are more flexible but also more expensive whereas high volume systems are rigid but produce products at a low cost due to economies of scale (see **Process**).
- *Variety*: This means the variety of products that a system has to process. High product variety means highly customised, one-of-a-type products whereas low product variety means highly standardised products with only minor 'cosmetic' variations. Products based on a standard platform which receives several possible types of finishing are in the middle of the spectrum (see **Platform**).
- *Stability*: Is the demand pattern stable or highly variable? Examples of unstable demand are seasonal forms (Christmas, summer, winter seasons), and demand laws which are highly dependent on economic cycles.
- *Variability*: Variability refers to the feasibility of changing design specifications, and it should not be confused with variety. For example, modern automotive producers are characterised by high-variety as they offer a great number of options on standard platforms. However, their system is also characterised by low-variability as customers do not have the option to order a product which is not listed in an official catalogue. Hairdressers, on the other hand, are low-variety systems (they only cut hair) but high-variability systems (what they deliver is unique for each customer). High-variability systems are often referred to as *engineered-to-order* systems. Low-variety and low-variability systems are *make-to-stock* systems, whereas high-variety, low-variability systems as *make-to-order* or *assemble-to-order* systems.

- *Service weight*: The extent to which the product delivered is a pure good, a pure service, or a mix of both.
- *Clock speed*: The extent to which competition forces frequent releases of new products. The computer industry is an example of an industry with a high clock speed as new generation processors are released very often. The restaurant industry is an example of an industry with a lower clock speed, as restaurant innovations are rare and tend to remain marginal.

Systems control: the feedback loop

In Figure 2, feedback loops are the arrows going from the end of the transformation process to either the beginning of the process or to the resource box. A feedback loop indicates that an operations system is capable of self-adjustment. Feedback or system adjustment is triggered in control nodes where managers check that products conform to specifications (the trigger points are shown by circles in Figure 2).

For example, McDonald's pioneered the fast food industry by guaranteeing rapid service. If a restaurant manager notices that customers on average wait 20 minutes before being served, there is something wrong with the transformation process! It may be that staff at the counter and in the kitchen are too slow, in which case the restaurant is missing essential resources. Courses of action may be to hire more staff, or to initiate more training to make sure that all staff are aware of McDonald's standards. Another reason may be that the manager never planned adequately for the volume of demand at a specific time of the day, for example lunchtimes. In this case the resources are available but insufficient. Opening additional service counters may solve this problem. Note that in this example we are adjusting resources. In other cases it will be the input of the process which will have to be adjusted. For example, a car may be defective because it has been fitted with defective tyres: in this case, the only adjustment which is required is to source better tyres.

Systems boundaries

The upper half of Figure 2 displays three connections between the operations system and the external environment. These connections are represented by triangles symbolising either a transfer of control from the operations system to the environment (an upward triangle) or from the environment to the system (a downward triangle).

system

System supply

Vertically integrated systems involve all the processes from the extraction of raw material to the manufacture of a final consumer good. Through experience with specialisation, firms have learnt that it is often impractical to cover an entire **supply chain**. For example, it would not be practical for an accountancy firm to manage a paper mill to make sure that it always had an ample supply of paper to hand! Instead, the accountancy firm will purchase paper from a specialist supplier. In doing so, the firm's performance becomes dependent on the performance of that supplier. The first upward triangle in Figure 2 symbolises this dependence, i.e. the fact that an operations system's performance depends on suppliers.

Using outputs

Once products are sold or service provisions completed, customers will form a value judgment on them. Although a product or service may be designed with clear specifications, they might be perceived differently and used differently by customers. The second upward arrow in Figure 2 symbolises the transfer of control from the system to its customers.

For example, MacDonald's decision to use polystyrene packages to hold cooked burgers most probably originated with the desire to guarantee a high quality service and to avoid serving cold hamburgers to customers. When this decision was made, no-one within the operations system forecasted that some customers would react very negatively by pointing out that this form of packaging was not environmentally friendly. In other words, McDonald's destructed value where it thought it would be creating it. This example illustrates the complexity of the transfer of control from operations system to customers as this transfer is about the formation of value judgments about outputs. This is discussed in more detail elsewhere (see **Customers**).

Specialist process, marketing risk, and social responsibility

The external environment – which comprises customers, regulators, and the public at large – also implicitly transfers a number of control rights to business organisations. This transfer is symbolised by the downward arrow in Figure 2. Examples of these interactions are:

- By switching to a new technology, an industry can indicate to a company that it is time to update its operating resources.
- Customers implicitly trusting that processes will be managed according to standard national expectations. For example, pollution levels should remain low and no child labour should be employed. When this implicit trust erodes, control mechanisms might be put in place (e.g. third party compulsory environmental audits). Governments typically assume that companies should conduct business according to regulations and should also pay all relevant taxes. Again, should trust erode, further control mechanisms will be set up.

Whereas from the Industrial Revolution onwards the external environmental of operations systems has been one of lenient control, the reality of today's operations system is that more and more external regulations and controls are applied. Although these actions are usually implemented as the result of a real need, and while they usually seek the betterment of society, they usually make operations management more complex. The food and health industries are examples where operations management has to go hand in hand with strict statutory compliance.

REFERENCES

Barney, J. (1991) 'Firm resources and sustained competitive advantage', *Journal of Management*, 17(1): 99–120.

For a more detailed review of the origin, components and ways to measure intellectual capital, see: Joia, L. (2000) 'Measuring intangible corporate assets: linking business strategy with intellectual capital', *Journal of Intellectual Capital*, 1(1): 68–84.

Hall, R. (2000) 'What are strategic competencies?', in J. Tidd (ed.), *From Knowledge Management to Strategic Competence*. London: Imperial College Press, pp. 26–49.

Hamel, G. and Prahalad, C.K. (1990) 'The core competence of the corporation', *Harvard Business Review*, 68(3): 79–91.

Hopp, W. and Spearman, M. (2000) *Factory Physics*. New York: McGraw-Hill.

Schroeder, R., Bates, K. and Juntilla, M. (2002) 'A resource-based view of manufacturing strategy and the relationship to manufacturing performance', *Strategic Management Journal*, 23: 105–117.

Von Bertalanffy, L. (1968) *General System Theory*. Revised edition. New York: George Braziller.

An output is the conceptual description of the tangible or intangible end result of the act of producing through an operations system.

OUTPUT AND PRODUCTIVITY

Operations management is goal orientated: its purpose is to make sure that a **system** is used to produce an *output* from inputs. The production of outputs, however, is usually not without constraints. There may be several restrictions on inputs or resources used to generate the output. In the business world, a universal constraint is the cost of inputs and resources. This constraint is captured by the *productivity* ratio. Productivity is obtained by dividing outputs (e.g. in units or currency) by inputs (e.g. in units or currency, respectively). Operations management is about producing output with maximum, or challenging, productivity targets. In order to raise productivity, operations managers can:

- Find ways to produce more outputs with the same quantity of inputs.
- Maintain output levels but decrease inputs.
- Combine an increase in outputs with a reduction in inputs.

FROM MANUFACTURING MANAGEMENT TO OPERATIONS MANAGEMENT

This output, or 'product', can take many forms but it is common to differentiate two types: goods and services. A *good* is a tangible manufactured output (i.e. something that can be touched) such as a computer, a book or a bicycle. A *service* is the provision of an intangible output (i.e. the provision of something which cannot be touched). Instead it may be felt, experienced, heard, smelt or appreciated. Examples of services include hairdressing, transport services (goods and persons) and dog training.

Historically, operations management emerged in the manufacturing sector. After the Industrial Revolution, factories used a variety of

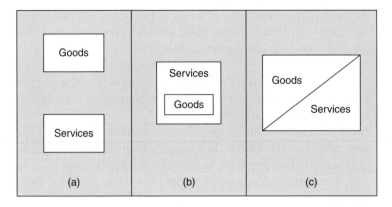

Figure 4   The three perspectives on goods and services

technological and managerial innovations to expand the scale of their operations. This scale became such that it was necessary to assign specialist managers to the task of managing operations. This specialty was named 'Production Management' or 'Manufacturing Management'. When these functions emerged, with their organisational departments, managers and staff, the service sector was, in comparison, small and marginal. For example, hotels were still small family-run businesses, rather than the 'giant' hotel chains of today which can often individually accommodate more than 2000 guests per night.

GOODS AND SERVICES

In the last two decades, operations management as a formal academic discipline has slowly evolved to embrace the problem of managing operations for the provision of goods *and* services. Figure 4 describes the three perspectives which have been used in this shift from 'production management' to the broader concept of 'operations management'.

A first school of thought is to consider that goods and services are fundamentally different and thus that their provision processes are also so different that they cannot possibly be compared. This position is usually supported by stressing the key characteristics of services which goods do not possess as illustrated in Table 1. This usually results in the belief that production management and service operations management are two different fields.

The strong distinction between goods and services suggested in panel (a) of Figure 4 is, at best, a moot point when one considers the following examples of intertwined goods and services:

- Some services, for example car repair, do not demand a customer presence. In that respect, running a repair shop is not very different from running a manufacturing job shop.
- Some business consultants specialise in providing off-the-shelf business solutions: the advice they sell is pre-typed, pre-thought and only needs to be customised to their client's specific context. In this case, intangibility does not affect the capacity to store the service offering.
- In the custom capital goods industry (e.g. assembly machines), customers and manufacturers interact a great deal during the design and manufacturing phases. In fact, it is common in this industry to send design engineers to work full time at the customer's site, and to invite a project manager from the buying company to work in a project team at the manufacturer's site. This exchange of workers helps to make sure that knowledge about how the capital good works is transferred effectively. Although labelled a 'manufacturing' transaction, this arrangement has a fundamental service dimension.

Given the variety of configurations within manufacturing and service operations, a clear-cut distinction between goods and services is only likely to be a gross generalisation. Table 1 is useful in simple cases, as for comparing car manufacturing with the provision of beauty services, but in the more complex cases, it would be more misleading than helpful.

A second school of thought (shown in panel (b) of Figure 4) is to observe that there are often similarities between the provision of services and goods, and that, more and more, these are provided simultaneously in a *bundle*. Take, for example, the case of *facilitating services*. These are services offered to customers which support the sale of a product, as for example a telephone support hotline linked to a computer purchase.

The distinction between services and products can actually become very difficult to make:

- Imagine purchasing a car with a full maintenance agreement (a facilitating service).

Table 1   Goods versus Services

	Goods	Services
Intangibility	Are highly tangible – quality can be assessed against objective specifications.	Are highly intangible – assessment of quality is difficult before purchase. Assessment is perceptual and subjective.
Heterogeneity	Are highly standardised.	The service experience may vary.
Inseparability	Are produced in facilities which do not involve the customer.	Provision requires high levels of skilled customer–seller interactions.
Perishability	Goods can be stored.	Services cannot be stored.

- Or purchasing an operating lease, i.e. a service agreement through which you will lease (rent) the car, but all maintenance, repairs, taxation and insurance will be handled by the leasing organisation.

In these two examples what is provided is a product with a facilitating service or a service with a facilitating product. Practically, however, the product bundle that is offered to customers is almost identical.

Although this second point of view is a reality in several economic sectors, pure services and pure goods provision still exist today. This is why the perspective presented in panel (c) of Figure 3.1 is a more robust description of the different contexts in which operations managers have to work. Business organisations can provide a variety of product bundles, ranging from pure goods to pure services, with any possible mix in between.

FURTHER READING

Parasuraman, A. and Varadarajan, P.(1988) 'Future strategic emphases in service versus goods businesses', *Journal of Services Marketing*, 2(4): 57–66.

output

> *Service science is the application of inter-disciplinary scientific methods to design and manage better service provision systems.*

THE SERVICE REVOLUTION

As discussed in the previous concepts, operations management is a discipline that originated in the field of manufacturing management. Although some economies today still rely extensively on manufacturing sectors for their wealth, the service sectors in the vast majority of modern economies now dominate in terms of employment figures and contributions to Gross National Product (the service sectors of economies such as those of the UK or the USA typically employ more than 75 per cent of their national workforce). This phenomenon is referred to as the *service revolution*, and it sometimes requires acute adjustments at all levels within national economies. For example, old manufacturing management university degrees have to be replaced with service management degrees. This implies that researchers, lecturers, and textbooks must all adjust to new economic realities. Similarly, workers leaving a declining manufacturing sector in terms of employment opportunities have to reconvert their skill sets to new forms of employment. Even the legal aspects of businesses have to be rethought to match the new service-based economy (e.g. new e-commerce legislation).

In Occidental countries, the service revolution started in the late 1970s and service sectors have experienced constant growth since then. In terms of resource adjustments, the process is still continuing however, as changing resources such as skills sets, knowledge and best practice can be time consuming. As one might expect in a phase of economic transition, uncertainty and speculation are usually high and managing a business can often turn out to be a major challenge. Take for example Webvan, a major investment initiative by the US bookseller Borders in the sector of internet-based groceries retail. Webvan ended up as a major business failure along with many other 'dot.com' companies which were launched in an over-enthusiastic response to the 'internet service revolution'. Although the societal and economic changes that have taken place since the Industrial Revolution and until today's service revolution have indeed been remarkable, it is important to remember that there are real economic forces at play, and that business and operations managers should take these into consideration.

THE THREE SECTOR HYPOTHESIS AND BEYOND

The fact that the service sector would become more important than the manufacturing sector was foreseen by two economists (Colin Clark and Jean Fourastié) and is often called the *three sector hypothesis*. Simply stated, the three sector hypothesis stipulates that with time, employment and the economic contribution of the primary sector (agriculture and mining) will decline and shift to the secondary sector (manufacturing). Eventually, employment and economic weight will shift from the second to the third sector, i.e. the service sector.

It is worth highlighting the role that operations management plays in this economic transformation process. Take, for example, the transition from the secondary to the tertiary sector: at the beginning of the twentieth century, the manufacturing of a consumer good (e.g. a tool, a car) was a complex affair due to a lack of knowledge and technology. For example, the assembly of a car back then could take a couple of years, making this an extremely expensive good, and also making car assembly a viable operation only if a cheap workforce was available (as was the case in the nineteenth century where productivity improvements in agriculture meant that many unemployed agricultural workers were coming to the industrial urban areas in search of employment).

With operations management, this relatively inefficient form of production could be improved to the modern manufacturing standard that we know today. Note that the three sectors hypothesis does not say that the manufacturing sector will disappear (there are still many car factories in the UK, for example) and neither does it say that manufacturing will become an unprofitable activity. What it does say is that due to operations management knowledge, the productivity of these factories became such that only a handful or workers in a handful of factories are now needed to do the work that hundreds used to do. As a consequence, workers must exit the industry and seek employment in other sectors – typically sectors where productivity is still low and not mastered, or where labour is needed to offer new, or better, services.

There is considerable debate regarding what happens beyond the tertiary sector. Some suggest the existence of a fourth sector, the *information economy*, dealing with the creation and diffusion of knowledge that therefore includes information management, education and research and development. Others advance the existence of a fifth sector, described by some as the government (health, police, etc.) and the not-for-profit sector. Yet others put forward as a fifth sector the *experience economy* (experience is defined by the quality of emotions and feelings experienced by customers). Clearly, although it is evident that these three additional sectors are indeed growing quickly, it is not certain as yet which of these will grow faster than the others. What is known, however, is that in each of these sectors there should be important efforts to apply operations management as a discipline in order to improve productivity and generate wealth.

SERVITISATION

The service revolution is also having an impact on the manufacturing sector. Similar to the quality revolution which took place in the 1980s when companies had to adopt quality as a competitive weapon, modern manufacturing firms cannot survive without embedding services within their products. The trend is known as *servitisation*: the idea that manufacturing firms should be managed as service providers rather than as producers, as value to customers lies in the overall service provision and not just in the acquisition of a product.

SERVICE SCIENCE

Service science is the ongoing response to a desire to improve productivity in the service sector. Initially an approach developed by IBM, service science, or 'service science, management and engineering' (SSME), is an interdisciplinary approach attempting to bring to services the rigour that work study and operations management brought to work methods in manufacturing. Due to the specific intangible, emotional and perishable aspects of services, service science requires the integration of theories from management science, the social sciences and the engineering sciences. The emergence and popularity of call centres is a typical example of the outcomes of service science: call centres and the provision of telephone banking services are good examples of the application of the standard operations management principles – standardisation of tasks and processes, standardisation of scripts to guide customer contact, establishment of standard times to achieve performance targets, etc. Hefley and Murphy (2008) provide an extensive review of this emergence and of the best practices in service science.

FURTHER READING

Vandermerwe, S. and Rada, J. (1988) 'Servitization of business: adding value by adding services', *European Management Journal*, 6(4): 314–324.

REFERENCES

Hefley, B. and Murphy, W. (2008) *Service Science, Management and Engineering*. Berlin: Springer-Verlag.

Customers

> *Customers are the ultimate recipients of the provision of a good or service by an operations system. They can be close to, or remote from, an operations system, but in all cases their demands and needs are the prime inputs for the design of an operations system.*

CUSTOMERS AND RELATIONSHIP CAPITAL

As an operations manager, in what ways should you think of customers? Customers form judgments about the value of the output of operations systems and in doing so they exert a direct or indirect pressure on an operations system. Customers could be seen as troublesome, as it is from them that complaints, excessive demands or pressures to operate in different ways will stem. Alternatively, customers and their needs are the only reason why an operations system exists in the first place. If customers only expressed a need for luxury travel, low cost airlines would disappear. If customers desire cheap travel, low cost airlines will thrive.

In a free market economy, it is essential that an operations system's output matches customer expectations. This is why many of the operations management frameworks described in this book (e.g. **TQM** and

Six Sigma) will take customer satisfaction as the starting point for any corporate improvement initiative. The central importance of customer satisfaction in operations management is explained by the fact that a positive relationship between a firm and its customers is a resource (relation capital, see **System**) by which the system performance can be increased. Berry and Parasuraman (1997) use factor analysis to classify the various behavioural intentions of customers as follows:

- *Customer loyalty to the company*: for example, a loyal customer may encourage friends to do business with a company. Loyal customers are happy to commit to more business with this company. Non-loyal customers will do the opposite.
- *Propensity to switch*: customers may be reluctant to switch (a source of capital) or may always be switching (for example, for better one-off deals).
- *Willingness to pay more*: this can be observed for example when products are priced higher than those of the competition whilst remaining bestsellers.
- *External response to a problem*: should a problem occur during a transaction, would the customer complain to a regulator, engage in legal action, or divert their business to a competitor?
- *Internal response to a problem*: the customer will attempt to solve problems by contacting the company's employees.

It may come as a surprise that operations management will directly concern itself with customer needs as these are by definition the specialist area of marketing. The distinction between operations management and marketing as business functions is an example of the principle of division of labour at work. Specialisation, however, requires co-ordination. This means that when operations managers concern themselves with customers, they are not trying to compete with their marketing departments. Instead, they are making sure that the interface between marketing and operations management is working effectively. There are three ways in which operations managers can, along with marketers, participate in managing the relationship with customers:

1 *Listening to customers* involves a number of tools and techniques used to translate external performance specifications into internal specifications (see **Performance** for more information on performance management).

2 Many service provisions require the involvement of contact person-nel. *Customer contact* refers to a set of specifications and guidelines for the effective co-production of services.
3 *Personalisation* in operations management is a set of capabilities used to provide a customised service to large customer segments.

LISTENING TO CUSTOMERS

Listening to customers can be a challenge in operations management for a variety of reasons: they may not be in contact with the system (e.g. manufacturing), or there may be contact but there is variability between the needs of customers (e.g. in a doctor's practice), or customers may not know exactly what they want (e.g. a consultant facilitating a strat-egy analysis meeting for a corporate client).

Throughout the concepts in this book, you will find references to cus-tomers and customer satisfaction, a reminder that organisations will often have multiple goals. A business firm, for example, will seek prof-itability and customer satisfaction. A government agency will seek pub-lic utility and stakeholders' satisfaction.

Berry and Parasuraman (1997) go further and argue that listening to customers should be made a more formal and structured activity by introducing the concept of a *service quality information system*. They therefore provide an exhaustive list of the mechanisms through which organisations can listen to their customers (surveys, focus groups, mys-tery shopping, service reviews, etc.) and they also summarise the goals of an effective service quality information system:

- Take into account the voice of the customers when making decisions.
- Reveal customers' priorities.
- Identify improvement priorities and guide resource allocation.
- Track company performance along with that of competitors.
- Disclose the impact of service quality initiatives and investments.
- Provide a database to be used to correct poor service and to recog-nise and reward excellent service.

Customer Relationship Management (CRM) systems are computer-based systems that allow large firms to build a database and to interact with customers, as for example through the management of loyalty card schemes. CRM systems attempt to maintain a feeling of personal care and a relationship when the volume of customers is such that maintaining personal contact would not be feasible.

In the rest of this section, we discuss two techniques used in operations management to listen to customers at the stage of designing products and services: customer-perceived value and quality function deployment.

Customer-perceived value

Miller and Swaddling (2002: 88) define customer-perceived value (CPV) as 'the result of the customer's evaluation of all the benefits and costs of an offering as compared to that customer's perceived alternatives. It's the basis on which customers decide to buy things'.

Miller and Swaddling argue that customers go through a cost-benefit analysis when they decide to acquire a product. Benefits include the financial impact of purchasing the product (e.g. increased revenues or reduced costs), time savings, increased safety, and prestige derived from ownership. Costs include the purchase price, the training required for the user, the process changes required from the adoption of the product, and tax and insurance considerations. Customers will only acquire a product if perceived benefits exceed perceived costs.

Miller and Swaddling further posit that:

- *Customer value is market-perceived*: This means that like beauty value lies in the eyes of the beholder! A product which is technologically superior will not necessarily be a bestseller. This is why companies should focus on understanding how customers make value judgments in the marketplace.
- *Customer value is complicated*: There may be many variables at play in a customer's mind when making a decision.
- *Customer value is relative*: Value is assessed relative to the alternatives the customer perceives they have. Companies should endeavour to discover what these alternatives are.
- *Customer value is dynamic*: Customers' perceptions of value are permanently evolving with their changing circumstances or with changes in the marketplace.

The recommendation in Miller and Swaddling's work is that significant research resources should be devoted to **New Product Development** (NPD) and **New Service Development** (NSD) to understand customer-perceived value. Researching customer-perceived value can be achieved through using tools and techniques which will focus on customers, such as lead users methodology and ethnographic design (an approach where the design is preceded by studying the 'persona' of customers). Other techniques include one-to-one interviewing, focus groups, customer advisory panels, customer role playing, and the organisation of customer events.

Quality function deployment

Quality Function Deployment, or *QFD* (Akao et al., 2004), is a technique that was developed in Japan in the late 1960s in order to make sure that design activities would balance the engineering perspective with the 'voice of the customer'. The driving idea behind QFD is to take into account customer needs before a product is designed and built, not afterwards. QFD can be used in any design activity: new product development, technology selection, service development, and process design.

One of the strength of the QFD methodology is its ability to co-ordinate decisions amongst different departments over time while maintaining the integrity of the initial customer specifications. For example, a QFD exercise included in the concept design can feed into another QFD exercise at the detailed design stage, which could in turn feed a process design QFD exercise. Thus, QFD is one way of achieving cross-functional **integration** and **co-ordination**.

CUSTOMER CONTACT

Customer contact is the extent to which the customer will be part of the execution of a process. In manufacturing settings, operations managers are rarely in direct contact with customers. To deal with the complexity of dealing with an end customer, specialists in sales and marketing will intervene. This practice has been described by organisational theorists as 'buffering the technical core' (Thompson, 1967). Buffering this technical core, i.e. trying to isolate the core of the firm from the end customer, is also called *decoupling*. By introducing an interface between the customer and the technical core staff, each party deals with a simplified problem. For example, a factory is protected from demand fluctuations by an inventory buffer. Similarly, process engineers are protected from a direct interaction with end customers by the sales department. In manufacturing operations, decoupling is systematic.

Chase (1981) suggested that decoupling has been almost a systematic practice in manufacturing because customer contact has a negative impact on efficiency:

$$\text{Potential facility efficiency} = \frac{f\,(1 - \text{Customer Contact Time})}{\text{Service Creation Time}}$$

According to Chase's formula, activities which involve customer contact time are inherently slowed and maximum efficiency can only be achieved if contact time is eliminated.

In the service industry, however, customer contact is the norm. Babbar and Koufteros (2008) highlight that, initially, customer contact in operations management simply meant the presence of a customer in the operations system. It was then recognised that an operations manager should pay attention to the actual interaction which takes place between the service provider and the customer. This interaction is often called the *service encounter*. In the most complex cases, the customer is actually involved in the definition, design and delivery of the service along with the contact personnel: this is referred to as *co-production*. A side issue in the days when manufacturing dominated the economic scene, customer contact has increasingly been recognised as a fundamental research issue in operations management. This has resulted in the formulation of 'contact theory', that Babbar and Koufteros (2008: 818) define as recognising 'the interface between the firm and customer to be a seminal element of consideration for service firms and contact employees as providing service-delivering firms valuable opportunities for responding to the needs of customers, satisfying them, and helping to build a relationship with them'.

The legitimacy of contact theory was established by Soteriou and Chase (1998), who were the first researchers to demonstrate empirically the existence of a relationship between customer contact and perceptions of service quality. Moreover, providing excellent customer contact can also have other impacts on performance besides service quality. High levels of customer contact can supply opportunities for marketing the firm and its other services (Chase et al., 1984) or for building trust and confidence between the firm and its customers. For example, although the computer manufacturer Dell was once famous for its outstanding level of customer service, it went through a phase of decline which culminated with negative sentiments toward Dell being held by 48 per cent of its customers. When Michael Dell returned to the company in

2007, one of his first campaigns was to re-establish customer contact. Dell employs a team of 42 employees who spend their days interacting with customers on social networking web sites such as Facebook in order to feed the information that they collect back to the company's designers. As a result, negative sentiment toward Dell dropped to 23 per cent in 2008 (Fortt, 2008).

Customer contact and design of service system

High contact service systems and low contact service systems are very different in terms of system requirements. In addition to being able to distinguish between the design requirements of high and low contact systems, operations managers should also understand what it is in their respective industry that creates a good contact experience. For example, Babbar and Koufteros's (2008) research shows that the perception of airline service quality in the USA was based on customer contact as measured by personal touch. Personal touch was defined as individual attention, helpfulness, courtesy and promptness.

When should we decouple operations?

A key systems design issue is deciding at what point a process must become decoupled from this interaction with customers. Different service sectors will require different (or will not lend themselves to) ways of decoupling.

According to Chase (1981), services can be categorised as:

- *Pure service*: where contact time is unavoidable (e.g. medical services, restaurants).
- *Mixed services*: where decoupling takes place. The customer end of the service is called a *front office*; the part of the service which is decoupled is called a *back office*.
- *Quasi-manufacturing*: there is no customer contact, e.g. a distribution centre.

Chase suggests the following procedures for analysing which contact strategy should be followed for a service:

1 Identify those points in the service system where decoupling is possible and desirable.
2 Employ contact reduction strategies where appropriate.

3   Employ a contact enhancement strategy where appropriate.
4   Employ traditional efficiency improvement techniques to improve low contact operations.

PERSONALISATION

From mass production to mass customisation

The Industrial Revolution and the societal changes that came with it were made possible due to the development of new technologies and the exploitation of economies of scale. Mass production, however, has a drawback. Through its focus on reducing costs and intensifying the pace of production, it does not allow for the customisation of products. Henry Ford, for example, was famous for his statement that a Model T could be ordered in any colour, provided that this colour was black! There is a simple production explanation for this policy: back in the 1910s, the technology did not permit a rapid change of colour in the painting shops. Switching colours in a painting room might have required several hours for cleaning equipment. These hours represented precious time lost that would lead to a decrease in productivity and profitability.

Henry Ford's first competitive challenge came in the 1920s from General Motors: recognising the need for more diverse products in the market, General Motors built four separate factories producing four different models, each available in different colours and versions. In terms of costs, these factories could not compete with Ford: the scale and variety of products on offer were such that their cars were much more expensive. However, a demand existed for differentiated cars and General Motors thrived in this business, eventually forcing Ford to abandon production of the Model T and to release a new product, the Model A.

At a small scale, the competitive battle between Ford and General Motors in the 1920s was the ancestral version of the rise of *mass customisation* in the 1980s. Competing via cost is only a powerful competitive strategy if customers value cost and no other performance dimension (see **Performance**). After World War II, most industrial developments took place in a climate of economic reconstruction and therefore customers could not afford to be too specific in their demands. Ordering a customised product was always possible, but it came at a premium price and with a very long lead time. However, the nature of demand gradually evolved toward more and more differentiation of needs. When marketers used to specify products on the basis of the average of a distribution, they started to look at the shape and range of the distribution. They recognised that different segments existed under a demand distribution, and throughout the years that followed, the notion that firms may be able to serve a 'segment of one' started to gain ground. The resulting idea, which was documented in the early 1980s, was called mass customisation. Hart (1995: 36) defines it as: 'the use of flexible processes and organisational structures to produce varied and often individually customised products and services at the low cost of a standardised, mass-production system'.

Mass customisation strategies

Gilmore and Pine (1997) have identified four approaches to implementing a mass customisation strategy:

- *Collaborative mass customisation*: The customer is directly involved with the co-specification of the product, and potentially in its co-production.
- *Adaptive customisation*: This corresponds to a slightly different need, as the customer can adapt the product or service to match his or her changing needs. In other words, the provider recognises that customer needs fluctuate (with weather, mood, etc.) and builds into the product the possibility of adapting it to circumstances.
- *Cosmetic customisation*: This strategy focuses on the appearance or packaging of the product, which is usually the last stage in production. The customer will select an appealing product from a very wide range of combinations, or can buy different panels or 'fascias' to customise their products later on during consumption.
- *Transparent customisation*: In this approach, the customer cannot or does not have the time or knowledge to specify the exact nature of their needs. As a result, the supplier takes control and provides a customised product or service without the customer being aware of this fact.

Mass customisation: the process side

The key challenge of mass customisation is not to personalise the provision of products or services, but is to do so whilst keeping costs at similar level than is the case for mass production. There are number of capabilities and process innovations that can be implemented to support a mass customisation initiative, from the operations side. It goes without saying that marketing should also be involved in the process, as this will play a key role in eliciting, capturing, and documenting customer preferences. Key operations capabilities supporting mass customisation are:

- *The use of modules in product designs:* This means that customising the product becomes a simple matter of assembling it from different modules, rather than redesigning the product every time. (Platform technology and the use of modules are described in more detail in **Platform.**)
- *The use of flexible processes:* This allows a single facility to handle 'batch sizes of one', and therefore to achieve a smoothed production of mass customised products (see **Flexibility**).
- *Responsiveness:* This is a requisite and especially important in the apparel industry, where point of sales data systems can capture in real time the fact that a specific product version is proving successful. Through quick response supply chains, production of this version can be scaled up so that more adequate quantities can be supplied to the stores (see **Responsiveness**).
- *Postponement:* This is another key capability in mass customisation (Feitzinger and Lee, 1997). A product can be decomposed into a common core and customisable elements. The idea of postponement is to delay the provision of customisable elements until the latest possible stages of production, in order to allow upstream production stages to experience economies of scale.
- *Use of technology:* Thanks to information technology, it may be possible to offer customised services at a minor cost. Airlines and some ferry companies, for example, have uploaded diagrams of their seating arrangements on the internet to allow customers to choose their seats if they desire to do so.

MASS CUSTOMISATION OF SERVICES

Mass customisation in the service industry is a puzzling affair. Historically, the service sector has been famous for naturally high levels of service personalisation, an important competitive capability derived primarily from the quality of contact personnel. Take the example of personal banking services up until the mid 1980s. The typical organisational design of a retail bank was that each customer would be allocated a personal advisor, who could be contacted when customisation was needed. Non-customised services were delivered over the counter.

Instead of going through a mass customisation revolution, the retail banking industry went through a mass production revolution. Many of the banking innovations of the 1990s and early 2000s had to do with cost cutting and productivity enhancement: the use of call centres and telephone banking, the retirement of personal advisors, etc. When the need for a customised service appears today customers will still be offered a personal consultation, but with an employee who will have no previous contact or history with that customer. As a result, most of the relational advantages that existed in the old configuration have disappeared.

In a survey of the UK financial sector, Papathanasiou (2004) showed that a majority of respondents saw a strong potential in mass customisation to improve the personalisation of services and recognised the internet as the most promising medium to do so. For example, Amazon's personal recommendation service, which is based on the data mining of a very large transaction database, shows how by using technology a firm can maintain on a large scale the 'feel' of a relation. Similarly, Yahoo! Launch radio is an internet-based personal radio channel that plays music based on the rankings previously entered by each user.

The idea that the internet-based or technology-based mass customisation of services has a bright future is beyond debate. It is indeed a promising avenue for competitive improvement. A question remains, though, regarding the service industry's past practice of dismissing human-based mass customisation. Note that when the manufacturing sector adopted mass customisation, the specification was to increase customisation while maintaining cost performance. The service sector could, in comparison, be accused of having increased cost performance while reducing customisation.

REFERENCES

Akao, Y., King, B. and Mazur, G. (2004) *Quality Function Deployment: Integrating Customer Requirements Into Product Design*. New York: Productivity Press.

Babbar, S. and Koufteros, X. (2008) 'The human element in airline service quality: contact personnel and the customer', *International Journal of Operations and Production Management*, 28(9): 804–830.

Berry, L.L. and Parasuraman, A. (1997) 'Listening to the customer – the concept of a service quality information system', *Sloan Management Review*, Spring: 65–76.

Chase, R. (1981) 'The customer contact approach to services: theoretical bases and practical extensions', *Operations Research*, 29(4): 698–706.

Chase, R., Norcroft, G. and Wolf, G. (1984) 'Designing high-contact service systems: application to branches of a savings and loans', *Decision Science*, 15(4): 542–56.

Feitzinger, E. and Lee, H.L. (1997) 'Mass customization at Hewlett-Packard: the power of postponement', *Harvard Business Review*, January–February: 116–121.

Fortt, J. (2008) 'Michael Dell "friends" his customers', *Fortune*, 15 September: 35–38.

Gilmore, J.H. and Pine II, B.J. (1997) 'The four faces of customization', *Harvard Business Review*, January–February: 91–101.

Hart, C.W.L. (1995) 'Mass customisation conceptual underpinnings, opportunities, and limits', *International Journal of Service Industry Management*, 6(2): 36–45.

Miller, C. and Swaddling, D. (2002) 'Focusing NPD research on customer-perceived value', in P. Belliveau, A. Griffin and S. Sommermeyer (eds), *The PDMA Toolbook for New Product Development*, Product Development & Management Association.

Papathanasiou, E.A. (2004) 'Mass customisation: management approaches and internet opportunities in the financial sector in the UK', *International Journal of Information Management*, 24: 387–399.

Soteriou, A. and Chase, R. (1998) 'Linking the customer contact model to service quality', *Journal of Operations Management*, 16(4): 495–508.

Thompson, J. (1967) *Organizations in Action*. New York: McGraw-Hill.

Technology

> **Technology is the application of scientific knowledge to the change and manipulation of the human environment.**

DEFINING TECHNOLOGY

The term technology is a combination of the Greek *technē* ('art', or 'craft') with *logos* ('word', 'speech') meaning a discourse on the arts, both fine and applied. In other words, it means the application of scientific knowledge to the change and manipulation of the human environment.[1] Technology, therefore, refers to the know-how – techniques – which are combined into a process to be executed. The term includes hardware

---

[1] The author is indebted to Professor David Bennett, Professor of Technology Management at Aston Business School, for this definition.

technologies (e.g. computers, the internet), software technologies (e.g. a web browser), and 'human-ware' (for example the tacit knowledge of the execution of a process, e.g. the skills displayed by a top chef).

TECHNOLOGY IN MODERN OPERATIONS MANAGEMENT

The association of technology with operations management is a fundamental tenet of the 'age of enlightenment', where the betterment of life and of consumers' experiences is continuously sought. One fundamental aspect of progress in 'modern' operations management is the law of technology, which stipulates that efficiency can be derived from the adoption of technologies performing specialised tasks. Although many concepts in this book make reference to the principles of the division of labour as one of the foundations of operations management, it is important to realise that technology has played an equally important role in the shaping of modern operations systems. As captured by the definition given above, technology is not only used to refer to plant and equipment but also to other resources such as process capital (ways of doing things), innovation capital (the ability to integrate new technologies into existing product platforms), and organisational capital (new ways of organising).

Technology has been such a prevalent factor in changing the practice of operations management since the Industrial Revolution that it is impossible in one short paragraph to provide an exhaustive list of all the underpinning 'revolutionary' technologies. Examples include the steam engine, transport technologies, just-in-time production methods, standards of tolerance for mechanical parts, and intelligent manufacturing. Along with many others, these technological innovations have shaped what manufacturing and service companies can and do achieve.

How technology shapes operations systems and entire business firms is a long-established research stream in organisational theory. Amidst the key pioneers was Woodward (1958), who showed that depending on the degree of technical complexity in the workplace certain patterns of structure and work practices were most suitable. Woodward's work is famous for her classification of 100 British manufacturing firms based on patterns of structure and technology.

Thompson (1967) is another pioneer of the so-called technological determinism school: instead of looking at technical complexity, he studied patterns of interdependence implied by technology at work. His work is highly relevant to operations management as each type of interdependence pattern corresponds to specific operations management approaches in terms of designing and planning work processes. Thompson's work is also frequently cited in **supply chain** management research. The third contributor of technological determinism here is Perrow (1970) who classified various technologies into four categories as a function of task variety and predictability at work. Again, the contribution is to explain viable patterns between work context, technologies, and structure.

TECHNOLOGY-INDUCED BUSINESS TRANSFORMATION

It is important is to appreciate just *how* technology affects operations. A good example is provided by Venkatraman's (1994) study of the impact of information technology on business practice. Through a review of the investments in IT of major US corporations, Venkatraman identified five ways in which IT can transform business operations:

- *Localised exploitation*: These investments are isolated systems solving specific productivity problems. Inventory management systems, for example, are used to automate a task but do not imply a redefinition of work processes.
- *Internal integration*: These investments have two purposes. The first is to guarantee technical interconnectivity, so all users in a firm can access the same technological platform. The second is to integrate business processes so that roles and responsibilities are clear and understood by all (see **Integration**). Duplicate or conflicting roles, for example, have to be eliminated before any corporate-level improvement can be applied.
- *Business process redesign*: Following the technological determinism school, Venkatraman argues that most business processes were developed because of technological and environmental constraints. When IT technologies are introduced at work, process analysts can free themselves from legacy constraints and find new, more efficient, ways of working. In this case, IT adoption leads to the redefinition of operations systems.
- *Business network redesign*: The previous idea can be applied beyond the boundaries of an organisation to the business network that it belongs to. Through appropriate information systems and IT platforms, distribution specialists can redesign distribution channels. Direct sales channels from manufacturers to customers or from

wholesaler to customers (e.g. Amazon.com) are examples of business network redesign.

- *Business scope redefinition*: At the highest level, IT technology developed in-house may be deployed to enter completely new markets. Airline reservation systems and e-business models are examples of IT technologies that first movers have been able to sell to other commercial sectors.

The impact of technology on operations is so important that most large corporations will employ specialists – technology managers – to help them identify which technologies they should invest in (see **Technology Management**).

TECHNOLOGY, SOCIETY, AND FUTURES

The pioneering school of technological determinism laid the foundations for the investigation of *how* technology affects society and how society affects technologies. Operations managers usually concern themselves with technology management, but it is important to appreciate that there is an ongoing and healthy debate surrounding the concept of technology beyond its use in operations systems. Webster (1992) and Johnson and Wetmore (2008) are examples of authors who are exploring the wider question of society and technology.

In particular, the school of *socio-technical systems* argues that there must be a fit between social arrangements and technical systems. Socio-technical system theory has implications when designing work and processes.

TECHNOLOGIES AFFECTING THE FUTURE OF OPERATIONS MANAGEMENT

To conclude this concept, it is relevant to highlight that one of the responsibilities of an operations manager is to keep abreast of technological developments in order to identify which technologies, will transform operation systems in their particular industry. Examples of current key transforming technologies include:

- Bio-engineering where new products are designed by combining principles from mechanical engineering and biology.
- Nanotechnology for the design and manufacture of very small (the scale of a few microns) mechatronic products.

technology

- E-commerce technologies that have resulted in a new field of study, e-operations, within the discipline of operations management. These have an especially strong impact on service operations management, such as the provision of online banking services.
- Space commerce which was once the restricted domain of highly-funded government agencies, but more and more corporations are entering the arena. The company Virgin Galactic even offers (wealthy) customers trips in a space shuttle. At the time of writing this book, there is no specialist 'space operations management' publicly-available body of knowledge, but as space commerce grows it is clear that this body of knowledge will emerge.

REFERENCES

Johnson, D.G. and Wetmore, D.M. (eds) (2008) *Technology and Society: Building our Sociotechnical Future*. Cambridge, MA: MIT Press.

Perrow, C. (1970) *Organisation Analysis*. London: Thompson Learning.

Thompson, J.D. (1967) *Organisations in Action*. New York: McGraw-Hill.

Venkatraman, N. (1994) 'IT-enabled business transformation: from automation to business scope redefinition', *Sloan Management Review*, 35(2): 73–87.

Webster, A. (1992) *Science, Technology and Society: New Directions*. Basingstoke: Palgrave-Macmillan.

Woodward, J. (1958) *Management and Technology*. London: HMSO.

Co-ordination

Co-ordination is the alignment and synchronisation of people, processes, and information within operations systems in order to maximise productivity.

CO-ORDINATION

One of the consequences of seeking performance through specialisation is the need for co-ordination. The ability to co-ordinate, thus, is a core activity of operations management. Simply put, the challenge of operations managers is to make sure that all resources, inputs, and processes are available in the right quantity, in the right place, at the right time, in order for productive activities to take place.

Mintzberg (1983) was one of the first academics to write about co-ordination. He listed the following ways through which work could be co-ordinated:

- *Mutual adjustment*: Co-ordination is achieved by informal communication between the people doing the task, as for example when two canoeists paddle along a river. Although operations management co-ordination tends to use more formal mechanisms, certain cultures favour this type of co-ordination. Japanese work production teams, and the self-managed teams recommended by the socio-technical systems approach (popular in Scandinavian work systems, see **Work**), are examples of co-ordination through mutual adjustments. Research on behavioural operations management deals with this type of co-ordination.
- *Direct supervision*: Direct supervision is more of a management issue than an operations management issue. How a person is made responsible for the work of another, and how a person manages this relation, are the prime responsibility of a line manager.
- *Standardisation of work processes*: This has been the main battlefield for operations management, especially through the scientific management movement. Its modern descendant is the field of process management (see **Process Management**).
- *Standardisation of outputs*: This is done through the planning function, where levels of outputs (quantities, costs, quality levels) are set, and resources are allocated accordingly. Co-ordination through planning is discussed in **Planning and Control**.
- *Standardisation by skills and knowledge*: When workers are given specific roles that use their specific (and standardised) skills, co-ordination is automatically achieved. Examples are legal offices and academic departments, where each individual knows his or her respective role and acts only in ways prescribed by a professional code of conduct.

CO-ORDINATION THEORY

Many business and non-business disciplines concern themselves with co-ordination. This is not surprising as the reality of modern organisations, (see **Operations**) is one of high interdependence within large, potentially dispersed, networks of specialists. Malone and Crowston (1990) observed that although there is a lot of research done about co-ordination in different fields, there is little if any effort to integrate the different research streams together. Through a multi-disciplinary review of the literature, they propose a theory of co-ordination, which they define as the *body of principles about how activities can be co-ordinated, that is, about how actors can work together harmoniously.*

Their theory first identifies the components of co-ordination, which are: *goals, activities, actors,* and *interdependencies.* The purpose of co-ordination theory is to manage interdependencies so that actors can complete the required activities in such a way that goals are attained. Should goals be changed, activities, actors and interdependencies may have to be adjusted. This is the case for any of the four components.

Malone and Crowston (1990) then investigated the different types of interdependencies, and found themselves following the path of the technological determinism school (see **Technology**). They do not provide a full taxonomy of interdependencies and instead give a preliminary list of different kinds of interdependence. These examples include:

- Prerequisite: The output of an activity is required by a downstream activity.
- Shared resources: Different activities utilise the same resource.
- Simultaneity: Two or more activities should be completed at the same time.
- Manufacturability: what the design department produces should be manufacturable, i.e. process engineers should be able to design a manufacturing process.
- Customer relations: Two or more actors deal with the same customers, for example a salesperson and a field technician.

Finally, Malone and Crowston (1990) listed the processes underlying co-ordination. The first category grouped pure co-ordination processes. These can be applied to the four components of co-ordination. Pure co-ordination processes include identifying goals, ordering activities, assigning activities to actors (scheduling), allocating resources, and synchronising activities. All of these are typical operations management processes and are discussed in more detail throughout this book.

Group decision making is a second class of co-ordination processes and is about making collective decisions. This includes proposing alternatives, evaluating alternatives, and making choices.

Communication is another class of co-ordination processes and is about establishing common languages, routing information flows, and diffusing information within an organisation.

Finally, the last class of co-ordination processes is about the perception of common objects. It is important that actors see objects (products, customers, plans, etc.) in the same way so that any decisions made are not based on different interpretations of the facts. This is where standards, training, or the use of shared databases come into play.

REFERENCES

Malone, T.W. and Crowston, K. (1990) 'What is co-ordination theory and how can it help design cooperative work systems?', *CSCW 90 Proceedings*, ACM: 357–370.

Mintzberg, H. (1983) *Structure in Fives: Designing Effective Organizations*. Upper Saddle River, NJ: Prentice-Hall.

Planning and Control

> *Planning is the organisational process which is used to set, discuss, validate, adopt and revise goals and objectives.*
>
> *Control is a feedback process through which operations managers adjust their plans, actions and knowledge.*

PLANNING AND CONTROL AT WORK

Figure 5 illustrates planning and control in action. It shows that planning is a *feedforward* process (the downward arrows in Figure 5), whereby operations managers attempt to anticipate the future, design adequately co-ordinated operations systems, and efficiently utilise these systems.

Organisations attain their goals through *controlled performance*: this means that organisations use control processes to verify that plans are being followed or that adequate actions are being taken in the opposite case. Control is a *feedback* process (indicated by the upward looping arrows in Figure 5). Although control sometimes carries a negative connotation – as for example when thinking of control as surveillance or control as a lack of trust – it is important to note that in operations management, as in systems theory, control is a positive mechanism: it is a way to highlight issues, to trigger analysis, to learn, and to stimulate the improvement of operations systems. It shows that the desire to anticipate future needs and demands is what drives organisations to plan. At a corporate level, understanding future demand has two dimensions:

- Future demand should be estimated qualitatively, that is in terms of the future specifications of the product and services which will be demanded. This is one of the responsibilities of the marketing function.
- Understanding future demand quantitatively is a general corporate concern which is addressed through forecasting (see **Forecasting**).

Given an estimate of future demand, operations managers then apply their know-how of the business to set goals for their operations systems and select the resources that they will need to attain these goals. When the plan focuses on the timing of actions to implement, this is referred to as a schedule. When the plan incorporates cost elements, this refers to a budget.

A plan is basically a structured presentation of how a goal will be attained. Who will do what, and when? What technologies will be used? How will production be gradually increased? Will learning curve effects lead to automatic increases in productivity? These are only a few examples of the numerous questions which have to be answered in planning.

Once a plan is completed, it is communicated to all interested parties so that during the execution everyone in an organisation will know when action is needed and how different actions fit together.

There are two mechanisms by which the difficulty of producing realistic plans can be addressed. First, planning is usually a group rather than an individual process: because of the breadth of knowledge required, it is necessary to tap into the expertise of several specialists rather than one individual. Second, planning is an iterative process: in (common) cases where planning is very complex, a first plan is produced and executed. A first plan, designed using a blank piece of paper, is generally unlikely to be very good. By monitoring its execution, operations managers can discover where the plan is going wrong, understand why this is so, and decide what they should do about it.

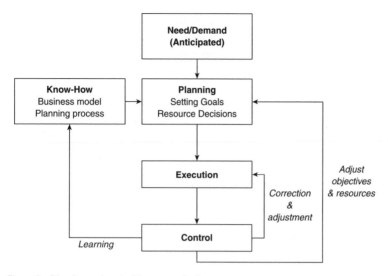

Figure 5   Planning and control in an organisation

It is through effective control systems that operations managers can:

- Detect that the plan is not being followed and take immediate corrective action.
- Appreciate that the goals are unrealistic or the resources inadequate; again corrective actions can be implemented.
- Learn that the planning data (or assumptions) were erroneous and need to be improved.

MATCHING DEMAND WITH SUPPLY

Planning and control are not the sole responsibility of operations managers. Within organisations, all business functions play a role in the planning and control cycle depicted in Figure 5. Accountants, human resource managers, and marketers all have to plan and control both within their departments and across their organisation. Each business function, however, focuses its planning and control processes on its specialist area. For example, accounting and finance departments focus on planning and controlling for funds and profitability.

The operations function's prime planning and control concern is to make sure that the organisation can match demand with supply. As operations managers are ultimately responsible for the design and operation of a firm's resources, they are also responsible for making sure that these resources deliver products and services of the right specifications, to the right customer, at the right time.

PLANNING HORIZONS

A common distinction, made in all planning disciplines, is to differentiate the nature of planning and control activities on the basis of planning horizons (Anthony, 1965).

Long-term planning is concerned with the distant future. In general, long-term planning means planning for the next two to ten years. What constitutes the 'long term' is a function of the operating cycle of an industry. For example, in the car industry new models are released every three years, whereas major platform redesigns occur about every five to seven years. In the forestry industry, exploitation cycles can be very long: in Northern Europe the growth cycle of pine trees is about twenty years, whereas hardwood species need one hundred years between plantation and harvest. Thus, forestry planning tends to be based on much longer time horizons than most industrial sectors.

Long-term planning is also often called *strategic planning*, as it focuses on declining the strategy and long-term goals of the organisation into quantitative plans. At this level, demand is estimated as an aggregate. A computer manufacturer will estimate the number of computers to be sold (without detailing the exact models or version which will be sold), or it may set target sales for key models (but still exclude some versions). Similarly a consulting firm will estimate its total hours to be sold, without decomposing the hours in key types of consulting products. In operations management, strategic planning is achieved through **operations strategy**, system design and resource decisions.

Medium-term planning, or *tactical planning*, is concerned with planning for the next six to 24 months. Key resources are now fixed: it is impossible, for example, to double the capacity of a factory in six months. Strategic planning (the past decision made about capacity) *constrains* medium-term planning. It is within the perimeters of existing resources that managers must match expected demand. The strategic stage sets an average capacity level in units per month. Based on market observations, economic conditions and between months variations (seasonality), managers now have to come up with *tactics* to match demand. In accounting, medium-term planning is often called *management control* to highlight that it is a phase where managers adjust objectives and resources, or correct the execution, on the basis of evolving market conditions. In operations management, medium-term planning is called *aggregate production planning* (APP).

Finally, *short-term planning* deals with planning and control activities for the next six to 12 months. The output of short-term planning is a schedule which is often broken down into very detailed specifications of future activities per month, per week, per day, and eventually per hour. At this level, plans are prepared on the basis of completely disaggregated data. Plans are still constrained by the decisions which were made at the strategic and tactical level. Control is a key activity, as it is needed to detect departures from the plan and to direct the attention of managers onto those areas that need immediate action.

PLANNING FLEXIBILITY

What happens, in the hierarchical planning process described above, if one of the high-level strategic decisions turns out to be a mistake? As discussed above, control mechanisms are here to detect non-conformance to the plan and to trigger corrective managerial actions.

However, adjustments are only possible to a certain extent. For example, corrective actions may not able to reverse the negative consequences of having invested in the wrong resource. To avoid those situations, planning can be improved by considering the concepts of *robustness* and *options*.

Driouchi et al. (2009) describe robustness analysis as the process of distinguishing within a resource decision:

- The part of the decision which has to be made now.
- The further decisional options which can be made at a later time.

Their recommendation is to select the now-decisions which, when analysed in several different likely futures, can offer advantageous decisional options to address potential future problems. A robust decision is one which leads to satisfactory outcomes in all possible futures.

The **real options** approach requires planners to consider all the managerial options associated with the acquisition of a resource. Can the project be abandoned? Can the project be postponed? Through financial valuation techniques, the resource with the highest option value is the one that offers the most flexibility, and thus, the one that should be preferred in contexts were uncertainty and variability are high.

REFERENCES

Anthony, R.N. (1965) *Planning and Control Systems: A Framework for Analysis.* Cambridge, MA: Harvard Business School Division of Research.

Driouchi, T., Leseure, M. and Bennett, D. (2009) 'A robustness framework for monitoring real options under uncertainty', *Omega*, 37: 698–710.

Integration

> *Integration is the capability of providing a real time seamless co-ordination of processes within operations systems.*

INTEGRATION SYSTEMS: FUNCTION AND FORM

Integration is a technology for **co-ordination**: the challenge of integration is to make sure that plans are executed smoothly, that any supporting information is exchanged at the right time without distortions, and that deviations from the plan are detected instantly, reported, and then acted upon. In the context of modern operations management, examples of high-level integration are best described through *Enterprise Resource Planning* (ERP) systems, which are large-scale, organisation-wide, information systems. They are the result of the parallel evolution of two distinct types of systems.

On the one hand, ERPs are planning and resource allocation systems: as such these are similar in function to operations management systems such as **Material Requirements Planning** systems (MRP) and Manufacturing Planning Resource (MRP II) systems. MRP II systems, in addition to planning work orders, 'book' manufacturing resources to make sure that a plan is always feasible in practice. However, MRP II systems only produce plans for the use of manufacturing resources and do not address planning in other areas: will sufficient distribution capacity be in place to distribute the manufactured products? Through the same principles behind the design of MRP II systems, logistical managers will build and use a Distribution Resource Planning (DRP) system, but the two systems are often used separately, i.e. they are not integrated.

On the other hand, information managers can recognise the loss of efficiency incurred when operating stand-alone information systems. The accounting department, for example, may be able to produce better budgets if it had real-time access to the plans in the MRPII system. Similarly, the logistical function would benefit from accessing the MRPII system, as would the marketing function in order to produce better marketing plans.

ERP systems are information systems designed to integrate on a real-time basis the planning and management of all organisational resources under one unique system. When any organisational department creates a resource, or plans to acquire one, the entire organisation is immediately made aware of this decision. ERP systems cut through functional boundaries and also through hierarchical boundaries, as they are designed to support simultaneously the needs of staff, line managers, middle managers, and top managers.

Key leaders in the ERP industry are SAP, Oracle, PeopleSoft, Siebel, and Bann. As ERP systems truly integrate all functional areas together, implementing an ERP is a large-scale project. The typical cost of implementing a full ERP solution for a large organisation requires a few million Euros in hardware, about 30 million Euros in software, and at least 200 and up to 500 million in consulting fees. Why this high cost of implementation? Consider what an ERP does: it links together all the resource decisions across an organisation. This means that before implementing an ERP, all organisational members need to agree on the common processes by which they can make resource decisions. Tchokogue et al. (2005) have documented an example of an implementation project at Pratt & Whitney Canada, and have stressed the organisational redesign which is necessary to achieve coherence and rigour across an organisation. Typically, organisations which do not have well integrated processes will experience major difficulties, or failures, at the implementation stage.

ERP AND PROCESS MANAGEMENT

Take the example of a firm where cost accounting and manufacturing processes have historically been separated. Manufacturing and accounting may have an ongoing dispute about estimates of production costs and they may use two different sets of cost formulas to guide their decision making. This is a typical scenario for an organisation with non-integrated processes. This means that an interfacing process should be designed, so that both functions can adequately feed data and information to each other. This is where ERP consultants come in. Their task is to map all the existing processes and to identify any gaps, redundancies and inconsistencies in this organisational-level process map. Once a reliable and effective process map is finalised, it can be formalised within the ERP system.

Some ERP consultants will go further and explain to clients that they are not purchasing an integrated information system, but a best-in-class set of processes. ERP consultants, through their various customers, can end up with a very good exposure to the variety of processes used by all competing firms within an industry. As such, it is easy for them to discover superior processes and to recommend these to firms in the same, or another, industries.

ERP: OPERATIONS MANAGEMENT ISSUES

We have already seen that ERP systems deal with planning for resources and with designing the best processes for the utilisation of these resources: resource planning and process management are two central areas of operations management, and thus, the ERP-enabled organisation will have a great degree of its operations expertise embedded into their ERP system.

Beyond the question of process choice and planning capability, an often overlooked aspect of an ERP system is its natural control capability. An ERP system includes a detailed specification of all the work processes within a firm. For example, when a sales office accepts an order into the system, information about that order is passed immediately to accounting and production. When a production schedule is established information flows back to accounting and sales. When production is launched, this is entered into the system. When it is completed, this is again captured in the system, and all relevant parties are informed of its completion. This high level of real-time process visibility would be difficult, if not impossible, to achieve without an ERP system. Therefore, in addition to its planning capability, an ERP system is also an extremely powerful monitoring and control device. Control is an important step by which managers can address emerging problems and learn how to improve their plans, and therefore, one should expect that an ERP system would improve an organisation's responsiveness, synchronisation of actions, and planning skills.

At a management level, the large (integrated) databases that ERP systems use have also changed the degree to which real-time *detailed* information is available. In a traditional non-integrated information system architecture, the conventional wisdom was that line managers would work from detailed data and prepare summary reports. Middle managers would then work from the summary reports and prepare their own performance reports displaying only key performance indicators. These reports would then be sent to top managers. Not only can this reporting and aggregation of data be automated through an ERP system but also top managers then have the possibility of 'drilling down' onto detailed data at the click of the mouse to understand the root cause of a disappointing value for a performance indicator. For example, a top manager at the headquarters of a large multinational with 25 factories across the globe is now able to drill down to daily or hourly production and quality data from all those factories. Without an ERP, obtaining this type of data could have taken weeks.

Although the potential benefits of ERP from an operations performance perspective are impressive on paper, a word of caution is still necessary. Trott and Hoecht (2004) question the potential impact of the implementation of a rigid ERP system on innovation capabilities. They stress that limiting options to those available through a 'pull-down' menu could be very limiting in creative work environments. Similarly, Lengnick-Hall et al. (2004) consider that many of the claims from ERP vendors are overstated. Although they recognise that ERP systems may be a necessity in order to co-ordinate very large and dispersed operations networks, they also argue that the capabilities attached to an ERP are not by themselves sufficient to guarantee that a firm will achieve a top competitive position in its industry. Their conclusion is that ERPs provide a platform for increasing social and intellectual capital but that in order to achieve a long-term competitive advantage, firms should do four things:

- Apply leverage to ERP connections to enhance the structural, relational, and cognitive dimensions of their social capital.
- Use their social capital to build their intellectual capital and thereby have a superior base of knowledge with which to compete.
- Be able to transform their ERP systems to conform to new insights or changes in the social system.
- Be able to transform their ERP systems to accommodate new avenues for competitive value that originate beyond current operations.

REFERENCES

Lengnick-Hall, C.A., Lengnick-Hall, M.L. and Abdinnour-Helm, S. (2004) 'The role of social and intellectual capital in achieving competitive advantage through enterprise resource planning systems', *Journal of Engineering Technology Management*, 21: 307–330.

Tchokogue, A., Bareil, C. and Duguay, C. (2005) 'Key lessons from the implementation of an ERP at Pratt & Whitney Canada', *International Journal of Production Economics*, 95: 151–163.

Trott, P. and Hoecht, A. (2004) 'Entreprise resource planning and the price of efficiency: the trade-off between business efficiency and the innovative capabilities of firms', *Technology Analysis and Strategic Management*, 16(3): 367–379.

Risk

> *Risk is the set of events and consequences, foreseeable or not, that occur, within or beyond the boundaries of an operations system, in reaction to the implementation of a plan of action.*

RISK MANAGEMENT

Industrial engineering has always included in its subject matter the subject of product reliability and of product liability. At the moment *risk management* has become a 'hot' topic in business studies, a topic which has grown quickly especially in the field of finance. Simply put, *modern risk management is concerned with organisational exposure to volatility*. For example, a manufacturer may suffer from fluctuating raw materials prices, or a banker may suffer from fluctuating default rates on loans.

Operations management, quite surprisingly, has never been overly concerned with risk, at least from a theoretical perspective. There is indeed the industrial engineering heritage of product reliability and product liability, but these topics are often overlooked by lecturers and are not under the spotlight in operations management circles. This decline of product-related risk topics may be explained by the fact that the technical origins of operations management meant that a lot of operations management theory has been primarily concerned with optimisation. Optimisation can take into account uncertainty, as for example when we add a safety stock (a probabilistic estimate) to an optimal inventory ordering policy. Lewis (2003) was the first operations management scholar to highlight that this variance approach to risk management is an oversight of operations management as a discipline. A safety stock gives a certain level of confidence that an organisation will not run short of inventory. However, it does not tell us what that organisation will do if it actually happens to run short of inventory. As Lewis (2003) points out, this later concern is more akin to a service quality problem, and represents the type of reflection that all operations managers should engage in.

A MODEL OF OPERATIONAL RISK

In order to address the limited coverage of risk issues in operations management, Lewis (2003) uses four case studies to validate and improve a model of operational risk. The key elements of his model are causes, consequences, and control.

Causes are the events that can take place and have an impact on the performance of an operations system. Causes can be external or internal to an organisation. Lewis's research shows that causes are rarely independent and unique events. The failure of an operations system is more often explained by a chain reaction of events, which when taken together will cause an operational failure. Reconstructing or forecasting these possible chain reactions is an important aspect of risk management. Consequences are the outcomes of the causes. Lewis's case studies show that such consequences are dynamic rather than static, i.e. they evolve over time: a consequence may lead to more consequences later on. Finally, consequences will affect a variety of stakeholders as these can be internal (e.g., a machine breakdown) or external (e.g., they can have an impact on the customer, the parties connected to the customer, or other parties such as the local community).

Controls are the mechanisms that operations managers can use to implement a risk management initiative. Lewis (2003) distinguishes three types of control: *ex-ante*, in process, and *post-ex*. *Ex-ante* controls are preventive risk management controls. They try to anticipate the occurrence of risky situations. The use of safety stock for inventory, design validating schemes such as value engineering and failure mode effect analysis (FMEA), the project risk analysis management (PRAM) framework, the use of options thinking (see **Real Options**), quality assurance certifications, and suppliers audits are all examples of *ex-ante* controls.

In-process controls are mechanisms to address a risk occurring live in an operation system. As it is too late to prevent the risk event, the purpose becomes to mitigate the potential negative consequences of that event. The inspection of incoming goods is an example of an in-process mechanism. Switching options is another example. A switching option gives a facility the possibility of switching inputs (for example, for a cheaper raw material), processes (for example, for a factory where favourable exchange rate conditions increase cost efficiency), or outputs (for example, the ability to stop producing a low demand item to produce a more popular item). Operational policies should incorporate guidelines for dealing with incidents such as fires, earthquakes, or other catastrophes having an impact on the operations of an organisation.

Finally, *post-ex* mechanisms correspond to the notion of service recovery in service quality management. The concept of service recovery can be extended to potentially more serious interventions such as a product recall or the abandonment of a project. An important area for *post-ex* mechanisms is *disaster recovery*.

REFERENCE

Lewis, M. (2003) 'Cause, consequence and control; towards a theoretical and practical model of operational risk', *Journal of Operations Management*, 21: 205–224.

Theory

key concepts in operations management

Theories are tools composed of a set of laws used to make sense of a phenomenon.

THEORY IN OPERATIONS MANAGEMENT

Schmenner and Swink (1998), among others, are two authors who have expressed concerns about the apparent lack of theory in operations management. However, they suggest that operations management researchers may have been too harsh on themselves as an examination of the operations management literature reveals a number of extant theories. The purpose of this section is to discuss two theoretical aspects of operations management. First, we discuss how operations management research uses, informs and complements economic theories. Then we draw up an inventory of operations management theories and indicate under which concepts they are discussed.

OPERATIONS MANAGEMENT AND ECONOMIC THEORY

In concept 1, we have developed a theory of operations management starting from Coase's theory of the firm. It is important to realise that in economics, there is not one unique theory of the firm. Over the years, economists have instead developed several 'theories of the firm'. These theories are presented in the following sub-sections. In each case, we indicate their relationship to operations management research.

The neo-classical theory of the firm

This theory is behind the standard view of the firm as a form of economic organisation seeking to maximise profitability. Kantarelis (2007) summarises the neo-classical theory of the firm by explaining that from the study of demand and supply functions, the theory makes predictions about the behaviour of markets and identifies optimal strategies for firms. Although this theory treats the firm as a 'black box', it describes many phenomena, such as economies of scale and economies of scope, which are central to many operations management decisions (such as operations strategy and capacity decisions). Moreover, it is because of that fact that the neo-classical theory of the firm treats the firm as a black box that operations management, a discipline which concentrates on the system within the box, can inform and enrich economics.

The managerial theory of the firm

The key contribution of this school is *agency theory*, where the differences between the principals (owners) and agents (managers) of the firm are explicitly recognised. Theories of contracting are important in this area and a lot of the research in **supply chain** management is based on agency theory.

The behavioural theory of the firm

Formulated by Cyert and March (1963), the behavioural theory of the firm challenges the neo-classical view and points out that managers have neither the omniscience nor the time to maximise the profits of the firm. In practice, managers have to act on incomplete information and instead of optimising they spend their time *searching* for better solutions and improvements. Instead of being the exercise of rational decision making, managerial decisions are the result of group behaviour. Powell and Johnson (1980) were the first to question the lack of behavioural variables in operations management research. They proposed an expectancy-equity model of productive system performance to show how behaviour variables can be taken into account. More recently, Bendoly et al. (2006) argued that the theory–practice gap in operations management is often explained by behavioural issues (how people perceive, react, and work in the workplace). Their literature review provides a summary of twenty years of research about behavioural operations management.

Transaction cost theory

Transaction cost theory (Williamson, 1985), the direct extension of Coase's ideas about the nature of the firm, deals with the choice of a mode of governance for economic transactions. Three alternatives for governance exist:

- Hierarchical governance: Where a firm prefers to internalise the production of an asset.
- Market governance: Where a firm prefers to rely on the price mechanism and market forces to source a product.
- The hybrid governance mode: Where a firm enters into a partnership or joint-venture with its supplier to secure the provision of an asset.

Transaction cost theory plays an important role in process strategy when operations managers are asked whether or not a process should be outsourced (see **Outsourcing**). Similarly, transaction cost theory plays an important role in understanding **supply chain** relationships.

Evolutionary theory of the firm

Departing from the static view of the firm in the neo-classical view, this theory holds that firms hold capabilities allowing them to deploy their resources in competitive markets. This means that in a response to change firms may design new capabilities (e.g. new processes) which will create entirely new economic sectors and industries.

Evolutionary matters are dealt with at two levels in operations management. At a practical level, a number of operations management concepts are about innovation and change (see **Innovation Management, Process Management** and **Kaizen**). At a theoretical level, the theory of evolution can be used to explain past changes and the current conditions within an industry structure. For example, Leseure (2000) presents the evolutionary history of operations management systems in the hand tools industry and its implication on manufacturing strategies.

THEORIES IN OPERATIONS MANAGEMENT

Key theories in operations management are:

- The theory of **operations** management.
- **System** theory.
- Contact theory (see **Customers**).
- **Co-ordination** theory.
- The theory of performance frontiers (see **Trade-offs**).
- The theory of swift, even flow (see **Just-in-Time Inventory**).
- The theory of constraints (see **Throughput**).

REFERENCES

Bendoly, E., Donohue, K. and Schultz, K. (2006) 'Behavior in operations management: assessing recent findings and revisiting old assumptions', *Journal of Operations Management*, 24: 737–752.

Coase, R. (1937) 'The nature of the firm', *Economica*, 4(16): 386–405.

Cyert, R.M. and March, J.G. (1963) *A Behavioral Theory of the Firm*. Englewood Cliffs, NJ: Prentice-Hall.

Kantarelis, D. (2007) *Theories of the Firm* (2nd edition). Geneva: Inderscience.

Leseure, M. (2000) 'Manufacturing strategies in the hand tool industry', *International Journal of Production and Operations Management*, 20(12): 1475–1489.

Powell, G. and Johnson, G. (1980) 'An expectancy-equity model of productive system performance', *Journal of Operations Management*, 1(1): 47–56.

Schmenner, R. and Swink, M. (1998) 'On theory in operations management', *Journal of Operations Management*, 17: 97–113.

Williamson, O. (1985) *The Economic Institution of Capitalism: Firms, Markets and Relational Contracting*. New York: Free.

Operations Strategy

Performance

Performance management is the managerial task concerned with identifying performance targets, communicating them, and making sure that
these targets are achieved.

INTERNAL VERSUS EXTERNAL PERFORMANCE

Organisational performance is difficult to manage because managers
only partially control those factors by which markets will assess a
firm's performance. Figure 6 makes a distinction between internal and
external performance. Managers can exert direct control over internal
performance measures: by investing, training, staffing, and motivating,
they can improve performance along one of the internal dimensions. In
contrast, the external performance of a firm is assessed by several different and independent parties through a process of value perception (see
Customers).

The internal performance of an operations system has traditionally
been described along five dimensions:

- *Cost*: Refers to the ability of an operations system to deliver an output at minimum cost. This may be achieved by offering a 'no-frills'
  product or by targeting a lower cost than competitors, given a certain
  quality standard (value for money).
- *Quality*: Refers to the ability of an operations system to deliver
  an output of a higher quality than a competitor's. This can be
  achieved either by offering an output with specifications which
  perfectly match the customer specifications ('fitness for use') or by
  offering an output that exceeds customer expectations ('delighting
  the customer').
- *Dependability of delivery*: Refers to the ability of an operations system
  to deliver an output to a customer on a due date.
- *Speed*: Refers to the ability of an operations system to deliver an output faster than a competitor, or in a short time frame which matches
  a customer's requirements.

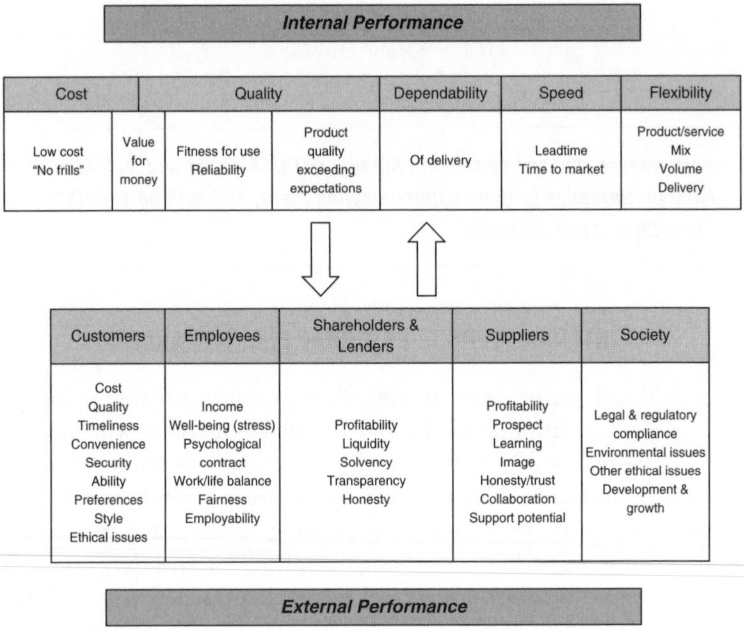

Cost		Quality		Dependability	Speed	Flexibility
Low cost "No frills"	Value for money	Fitness for use Reliability	Product quality exceeding expectations	Of delivery	Leadtime Time to market	Product/service Mix Volume Delivery

Customers	Employees	Shareholders & Lenders	Suppliers	Society
Cost Quality Timeliness Convenience Security Ability Preferences Style Ethical issues	Income Well-being (stress) Psychological contract Work/life balance Fairness Employability	Profitability Liquidity Solvency Transparency Honesty	Profitability Prospect Learning Image Honesty/trust Collaboration Support potential	Legal & regulatory compliance Environmental issues Other ethical issues Development & growth

External Performance

Figure 6   Internal vs. external performance

- *Flexibility*: Refers to the ability of an operations system to vary its outputs as demand dictates. Note that flexibility is both a performance measure and a capability (contrast this, for example, with efficiency – a capability which is used to achieve cost performance; see **Flexibility** for a discussion of the two facets of flexibility).

DYNAMICS OF PERFORMANCE MANAGEMENT

Figure 6 presents a static view of internal and external performance. In reality, the difficulty of aligning internal performance with external performance is compounded by the fact that market dynamics are far more volatile than resource dynamics. In most industrialised economies, competitors will introduce new products and higher levels of service on a permanent basis. Customer preferences and their spending habits can change with fashions, the weather, political and economic conditions. There are hundreds of variables at play, and all can contribute to an extremely dynamic, volatile, or turbulent market.

Unfortunately for managers, this is not the case for the acquisition and assimilation of new resources. New employees may need lengthy and expensive training before they can interact with customers. A new technology may take up to a year before it is fully deployed in a production system and several years before it generates financial returns.

This fundamental 'clock differential', which is illustrated in Figure 7, is explained by the fact that investments in resources are what economists call *commitments*. A commitment is an action by which a party commits itself in the long run. For example, by building a factory with a large capacity (i.e. by having a lot of excess capacity when compared to current demand) managers commit themselves to capture a large market share of a forecasted market. If the company eventually fails to secure this large market share, then it will have to operate its large under-utilised facility at a loss.

How can managers cope with, on the one hand, fast evolving markets and demand patterns, and on the other hand, internal systems which are slow and difficult to change and demand various commitments to achieve a minimum level of financial returns?

As shown in Figure 7, there are two solutions to this dilemma. The first solution is to develop strategic insight (i.e. the ability to build accurate forecasts of the evolution of a market in the future): this is the scope of *strategic management*. Its purpose is to direct and guide the firm toward a long-term strategic target. The resulting strategic intent is then used by top managers to reduce the uncertainty that a firm has to tackle, as resource decisions become an application of strategic directives.

However, hoping that strategic management alone is sufficient represents a leap of faith. Strategic insight and omniscience are two different things. This is why strategic insight needs to be coupled with management actions seeking to improve the *adaptability* of the firm. Adaptability is the ability of a system to evolve, more or less promptly and at a reasonable cost, when faced with complex and turbulent demand patterns (Katayama and Bennett, 1999). Adaptability, therefore, refers to the flexibility with which a firm can deploy, re-combine, and modify its resources to fit evolving needs. For example, assume that a company suddenly discovers that its strategic intent needs to be fundamentally changed as it was based on a faulty understanding of market requirements. If the firm's resources cannot be quickly reconfigured, it could be forced out of business.

Thus, strategic management and dynamic resource management are two distinct mechanisms used to better cope with the differences

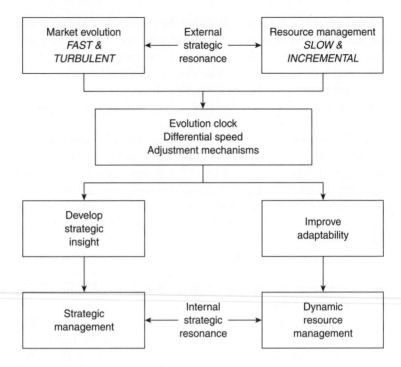

Figure 7   Managing long-term performance

between rapidly evolving business environments and slowly evolving internal resources. These should not work against each other, but should each contribute to facilitate the alignment of resources with market requirements.

When resources are aligned with market requirements, the firm is said to be in *strategic resonance*. Burgelman and Grove (1996) developed a framework to help managers deal with *strategic dissonance*, i.e. a situation where resources and requirements are not aligned. They identified two root causes of strategic dissonance:

- Divergence of the basis of competition and distinctive competence: This corresponds to the external strategic resonance arrow at the top of Figure 7. It means that resources, which form the firm's distinctive competences, are not aligned with those of its competitors that achieve a high external performance.

- Divergence between stated strategy and strategic action: This can be either because of a difference in timing (e.g. a strategy is to slow, or introduced too early, or resources do not follow) or because there is some dissent within the firm about the strategic intent or how resources should be combined. This corresponds to the internal strategic resonance arrow in Figure 7.

REFERENCES

Burgelman, R. and Grove, A. (1996) 'Strategic dissonance', *California Management Review*, 38(2): 8–28.

Katayama, H. and Bennett, D. (1999) 'Agility, adaptability, and leanness: a comparison of concepts and a study of practice', *International Journal of Production Economics*, 60–61: 43–51.

Operations Strategy

> *Operations strategy is the functional strategy derived from corporate strategy by which operations managers make sure that an operations system's resources are aligned with market and financial requirements.*

The purpose of this section is to focus on the content of operations strategy, i.e. the different decisions which need to be made. It also presents the various tools and techniques which are used to assist operations managers in making these decisions.

POSITIONING DECISIONS

Positioning decisions are concerned with internal performance objectives rather than resource investment decisions. External performance targets will typically be specified by the marketing function, but they might also be specified in terms which are difficult to translate into operations decisions.

operations strategy

Consider the example of a firm specialising in the design and manufacture of customised capital goods. This firm provides a specialist design service for capital goods which typically will be sold in 1, 2, or 3 units maximum, but which constitute, in all cases, a one-off project. Imagine that the marketing department has held focus groups with customers, and has found that they felt that the firm was systematically over-pricing. Thus, marketing could suggest to designers, engineers and project managers to use lower quality parts or adopt any other way to reduce costs. The operations people may reply to this suggestion that one-off projects are risky and expensive projects, and that they should not be compared with the purchase of standardised capital goods, a comparison which is often erroneously made by customers within this industry. Designing customised capital goods is an example of a product flexibility strategy: the firm's core competence is to design capital goods which have never been designed before. This demands resources which are not necessarily compatible with the notion of competing on cost. This is an example of a *strategic trade-off* (Da Silveira and Slack, 2001), i.e. of the idea that a firm can compete on one or a combination of a few internal performance dimensions, but not on all of them. Such a trade-off is illustrated in Figure 8.

Figure 8 shows that to increase cost performance, the firm should accept that it will have to decrease its flexibility, as it is impossible to achieve both high flexibility and low cost. Thus it is important that, given external performance targets, operations managers agree on what are the adequate targets of internal performance. Three techniques can be used to help managers make these positioning decisions.

1 Hill's (1989) *order-winning* and *order-qualifier* framework: For example, if the firm agrees that flexibility is an order-winner and cost an order-qualifier (i.e. an order is placed because the firm is able to provide a unique product, the cost has to be reasonable, but it is not a decisive variable), then cost reduction requests should be dismissed. Conversely, if the firm agrees that flexibility is an order-qualifier and cost an order-winner, the marketing feedback demands immediate action and a re-alignment of resources.

2 A second method is to prioritise the performance dimensions to communicate clearly within the firm which objectives take precedence over others. An example is provided in Figure 9. The figure should be interpreted as follows: the company needs to provide a minimum level of facilitating services (e.g. certification process, production launching assistance, provision of a users' manual) and

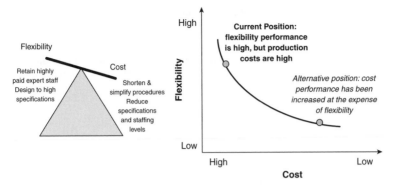

Figure 8   The flexibility–cost trade-off in capital goods design

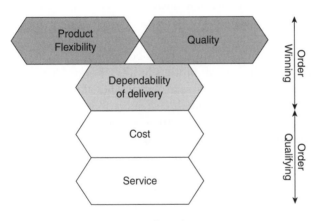

Figure 9   Priority hierarchy of performance dimensions

should keep costs within a certain bracket to enter the pool of competitive suppliers. Orders are won by the unique combination of high flexibility and high quality and the company will always avoid trading-off one for the other. Instead, it prefers to invest in additional resources to maintain this positioning. Dependability of delivery is important, but a secondary priority when compared with flexibility and quality. Thus resources improving quality and flexibility will always be preferred to resources improving dependability.

3 The final method to better understand trade-offs is to prepare *positioning tables*, i.e. to display in a table how a company and its competitors are positioned in terms of a trade-off involving two pairs of performance objectives. Table 2 provides an example.

Table 2 Example of a positioning table

		Flexibility/dependability of trade-off		
		Preference for flexibility	Balanced approach	Preference for dependability
Flexibility/quality trade-off	Preference for flexibility	C1, C2	C4, C5	C6
	Balanced approach	*Our Company*		C7
	Preference for quality	C3	C8	Not viable

Table 2 shows that the company's strategy has been to maintain a balanced approach between maintaining an activity of one-off projects (flexibility) with high quality. In terms of their ability to handle a truly unique project, competitors C1 and C2 would be more convincing, but the quality of their output will always be lower. In terms of offering the ultimate quality for one-off projects firm C3 is better positioned, but it has had a tendency to specialise in certain types of projects to offer such high quality levels. Therefore, if customers seek the best compromise between the ability to manage a truly one-off project and guaranteeing high quality levels, that company would win an order.

Table 2 is a useful guide for managers to give the direction in which the company should evolve. For example, there are no competitors in the centre cell of the table. Moving to this cell could be a winning strategy if a market exists for this positioning.

RESOURCE DECISIONS

Once a consensus has been reached about internal performance targets and about the extent to which a trade-off exists between these targets, operations managers will commit funds to developing certain resources. The different types of resource decisions that need to be made are those that correspond to the categories presented in the **System** section: inventory, plant and equipment, and intellectual capital. Investing in resources which correspond to physical assets is often called a *structural decision*. Deciding about developing the knowledge and experience of using structural resources is called an *infrastructural decision*. Infrastructural decisions are those related to the different components of intellectual capital: human capital, innovation capital, process capital, and relationship capital.

Table 3 gives a few examples of resource decisions, along with the types of decision variables which could be used to make these. There are several points about resource decisions which should be stressed:

- Resource decisions are broad and touch on all aspects of an operations system. It should be borne in mind that resource decisions are *strategic decisions*, i.e. they represent a form of commitment. This means that once made, they are difficult, costly, and sometimes impossible to reverse. For example, the decision to hire one additional welder for three months due to a peak in demand is a short-term resource adjustment operational decision. The decision to hire an additional welder on a fixed term contract of three years is a tactical resource adjustment decision. Only the decision to hire an additional welder on a permanent contract is a strategic human capital resource adjustment decision.
- The larger the commitment made, the less reversible the decision is. This non-reversibility is what economists call *path dependency*. Once the decision to build a large capacity factory has been made, a company has no other option but to gain a large market share in order to keep the factory utilised and profitable.
- There is great degree of interdependence between all resource decisions. For example, a facility location decision can be 'tied' to a human capital decision. Consider the example of an automotive manufacturer which has decided to build an assembly plant in Europe and has also made the decision that its new employees should have prior experience. Their investment is more likely to be in the UK's West Midlands, the north-east of France, or the north of Italy, regions known as the heartland of this industry, and thus, which will provide the desired labour pool.
- This degree of interdependence means that resource decisions cannot be considered to be one-off isolated decisions. Resource decisions form consistent patterns which are called *configurations*. A configuration of resources means a pattern of resources which is consistent across the board: there is a high degree of compatibility, or *fit*, between the different decisions that have been made.
- The techniques which are used to make the decisions can be very different in practice. In some cases the decision may be an optimisation

Table 3 Example of resource decisions

Type of resource	Type of decision	Description	Decision variable
Inventory	Stock level	How much inventory should be held?	Rate of stock withdrawal Cost of holding inventory Cost of stockout Cost of ordering
	Location of inventory in the value chain.	Where should inventory be located along the supply chain?	Demand variability
Plant & equipment	Location decision	Where should facilities be located?	Costs: labour, transportation Many others
	Capacity	What output level should be targeted?	Expected demand Economies of scale
	Replacement	Should we keep or replace a machine?	Cost Evolution of technology
	Own or operating lease	Should the or lease its productive assets?	Cost of lease Cost of self-maintenance
Process capital	Purchasing management	How should purchasing be organised? Which procedures should be used?	Location of facilities and suppliers Costs Risk of fraud and theft

problem, as for example inventory decisions where the objective is to minimise the total costs associated with inventory. In other cases, the decisions are made after a cost/benefit analysis. In the simplest scenario, a straight comparison of benefits against costs is sufficient, whereas in other cases discounted cash flow techniques such as the Net Present Value method (NPV) are used. Finally, the decision could require the use of decision analysis techniques to structure this, for example influence diagrams or decision trees.

RECONCILIATION DECISION

The decision variable column in Table 3 below shows that demand patterns, predictability, and variability are key issues when making resource decisions. Slack and Lewis (2001) have developed an operations strategy matrix to help operations managers verify that all operations decisions have been made properly and competently. Figure 10 below shows an example of how this matrix is used to describe the operations strategy of a dog kennel service. It displays a number of intersections between market requirements (translated as internal performance measures) and resources. Dark coloured cells indicate those which are critical to maintaining the positioning and performance of the company: in this case the focus is on selecting staff and developing working procedures so that customers believe that their pets are receiving the same amount of attention that they would at home. In particular, maintaining excess capacity to accommodate all existing customers in periods of peak demand (e.g. Easter vacations, extended weekends), keeping track of each customer's preferences, and providing detailed feedback about how the dog behaved during its stay are essential in terms of making sure that customers will return. Although cost control issues are not insignificant, they are, given the positioning of the company, relatively secondary. Figure 10 also shows that such a service does not require much capability to innovate: this is not surprising as the service has set specifications.

BEST PRACTICES

Developing a consistent pattern of decisions which forms a viable configuration of resources resulting in a competitive proposition is a complicated task. In order to assist operations managers, many researchers and consultants have formulated *best practices*, i.e. off-the-shelf, preconfigured patterns of resource investment decisions. The idea of best practices came as part of the *world class manufacturing* programme: the idea is to observe systematically how the best competitors in the world conduct their operations, and to imitate their best practices.

Best practices which are important in operations management are:

- *Benchmarking*: The systematic analysis of competitors' (or other firms') activities and their operations systems and performance achievements. The objective is to gain ideas to improve competitiveness.
- *Reverse engineering*: The dismantling of a competitor's product to understand how it was designed.
- *Extended enterprise*: The idea of managing an entire supply chain as if it were a one single, boundary-less enterprise.

Human capital, facilities, process capital and relationship capital are the dominant resources

Quality and flexibility of service provision positions
Kennel as a caring, dog-friendly operation
Price premium is justified

	Inventory	Facilities	Human Capital	Innovation Capital	Process Capital	Relationship Capital
Quality of service		Spacious, heated individual kennels & running fields	Retain high quality staff that love dogs		Check-in procedure. Include playing time.	Demand working contact number. Remember pet's name.
Dependability Availability of service at all times		Large capacity for peak times.	Use part-time workforce			
Flexibility Towards customer's demand	Stock all types of dog food.	Use some triple & double kennels	Accommodate all demands		Use name tags, and attach instructions on to each kennel.	Retain customers preferences. Give feedback on stay.
Costs Reduce operating costs		Designed for easy cleaning & disinfection			Working procedures help control costs	

▮ Critical Intersection   ▮ Important Intersection   ▯ Secondary Issue

Figure 10   An operations strategy matrix for a dog kennel

- Other well-known best practices: Just-in-time systems, total quality management, business process re-engineering, lean thinking, agility, quick response. These best practices are discussed in later concepts.

In theory, the idea of best practices is that the task of aligning a firm's resource with top performers should be facilitated. In practice, there is ample evidence that the adoption of best practices can fail. Companies have sometimes not succeeded in capturing all the benefits that they could have expected from their investments. There is also ample empirical evidence to show that a 'one-size-fits-all' best practice does not exist. This means that companies adopting best practices should be ready to exert judgment and analysis in order to customise these to specific operational contexts.

STRATEGY CHARTS

As an operations strategy is a pattern of decisions, both its formulation and implementation processes are difficult.

To facilitate the communication of strategic intent and the implementation of a set of resource adjustment initiatives consistent with this intention, a team of researchers from the University of Cambridge have

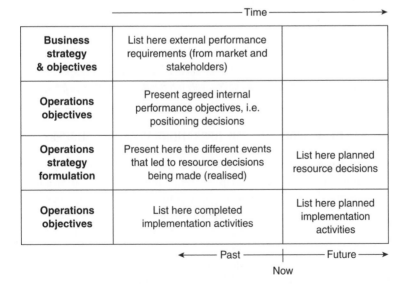

	Time →	
Business strategy & objectives	List here external performance requirements (from market and stakeholders)	
Operations objectives	Present agreed internal performance objectives, i.e. positioning decisions	
Operations strategy formulation	Present here the different events that led to resource decisions being made (realised)	List here planned resource decisions
Operations objectives	List here completed implementation activities	List here planned implementation activities

← Past ——|—— Future →
Now

Figure 11   Format of a strategy chart (adapted from Mills et al., 1998)

designed a pictorial representation tool called *strategy charts*. Figure 11 presents the typical format of a strategy chart – an updatable diagram which clearly shows how the realised strategy is justified by strategic intent.

REFERENCES

Da Silveira, G. and Slack, N. (2001) 'Exploring the trade-off concept', *International Journal of Operations and Production Management*, 21(7): 949–964.

Hill, T. (1989) Manufacturing strategy. Homewood, IL: Irwin.

Mills, J., Neely, A., Platts, K. and Gregory, M. (1998) 'Manufacturing strategy: a pictorial representation', *International Journal of Operations and Production Management*, 18(11): 1067–1085.

Slack, N. and Lewis, M. (2001) *Operations Strategy*. Englewood Cliffs, NJ: Prentice-Hall.

Operations Strategy Process

key concepts in operations management

78

> *The operations strategy process is the set of organisational processes by which many stakeholders can collectively formulate an operations strategy.*

A GENERIC MODEL OF THE OPERATIONS STRATEGY PROCESS

Figure 12 presents a generic model of the process of developing an operations strategy which is adapted from a model developed by a team of researchers from the University of Cambridge (Mills et al., 1995).

Developing an operations strategy is influenced by the external context of a firm. For example, in a hypercompetitive, rapidly evolving market, a firm will have a tendency to encourage processes which provide adaptability. Conversely, a firm operating in a stable market might decide to avoid seeking adaptability as they may question the cost/benefits of this approach. Similarly, the internal context of the firm will also influence the operations strategy process. For example, a firm which has historically relied on a top-down approach to strategy will react negatively to emergent ideas which do not come through official channels. The output of the operations strategy process is the **operations strategy** *content*, shown on the left-hand side in Figure 12.

Formulating an operations strategy is not an end of itself. To be of any value, an operations strategy should be consistent with the strategic intent of the firm and other functional strategies (e.g. an IT strategy). A degree of *fit* leads to functional strategic resonance – the fact that all functions within a firm are aligned toward one strategic purpose. A second level of fit is to align a firm's resources with market requirements: this is external strategic resonance. Finally, an operations strategy should be comprehensive, i.e. it should have covered every resource decision issue that is needed.

To summarise, Figure 12 shows that the process of formulating an operations strategy is influenced by both the internal and external contexts of the firm; that it results in a set of decisions being made about the resources of the operations system; and that these decisions should be comprehensive, internally coherent, and aligned with market requirements.

TOP-DOWN APPROACHES TO OPERATIONS STRATEGY

Historically, operations strategy was formulated with Skinner's (1969) top-down process. Skinner's model has since been adapted in a number of ways and Figure 13 below presents a consensus view of the top-down approach to operations strategy. The process begins with the definition of strategic intent by top managers. At this point, operations managers are not involved. Consistent with the market-driven view of strategy, the marketing function prepares a marketing strategy that outlines the external performance targets. At this stage, the operations function is still not involved. The operations function starts to be involved when the external performance targets, as defined by marketing, need to be converted into internal performance targets. The operations function (along with other functions) is then authorised to proceed with making the appropriate resource decisions and committing funds according to the agreed strategy.

The characteristics of this process are:

- *Point of entry*: Operations enter the strategic arena late in the process, and this entry is timed. With this type of process – associated with

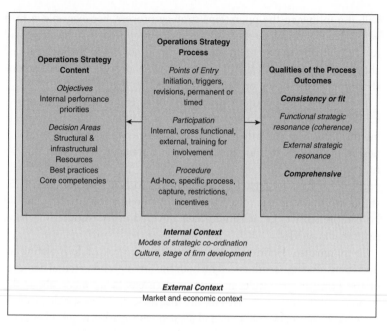

Figure 12   *A generic model of operations strategy (adapted from Mills et al., 1995)*

co-ordination meetings, the exchange of formal written documents and deadlines – the process initiation is probably infrequent, e.g. once or twice a year.

- *Participation*: This is staged and selective. The only participants are likely to be top, middle, and possibly line managers. Great emphasis is put on cross-functional participation, as the different roles of the function and the timing of interaction are planned for.
- *Procedure*: The operations strategy process is a managed sub-process of the corporate strategy implementation process. It involves stage gates and is associated with control procedures. Roles and timing tend to be specified in advance.

Another popular operations strategy framework is that developed by Hill (1989). Although essentially identical to the generic process shown in Figure 13, it possesses specific features:

- The use of order winners and order qualifiers to convert external performance targets into internal performance targets (see **Operations Strategy**).

- The suggestion that the formulation of a strategy may be an iterative process rather than a step-wise process as put forward by Figure 13. The iterativity of steps means that early decisions may have to be revised in light of implementation efforts. For example, it recognises that operations managers may encounter feasibility problems when making resource allocation decisions. Marketing demands may be 'too much' given current resources. In this case, an interaction with marketing and top management is necessary to make sure that plans and targets can be revised in a consistent fashion.

BOTTOM-UP APPROACHES TO OPERATIONS STRATEGY

In contrast with the top-down approach to strategy formulation, where strategic directions are set by top management, bottom-up strategy formulation processes recognise that employees, line managers and after-sales service representatives can all play a part in setting an operations strategy.

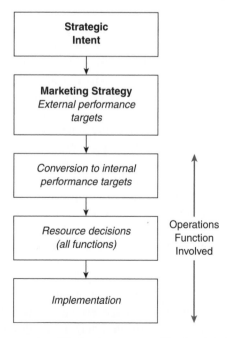

Figure 13   *A consensus view of the top-down process of functional strategy formulation*

If one takes Hill's idea of an iterative process and generalises it to the extreme, one ends up with the notion of *strategy as an iterative resource allocation*. Too much iteration, however, may be associated with chaotic and dysfunctional decision making. The purpose of bottom-up models is to show how iterations can be maximised whilst maintaining some form of structure in the strategy formulation process. Although there are several models which have been developed to describe the bottom-up approach, there is much less of a consensus view than in the case of the top-down approach.

Barnes (2002) proposed a model based on case study research in six small and medium enterprises. In addition to a top-down decision structure, the model leaves room for discoveries and adjustments to be made by all organisational levels. In other words, it combines the idea of formal strategy making with the possibility of emergent, 'discovered' strategies.

Other models of the strategy process are not necessarily specific to operations management. The Bower–Burgelman (B-B) process model (Tomo and Bower, 1996) of strategy making departs from top-down prescriptions of steps and focuses instead on the interactions between the different management layers: in particular, it highlights the role of reputation, credibility and influence in collective strategy formulation. Another model was developed by Pandza and his colleagues (2003) through case study research about three Slovenian companies. The key contribution of Pandza's model is to identify key epochs, or periods, during which specific links in a core model of capability adjustments to market requirements are more active than in other periods. For example, during an exploitation phase, the feedback from operations to the activity of adjusting capabilities is the dominant activity within an organisation. In contrast, marketing dominates organisational processes and especially the specification of market requirements during the 'initiating' phase. Finally, Weick's (1979) model of the social psychology of organising stresses the importance of group behaviour and social psychology in the discovery, formulation, selection and retention of ideas and practices.

Bottom-up models of strategy formulation share a number of common characteristics:

- *Point of entry*: There is no timed point of entry at which the strategy process should be initiated. The models suggest instead a web of permanent cycles which go through different episodes or epochs. As a self-adjusting and self-organising process, it is always at work with various degrees of amplitude. The notion of a permanent cycle does not however rule out the notion of a discrete output, e.g. the kick-off date for a new strategic initiative.

- *Participation*: This is all inclusive and self-organised. The interaction of a market-requirement voice with a resource-feedback voice is a common feature of these models. All management levels, and to some extent staff, are involved. In stark contrast with the top-down model, there is no clear-cut role prescription in these models. This is because they are all based on the notion of a participative equilibrium. Depending on the situation, participants should self-organise themselves so they can make the right decisions.

- *Procedures*: There are no set, defined and managed step-wise processes. Instead there is a collection of interlocking processes which are permanently iterating. Bottom-up models suggest the idea of a naturally-occurring cycle of sub-processes in equilibrium. Management actions and decisions are needed to maintain stability and continuity and to deal with situations of disequilibrium. Instead of making strategic decisions, the role of top management is either one of *steering* or of *troubleshooting*.

REFERENCES

Barnes, D. (2002) 'The complexities of the manufacturing strategy formation process in practice', *International Journal of Operations and Production Management*, 22(10): 1090–1111.

Hill, T. (1989) *Manufacturing Strategy*. Homewood, IL: Irwin.

Mills, J., Platts, K. and Gregory, M. (1995) 'A framework for the design of manufacturing strategy processes: a contingency approach', *International Journal of Operations & Production Management*, 15(4): 17–40.

Pandza, K., Polajnar, A., Buchmeister, B. and Thorpe, R. (2003) 'Evolutionary perspectives on the capability accumulation process', *International Journal of Operations and Production Management*, 23(8): 822–849.

Skinner, W. (1969) 'Manufacturing – the missing link in corporate strategy', *Harvard Business Review*, May–June.

Tomo, N. and Bower, J. (1996) 'Strategy making as iterated processes of resource allocation', *Strategic Management Journal*, 17: 159–192.

Weick, K. (1979) *The Social Psychology of Organising*. New York: McGraw-Hill.

operations strategy process

Trade-offs

> *A trade-off exists when an organisation cannot perform simultaneously on two performance dimensions: in order to increase performance on one performance dimension it has to decrease performance on the other dimension.*

THE STRATEGIC TRADE-OFF DEBATE

The concept of a strategic trade-off has been a controversial issue in operations management. For example, in the 1970s it was widely accepted that a cost/quality trade-off and a flexibility/cost trade-off existed in the automotive industry. Cheaper cars were of lower quality and high quality cars were expensive. Cheap cars came with no options and expensive cars had many options. This was challenged in the 1980s when markets witnessed the arrival of Japanese cars, which were available in more versions with more options, were of better quality, and were also cheaper! Needless to say, these products brought with them a dramatic level of competitive pressures for Western producers. For them, the Japanese approach was simply impossible: the previously held common wisdom was that it was not possible to perform well on *all* these performance dimensions!

For some operation managers, this was a clear message that strategic trade-offs did not exist. A famous proponent of this view is Schonberger (1996), who launched the *World Class Manufacturing* programme. The starting point here was to dismiss the idea of trade-offs. In his view, trade-offs were artificial, customary constraints put on operations managers. Instead, managers should be able to benchmark themselves with their best competitors in the world (hence, the world class label) and understand how and why they were able to perform so well. Finally, they should initiate investments to imitate the practices of world class competitors.

AVOIDING TRADE-OFFS THROUGH INNOVATION

To understand the ongoing debate about strategic trade-offs, it is important to make the distinction between a positioning decision and a *process innovation decision*.

A positioning decision is a recombination of existing resources to perform differently on a pair of performance dimensions. For example, in a high-street bank this would mean reducing staffing levels to reduce costs. The cost performance is increased, but the quality of service has been reduced (i.e. waiting time has increased).

A process innovation decision starts with the acknowledgment that the trade-off puts the company in a competitively untenable situation and that it has to devise new ways of doing things. For example, introducing state-of-the-art computer systems to assist clerks might increase their productivity to such an extent that a bank can reduce staff *and* maintain service standards. The difference between a positioning decision and a process innovation decision is illustrated in Figure 14. Note how the improvement in capability and know-how is indicated by raising the base of the 'pivot' of the trade-off (Da Silveira and Slack, 2001).

THEORY OF PERFORMANCE FRONTIERS

Schmenner and Swink (1998) proposed a theory to clarify the distinction between the concepts illustrated in Figure 14. They define a performance frontier as 'the maximum output that can be produced from any given set of inputs, given technical considerations'. The *theory of performance frontiers* stipulates that a firm has two performance frontiers. The first, the *asset frontier*, represents maximum performance under optimal asset utilisation, i.e. it describes reachable performance levels if assets are perfectly managed. The *operations frontier*, in contrast, represents achievable performance levels under current operations policies. The theory of performance frontiers argues that performance can be increased through two strategies. *Improvement* means adjusting processes to reach an operations frontier. *Betterment*, the second strategy, is about moving the operations frontier toward the asset frontier.

The theory of performance frontier is based on the following laws (Schmenner and Swink, 1998):

- *Law of Trade-offs*: An operations system cannot simultaneously provide the highest level among all performance dimensions.
- *Law of Cumulative Capabilities*: Improvements in certain operations capabilities (e.g. quality) are basic and enable improvements to be made in other operations capabilities (e.g., flexibility).
- *Law of Diminishing Returns*: As improvement (or betterment) moves an operations system closer and closer to its operating frontier (or its

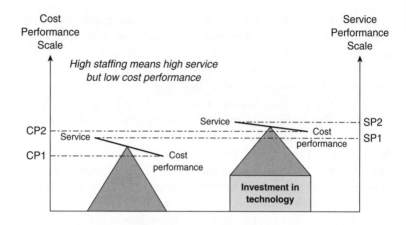

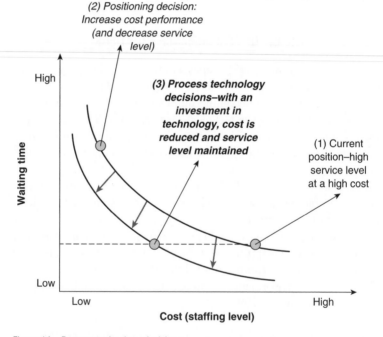

Figure 14   Process technology decisions

asset frontier), more and more resources must be expended in order to achieve each additional increment of benefit.

- *Law of Diminishing Synergy*: The strength of the synergistic effects predicted by the law of cumulative capabilities diminishes as the operations system nears its asset frontier.

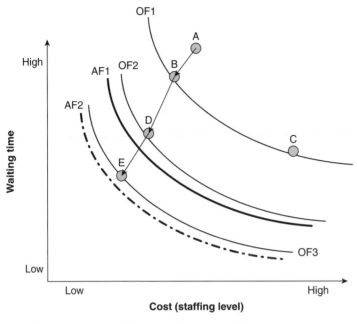

Figure 15   The theory of performance frontiers illustrated

Figure 15 provides an illustration of the theory in the case of the high-street bank already used in Figure 14. The bank begins at point A, where its service standard is poor (high waiting time) and the cost of providing the service moderately high. Through the improved management of operational practice, performance can be improved to reach point B on the current operating frontier (curve OF1). This indicates the maximum performance achievable with current operating policies and the current equipment. Note that when moving from point A to point B, operations managers have reduced waiting time and cost simultaneously: thus, they would conclude that trade-offs do not exist. The story is different at point B. Because the system has reached its operations frontier, there is no possible way to further reduce waiting time without increasing costs (in the direction of point C). Once at point B, operations managers would conclude that strategic trade-offs exist.

Through revised processes and policies (betterments), operations managers may be able, still with the existing assets only, to 'push' their operating frontier from OF1 to OF2. Note that OF2 is very close to the absolute performance frontier, the asset frontier AF1. The law of diminishing returns and diminishing synergy means that pushing OF2 closer to AF1 will be very difficult and expensive. Note, however, that once again, when moving from point B to point D, both waiting time and cost have been reduced. Through betterment, the trade-off between cost and service level has been temporarily eliminated. Once at point D, the trade-off is active again.

Finally, by investing in a modern IT system, the bank has the potential of shifting the asset frontier from AF1 to a new frontier, AF2. By revising the operations system accordingly, the bank can move from point D to point E (no trade-offs) to end up being faced by the usual strategic trade-off at point E.

REFERENCES

Da Silveira, G. and Slack, N. (2001) 'Exploring the trade-off concept', *International Journal of Operations and Production Management*, 21(7): 949–964.

Schmenner, R. and Swink, M. (1998) 'On theory in operations management', *Journal of Operations Management*, 17: 97–113.

Schonberger, R. (1996) *World Class Manufacturing: The Next Decade*. New York: Free Press.

Location

> *Location decisions deal with determining where a facility should be located.*

NATURE OF LOCATION DECISIONS

As there is usually some uncertainty regarding future demographic and economic cycles, the answer to a location problem is not always straightforward. The complexity of location decisions is due to several reasons:

- *The decision involves a number of quantitative (e.g. distance) and qualitative (e.g. quality of life at location) variables*: These need to be combined together for the best decision outcome. Although specific techniques can be used to overcome these issues and rank the different decision variables, there may be several problems when groups of managers have to make such decisions: personal preferences, different perspectives, different weights put on different decision variables, etc.

- *The decision is strategic in nature*: Whereas the location of the first facility of a company often has (but not always) no business rationales, further facilities should be chosen so as to be consistent with the strategy of the firm. A cost leader, for example, will seek locations in low labour costs areas, whereas a firm with a strategy of strong innovation will seek a location when knowledge workers and researchers are available.
- *There is a key risk taken when selecting a location*: As the company commits itself to using a site for an extended period of time, it is likely that the initial rationales as to why the site was chosen may erode over time. For example, a power plant that chose a location by a river ten years ago to take advantage of cheap cooling may have to invest massively today in order to respect new laws on the environment and industrial pollution.

Location decisions are not restricted to the study of where to locate a factory. Many service firms depend on a support facility to provide a service, as for example movie theatres, airports, resorts, and hairdressing salons.

DECISION STRUCTURE

Location decisions are made with a view to maximising the profitability of a firm under conditions of uncertainty (about the nature of future demand for example). The decision is informed by the operations strategy of the firm.

There are three generic steps to a location decision:

- *Framing the decision problem, or defining its scope*: At the strategic level, all decisions made are interdependent. For example, capacity decisions will have an impact on location decisions: is it better to open two medium-size supermarkets in two neighbouring cities, or to open a superstore between the two cities?
- Once the scope of the location decision has been specified, analysts usually start a search process in order to *identify a shortlist of potential sites*: For example, when BMW decided to built its first factory outside of Germany, a total of 215 potential sites were considered. These were narrowed down to a shortlist of four sites, out of which the site in Spartanburg, in North Carolina, was eventually selected.

- Once a list of potential sites has been established, a number of techniques can be used to *select the best location*: These techniques are described later in this section.

STRATEGIC FACTORS IN LOCATION DECISIONS

The key factors to consider are:

- *Logistical costs factors*: What are the costs of feeding the facility with supplies and of distributing finished products to customers? What are the travel costs of customers to a service facility? Can the logistical costs be reduced by creating a supplier's park?
- *International factors*: Are there any risks to be considered in the relocation decision, as for example political or cultural risks, or those due to the volatility of a foreign currency? Are there any tax advantages linked to a site, as is often the case with offshore economic zones?
- *Operations cost factors*: Will the cost of labour be cheaper in one location? This is important for an industry with a high labour content. However, the full cost of operations rather than the direct labour content may be more relevant, as one should take into account productivity differences between locations (Steenhuis and De Bruijn, 2004). There may also be other factors to consider, such as flexibility and a willingness to learn in future employees (Doeringer et al., 2004).
- *Access factors*: Does a location provide an advantage in terms of distributing products to a lucrative target market? Does it provide access to a specialist knowledge (e.g. working in Silicon Valley)? Or does it provide a right of access to natural resources?
- *Competitive factors*: Where are the competition located, and does this matter? In the comparison shopping retail sector (e.g. shopping for electronic and white goods, car dealers), it is common to co-locate with competitors to benefit from joint advertising and to be more attractive than in independent, isolated sites. In other industries, the strategy of saturation marketing is used. For example, Subway tends to open many shops close to each other in a city centre rather than try to open shops with different catchment bases.
- *Environmental, legal and workforce factors*: Do labour, pension, and social laws reduce or increase the cost of operations? Are the environmental regulations lenient or tight?

- *Local infrastructure*: Is the local infrastructure important? This includes the provision of electricity, roads, airports, and telecommunication. Steenhuis and De Bruijn (2004) distinguish integrated industries, which have high requirements for local infrastructure, from island industries, which can operate with limited local infrastructures.

LOCATION DECISION TECHNIQUES

Given the number of contexts for which location decisions are made, there is no universal technique used to support these decisions. Instead, operations managers and economic geographers have developed a portfolio of techniques, each specialising on a different class of problems. The most advanced location decision techniques dealing with multiple site location decisions are beyond the scope of this text, and thus, only the most basic and simple tools are described here.

Accounting cost–benefit models compare the respective profitability of two or more different locations. These are typically used for decisions where cost is the variable that matters the most. One drawback of cost–benefit models is that they often ignore the fact that cheaper solutions will often decrease the level of service provided to customers. For example, running two large warehouses in a UK distribution network is likely to be cheaper than running six smaller warehouses. With six warehouses, however, it will be much easier to guarantee next day delivery, a target that the two warehouse system may not be able to deliver.

Trade-off models are used to find an optimal trade-off between service level and logistical cost.

In the service sector, and especially the retail sector, travel time (or travel cost) to a location is a key concern as it directly impacts the demand for the service. In these cases, the objective of a location decision is to minimise the average distance travelled to the service facility. The *cross-median approach* provides the optimal solution to this type of problem. Unfortunately, an analytical solution to the cross-median problem formulation does not always exist.

An alternative to the cross-median approach is the *centre of gravity method*, whereby a location is selected as being the centre of gravity between different points, as weighted by the demand at each point around the facility. Although an intuitive solution, the centre of gravity method does not provide an optimal solution.

The *Huff model* of retail location is a gravity method which was developed specifically for the location of retail facilities, e.g. supermarkets. The model allows an analyst to compute the probability that a customer from area 1 will travel to store in area 2, whilst taking into account all the competing stores and their relative attractiveness. From this probability, and with demographic information, analysts can compute the likely turnover at one location, as well as the potential market share of a site.

Scoring models (also called the *factor rating method*) are the most pragmatic solution when a location decision does not only include cost or distance considerations. A scoring model requires a group of decision makers to list decision variables, assign weights to these variables, and then assign a score to each potential site on each variable. The best site is identified by computing a desirability index, i.e. the best aggregate score.

Geographical Information Systems (GIS) are information systems specifically designed to handle maps and geographical constructs. They can be an effective computer-based tool that can support both (1) the search for potential sites and (2) the selection of a site. By switching between views of production cost, the density of customers, and delivery times, analysts can manually – or through expert systems embedded in a GIS – discover new or best locations.

FURTHER READING

For more technical details on location decision techniques, see Chase, R., Jacobs, F. and Aquilano, M. (2006) *Operations Management for Competitive Advantage*. New York: McGraw-Hill. Technical Note 11, pp. 449–467.

For a more detailed discussion of location decisions in an international context, see Barnes, D. (2008) *Operations Management: An International Perspective*. London: Thomson, pp. 108–114.

For a more detailed discussion of location decisions for service facilities, see Fitzsimmons, J. and Fitzsimmons, M. (2008) *Service Management: Operations, Strategy, Information Technology* (6th edition). New York: McGraw-Hill. Chapter 10, pp. 225–254.

REFERENCES

Doeringer, P., Evans-Klock, C. and Terkla, D. (2004) 'What attracts high performance factories? Management culture and regional advantage', *Regional Science and Urban Economics*, 34: 591–618.

Steenhuis, H.J. and De Bruijn, E. (2004) 'Assessing manufacturing location', *Production Planning and Control*, 15(8): 786–795.

Capacity

Capacity planning is the set of management decisions that establishes the overall level of productive resources for a firm. In other words, it is the set of decisions dealing with how many units a facility should be capable of processing. Capacity decisions are difficult for one key reason: a capacity decision is the implementation of a long-term plan to meet an expected demand for a product or a service which, at the time of preparing the plan, may still only exist at the product concept stage or may not exist at all. Needless to say, this expected demand is subject to a great deal of uncertainty!

Let's assume, for example, that an automotive manufacturer predicts a demand of 70,000 units per year, when demand turns out to be 35,000 units annually. In this case, it is likely the manufacturer would have over-invested in capacity, i.e. that it would have built an expensive factory which will only be half used. The *irreversibility* of capacity decisions is what makes them a risky strategic decision. On the other hand, investing early on in a factory with a capacity of 70,000 cars per year could be a predatory strategy in order to be able to compete with other first movers in a given market segment. Such an aggressive capacity strategy means that when demand grows, the factory with the highest capacity is the one that can fill orders quicker and experience earlier economies of scale. A company with risk-averse decision makers, in contrast, is likely to only commit to a capacity if they are sure that it will not over-shoot demand.

MEASURING CAPACITY

When measuring capacity, the objective is to measure a level of activity. There are many ways of measuring capacity, and each industry has measures that are more suitable given their unique context of operations. For some companies, capacity measures are obvious: an automotive assembler, for example, will measure capacity in cars produced per year. Hospitals measure their capacity as their number of beds. In some systems, measuring capacity is difficult because products are non-standard. For example, precision machinists often describe their capacity in machine hours per month, although machine hours, selling price and costs can vary greatly between machines and process centres.

It is important to differentiate several concepts related to capacity:

- Planned capacity: This is the theoretical capacity of a system given some allowances (e.g. rest).
- Used capacity: This is the actual demand, or usage, of resources. If used capacity is less than planned capacity, this is a situation of *over-capacity*. If used capacity is higher than planned capacity, this is a situation of *under-capacity*.
- Efficiency: This is the degree to which production is as efficient as planned. Efficiency is typically measured as used capacity divided by planned capacity.

For example, a precision machinist has a planned capacity of 15,000 hours per month. In a given month, 16,000 hours were sold, but 3,000 hours were subcontracted out:

- The company is in a situation of under-capacity of 1,000 hours, as its sales (16,000 hours) exceed its ability to produce (15,000 hours).
- It is an example of 100 per cent utilisation, as the company works for as many hours as it can.
- The efficiency is 87 per cent (13,000/15,000), as when using all its resources, the company could only produce for 13,000 rather than 15,000 hours.

Some industries are infamous for their 'self-induced' economic recessions linked to over-capacity problems. This is the case for the automotive industry and airlines. In order to compete, companies in these industries try to offer better prices to their customers. One way to do so is by investing in capacity (producing more cars or flying more passenger-miles). The reasoning is seductive. What happens, though, when *everybody* in an industry thinks the same way? Every firm increases its capacity to the point that the total aggregate supply is way above the aggregate demand. This means that none of the suppliers can fully utilise their capacity, that economies of scale are not achieved, and that unit production costs are actually rising, thereby generating a severe profitability crisis.

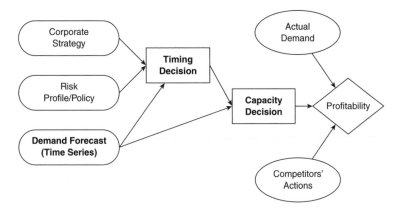

Figure 16   Capacity decision structure

DECISION STRUCTURE

Figure 16 displays the typical structure of a capacity decision. It shows that the key input for a capacity decision is a demand forecast. This demand forecast should be formatted as a time series, i.e. as a time-ordered series of demand figures (for example, a series of monthly demand for the next ten years).

The capacity decision itself is concerned with the size of the facility. The problem of sizing a facility, however, cannot be dissociated from the problem of when to build the facility. The timing decision, therefore, is a prerequisite of the capacity decision: based on the strategy of the firm, and on its risk profile, an investment in capacity may anticipate, chase, or follow demand. The timing decision also sets whether the firm should make a one-off capacity investment (to match the estimated future peak demand) or if it should stage the investment in a series of capacity expansion decisions.

Once a firm has decided on a timing strategy, the question of which capacity level to target should be answered. The key consideration is, given the demand forecast, what is the *best operating level*. Figure 17 shows the best operating level curve for a decision to open a new hotel.

The hotel chain considering the opening of a new facility has the choice of several different types of hotels, as shown in Figure 17. Facility A is a small motel type of facility, say with a capacity V_a=50 rooms. Facility B is a larger hotel with a capacity V_b=150 rooms. Facility C is a very large facility (e.g. a Hilton or Sheraton) with at least 300

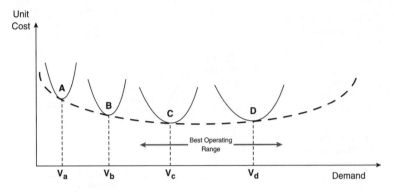

Figure 17   Best operating level curve

rooms. Facility D is an extremely large hotel, usually a full independent resort, which can include from 500 rooms up to several thousand rooms (e.g. Las Vegas hotels).

As Figure 17 shows, each hotel has its own economies of scale. For example, if the small motel A only has 20 customers a night, it is likely to lose money, as there are not enough customers to absorb the fixed costs of running the facility. At nearly its full occupancy, say 40 to 45 rooms, the hotel is at its optimal usage rate. When the hotel gets close to its full capacity, managing it becomes more difficult: extra staff may be needed, the restaurant kitchen may be too small to cater for all customers, etc. Additional costs will then start to appear to accommodate a full occupancy: these additional costs explain the phenomenon of diseconomies of scale.

Depending on which demand level the hotel chain is expecting at the new location, it should select the types of facility that can provide the cheapest unit cost. Most well-known hotel chains will try to position themselves in the 'best operating range' shown in Figure 17. On the low end of the range, it is common to find more entrepreneurial ventures rather than chain members. For example, bed and breakfasts are an extreme case of a facility with very low fixed costs, meaning that they can operate with very small capacities (three to six rooms).

ADJUSTING CAPACITY DECISION

Although capacity decisions are irreversible, some degree of adjustment of demand and supply is possible in the short and medium term. Supply adjustments are discussed in **Aggregate Production Planning** and demand-side adjustments in **Yield**. **Real options** thinking is also increasingly used a decision making framework to invite managers to avoid, wherever possible, full irreversible commitments in capacity.

FURTHER READING

More details about capacity planning with a focus on critically assessing a company's capacity strategy can be found in Slack, N. and Lewis, M. (2001) *Operations Strategy*. Englewood Cliffs, NJ: Prentice-Hall.

Process

> *A process is a set, documented, and repeatable method for executing an organisational task.*

Organisations need to align their processes with their strategic objectives. For example, if a company is positioned as a low cost manufacturer, it is important that it adopts processes that are cost effective. Process strategy is the area of operations management dealing with questions of *process alignment* and *capital intensity*.

PROCESS ALIGNMENT

In 1979, Hayes and Wheelwright proposed a framework called the *product-process matrix*. This framework links the type of product being manufactured to the type of process that should be used. Hayes and Wheelwright used two dimensions to describe product and processes: (1) the degree of standardisation of the product and (2) the volume of products that should be processed. Hayes and Wheelwright's contribution was to point out that a strategic trade-off exists between cost and flexibility. High volume processes produce cheap goods, but without any flexibility. At the other end of the spectrum, low volume products

process

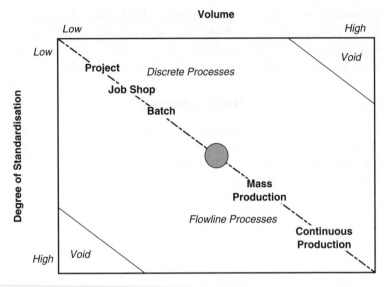

Figure 18   The product-process matrix

can be customised but their production will be costly. This trade-off is illustrated by the fact that profitable processes tend to be on the diagonal line of the product-process matrix, as shown in Figure 18. The extreme corners of the product-process matrix are shown as *Void*: in these regions, processes cannot be operated because of the cost–flexibility trade-off.

Figure 18 shows types of process systems, e.g. job shop production, which are well known archetypes of manufacturing systems. Production of a unique nature, or of a non-repetitive type, corresponds to project processes. The building of the Sydney Opera House is an example of a one-off project. Although it is a construction project, and thus is similar to other projects such as the construction of a hospital, it presents unique features which are unlikely to be encountered again (location, architectural design, environmental constraints, availability of materials, etc.). Job shop processes are very close to projects in nature. The distinction between the two is linked to the commonality between the different jobs that are being executed: in theory a project is viewed as a less standardised activity than a job. A cabinetmaker and a precision machinist are examples of job shop activities. It may be, however, that two machining jobs will have less in common than two houses built by the same contractor: this illustrates that the distinction between projects and job shops is sometimes difficult to make. A more useful and practical distinction is to use the terminology of 'project' when staff and equipment have to go to a project site, whereas in a 'job shop', it is the product that is moved to the staff and equipment.

Batch shops start to exhibit a higher volume of production and more standardisation. The term 'batch' is relatively vague, and can be used to refer to a production series of ten to a few thousand units. Although in terms of internal organisation and method of work, batch shops resemble job shops, they benefit from lower production costs as a result of *learning curves*.

Whereas projects, job shops, and batch process systems are quite similar to each other, mass production process systems belong to a clear and distinct category of processes, as symbolised by the central division circle in Figure 18. Discrete processes are sets of activities where each project/job/batch is a finite/discrete entity. In contrast, flow line processes deal with products that are so standardised that they can produce units more or less continuously, ideally with the same regularity than water flowing in a river. The distinction between mass production systems and continuous production is once again rather fuzzy. The typical example of a mass production system is an automotive assembly line. The typical example of a continuous production system is a brick factory or a paper mill. There is still some amount of potential variety in the former (different colours, engines, options) whereas in the latter, all the products are strictly identical. Clearly, a more 'fluid' flow is easier to achieve in continuous production systems rather than in mass production systems.

An important distinction between discrete and flow line processes is that discrete processes will usually include a product design stage, i.e. the products are either *engineered to order* or *made to order*. For example, each house built by a contractor has first to be designed. Flow line systems are more adapted to *made to stock* products. These are designed in successive generations, but each generation of products is produced on a large scale before its design is revisited. More importantly, in make to stock systems, the manufacturing company finances new product development. In the case of make to order systems, product development and design activities are paid for by the final customer.

What the product process matrix shows is that specific positioning decisions correspond to specific processes. A low cost strategy, for example, is associated with mass production systems. A high quality strategy is associated with job shop processes. It is essential that process strategists make sure that their process choices are compatible with their corporate strategy.

THE SERVICE PROCESS MATRIX

Process choices are a different matter in the service sector, and there have been many classifications of services published in the service management literature. A commonly used classification scheme in the service operations management literature is the service process matrix of Schmenner (1995), which is shown in Figure 19. The horizontal axis considers the extent to which all the services delivered by a firm are standard and the vertical axis uses the degree of labour intensity, which is computed as the ratio of labour costs to capital costs. Highly customised services are called professional services. As they are highly adapted to a client's need, they cannot be produced in a high volume and will rely on expensive contact time with an expert. Examples are a dentist's surgery and a garage car repair service. Service shops handle services that are less variable, and thus, can be provided at a more intensive scale. Examples are specialised car services (tyre fitting, exhaust replacement) and restaurant services. Mass services involve the provision of a unique, non-customisable service to a very large number of individuals whilst requiring extensive contact time: schools are one example. The service factory is less dependent on labour and more on capital costs, such as in the case of airlines or distribution services.

CAPITAL INTENSITY

A key consideration in process strategy is the degree of capital intensity of a process. By definition, a capital-intensive process requires a large investment of corporate funds that can only be recouped by producing and selling a large number of products. If the demand exists, capital intensity is a desirable strategy as it allows a firm to experience *economies of scale*.

Figure 20 shows that for two processes, A and B, the unit manufacturing cost of a product decreases as the quantity produced increases. This decrease can be explained by considering that total manufacturing costs (TMC) are made up of fixed costs (TFC, for example the plant and

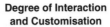

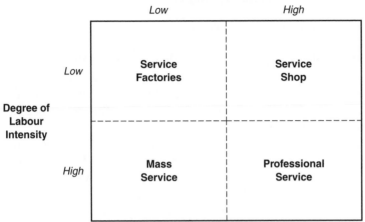

Figure 19   The service process matrix

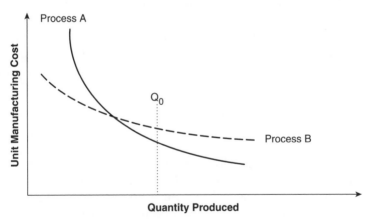

Figure 20   Economies of Scale illustrated

equipment depreciation expenses) and of variable costs (TVC, the cost of labour, raw materials, electricity consumed in production, etc.).

Assuming a simple cost function, total manufacturing costs *TMC* can be expressed as:

$$TMC = TFC + VC * Q$$

Here Q is the quantity produced and *VC* the variable cost rate per unit. Thus, the unit manufacturing cost of a product, *UMC*, is:

$$UMC = TVC/Q = VC + TFC/Q$$

This is the equation of the curves shown in Figure 20.

The interpretation of the phenomenon of economies of scale is straightforward: as more units (Q) are produced with the same fixed resources (*TFC*), the proportion of fixed costs (*TFC/Q*) allocated to each manufactured product decreases.

If the market is capable of absorbing a production of Q_0 (in Figure 20), then a process strategist should recommend the adoption of process A, as at this production level, each product made would be cheaper. Notice, however, that if the quantity to be produced were $Q_0/2$, the opposite recommendation would be made, as at this level, process B is cheaper.

In Figure 20, process A is more capital-intensive than process B. Processes that are not capital-intensive are labour-intensive: they typically involve complicated manual labour tasks that are difficult to automate.

A simple way to compare the capital intensity of two processes is to compute their break-even point, i.e. the level of production at which they generate zero profits. The break-even point of a process is given by computing:

$$Q_{BE} = \frac{TFC}{(P - VC)}$$

Here *P* is the selling price of the product.

If production (or sales) falls below the break-even point, then a company will incur losses. It is noteworthy that although capital-intensive processes are desirable as they allow companies to experience economies of scale, they are a risky investment as they could result in financial losses if demand goes below the break-even point. Conversely, labour intensive processes are less risky, but they provide limited and uncompetitive profit margins when demand is high.

REFERENCES

Hayes, R.H. and Wheelwright, S.C. (1979) 'Link manufacturing process and product life cycles', *Harvard Business Review*, January–February, pp. 133–40.

Schmenner, R.W. (1995) *Service Operations Management*. Englewood Cliffs, NJ: Prentice-Hall.

Layout

Layout decisions deal with the spatial arrangement of rooms, displays, machines and workers.

DECISION STRUCTURE AND CONTEXTS

Layout decisions are the direct implementation of the process strategy adopted by a firm (see **Process**). Each type of generic process strategy in the product-process matrix or the service-process matrix is associated with a generic layout.

In the case of manufacturing firms:

- Projects rely on project layouts, i.e. the workers go to the site of construction or assembly.
- Job shops and batch production systems use *process layouts*, i.e. layouts where machines and processes are grouped by family (for example, all the drilling machines are clustered together).
- Mass production systems and continuous systems use *flowline* types of layout, e.g. assembly lines, where machines and processes are grouped according the sequence of operations required to manufacture a product.

In the case of the service industry, layout decisions can vary greatly between sectors:

- Professional services' (e.g. doctors, solicitors) layouts will usually include a reception area, a waiting room, and a service room.
- Service shops (e.g. restaurants, garages) are usually similar in layout, but with a clear distinction between a front office and a back office. For example, customers are normally not expected to go inside the garage where their car is being repaired. In the case of restaurants, the dining area and the kitchens are usually well separated, although some restaurants, such as Japanese ones, are famous for the fact that the kitchen is in the centre of the dining area.
- Mass services layouts will depend on the industry. For example, airplanes have a more or less set layout regulated by international standards. Airport layout decisions, in contrast, are more difficult: the separations between travellers and non-travellers, between international transit and domestic traffic, and so on, are examples of constraints to be respected.

PROCESS (FUNCTIONAL) LAYOUTS

Figure 21 displays an example of a process layout. It shows that similar machines have been grouped in specialised zones, called process departments. In this type of production environment, different job orders follow different paths. For example, in Figure 21, jobs A, B, and C make very different uses of the various processes. The objective of process layout design is to arrange the departments so that the cost of transporting work in process inventory from department to department is minimised.

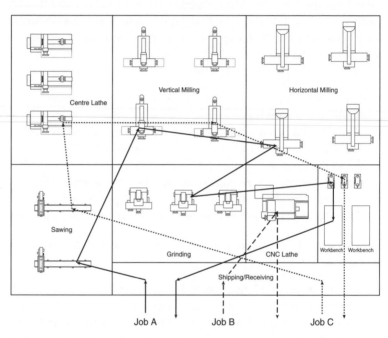

Figure 21   Process layout

Two methods are used to design process layouts. The first method, *block diagramming*, requires the full information about the number of parts which are carried between departments per unit of time. Each process centre is represented in a diagram by a 'block'. If two blocks experience heavy traffic they should be located close to each other. If two blocks have low levels of traffic they can be distant from each other. Finding a solution layout is either done manually using a trial and error process, or by adopting a mathematical optimisation, for example by formulating the layout problem as a linear programme.

In some cases, it will be difficult or impractical to compute the handling costs between departments. For example, the proximity of two departments may involve qualitative management considerations that cannot be easily translated in quantitative terms. In these cases, *Systematic Layout Programming (SLP)* is the technique to use. SLP uses a standard graphical convention to indicate the importance that two departments be adjacent on a 6-point scale ranging from 'absolutely necessary' to 'undesirable'. Analysts can then proceed by building a relationship table, summarising the specifications by pairing departments. The table is used to prepare a diagrammatic layout, which when fine-tuned is expanded by taking account of the real floor space requirements.

PRODUCT LAYOUT DESIGN: ASSEMBLY LINE BALANCING

The problem of designing a product layout is totally different from that of a process layout: instead of grouping machines by the function performed, machines and workstations are organised so that the product flows smoothly from a beginning to an ending workstation, as shown in Figure 22.

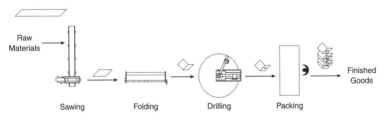

Raw Materials

Finished Goods

Sawing   Folding   Drilling   Packing

Figure 22   An example of a flowline

In the case of the simple product made in the example of Figure 22, the layout is easy to design as there are only four activities with a clear sequence. Consider, in contrast, the task of assembling a car: there are thousands of individual assembly jobs, each standing in a more or less complex precedence relationship with one another. The challenge of assembly line design is to order each of these activities in a workstation whilst respecting these precedence relationships, as is shown in Figure 23.

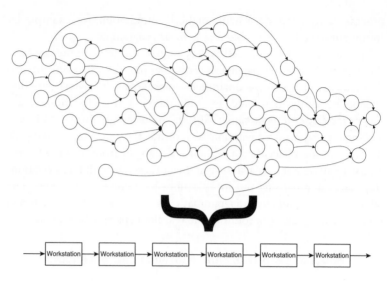

Figure 23 A product layout design problem

Figure 23 shows that the elementary activities form a complex network of precedence relationships. The problem is to regroup activities by workstation so that the layout of the factory is a flowline. The problem is complicated by the fact that each elementary activity will have a different task completion time, a fact which can result in the design shown in Figure 24.

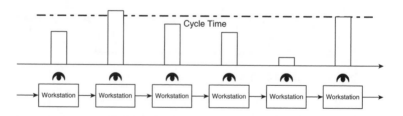

Figure 24 An unbalanced assembly line

The cycle time shown in Figure 24 is the time made available to each workstation in order to complete the set of tasks that they have been allocated. For example, if the cycle time is ten minutes, it means that every ten minutes each worker should complete his or her work sequence and pass the work to a downstream worker.

In Figure 24, each vertical bar indicates a workstation's *work content*, i.e. the time that it takes to complete the activities that have been assigned to this workstation. The difference between the cycle time and the workstation work content is the *idle time*. The layout design of Figure 24 can be criticised for several reasons: first, worker 2 cannot complete the workstation's tasks within the cycle time. It means that the facility will be unable to achieve its target output. Second, the line is *unbalanced*, i.e. different workstations have very different task completion times. For example, the worker 5 has an easy job whereas workers 2 and 6 are working on a full load. Figure 25 shows how a redistribution of the activities can result in a better *balanced* layout.

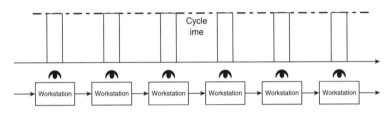

Figure 25   A balanced assembly line

Operations management textbooks will usually present a simple heuristics procedure to solve an assembly line balancing problem. A classification of the different balancing methods can be found in the survey by Erel and Sarin (1998). It is noteworthy that heuristics tend to be the preferred method for solving assembly line balancing problems, and that optimisation algorithms will exist only for the simplest problem formulation.

OTHER MANUFACTURING LAYOUTS

Process and products layouts represent two opposite 'end of the spectrum' archetypes of manufacturing layouts. To choose between the two is, at first sight, straightforward: if a company operates a make-to-order system, the variety of jobs that it has to process are such that it is better to design the layout by operating speciality, i.e. as a process layout. If a company operates a make-to-stock system then the layout can be product-based, as the products processed will nearly all be identical. In some contexts (where jobs are all different, products are not identical, etc.) other layouts can be used:

- *Cellular layouts*: Although a company may process a large variety of jobs, key families of jobs with very similar process requirements can exist. To increase efficiency, a process layout will be re-engineered as a cellular layout, where each cell is specialised for one family of products. Cellular layouts are very conducive to implementing team work by opposition to the non-team approach which would typically be used with a process layout. *Group technology* is the family of classification techniques used to regroup the products made by a company into cells.
- *Hybrid layouts*: These are used when a company processes large quantities of similar goods on a product layout whilst some delicate processes require that the rest of the factory be based on a process layout.
- *Flexible Manufacturing Systems*: Instead of processing identical products on a flowline layout, a company needs to process three versions of a product on a unique assembly line. A flexible line is the equivalent of three dedicated assembly lines merged into one.

SERVICE LAYOUT DESIGN

Many of the techniques used to design manufacturing layouts can also be used for the case of service systems. The systematic layout planning technique is a very general method that can be used for many layout problems, such as designing the layout of a restaurant or hotel. However, given the diversity of service operations systems, companies have developed many other specialised layout design techniques.

Consider, for example, the case of designing the layout of an airport. The legal and environmental constraints are so unique here that only a customised tool can be used. Examples of these constraints are: noise regulations, crossing runways, and the integrity of international transit and duty frees zones.

Traffic statistics, or sales potential, will often be a key variable in the design of retail layouts. The area next to the front door which all customers have to come through is a strategic layout zone where the company can promote its products. Supermarket layout design can also include design objectives such as maximising customers exposure to products. By locating frequently purchased items (e.g., milk, bread) at different corners of a store, supermarket managers can make sure that most customers will have to go along all the aisles, and will then potentially purchase more items spontaneously. The layout design can be complicated by taking into account different objectives, such as the evacuation time in the case of an emergency (e.g. a fire).

Finally, another consideration in layout design is Bitner's (1992) concept of a *servicescape*. Bitner showed that in the case of services, the physical surroundings can have an impact on how customers will approach (or avoid) a facility and how employees will approach (or avoid) work in the facility. Layout then is only one dimension to take into account when designing a service facility, along with ambient conditions (temperature, music, noise, etc.) and symbols (signage, artefacts, style of décor, etc.).

REFERENCES

Bitner, M.J. (1992) 'Servicescapes: the impact of physical surroundings on customers and employees', *Journal of Marketing*, 56(2): 57–71.

Erel, E. and Sarin, S. (1998) 'A survey of the assembly line balancing procedures', *Production Planning and Control*, 9(5): 414–434.

Technology Management

> **Technology management is the set of managerial decisions through which certain technologies are adopted, revised, improved, and abandoned by managers in order to implement their process strategy.**

AN OVERVIEW OF TECHNOLOGY MANAGEMENT

Technology management includes:

- *Technology roadmapping*: Analysts will identify which technologies a firm should invest in after having considered an exhaustive list of all the potential promising alternatives. Technology roadmaps are often prepared by industry associations or consortiums to identify in which areas of research and development firms should invest.

- *Technology evaluation*: This is the evaluation of technologies to determine if they are suitable given a firm's needs.
- *Technology selection*: This is the selection of the most suitable alternative amongst a set of feasible technologies. Technology selection is a managerial activity that involves: (1) strategic reflection, (2) a performance evaluation, and (3) a financial evaluation. The financial evaluation requires analysts to prepare estimates of the expected future operating cash flows if a technology is adopted, and the computation of a Net Present Value (NPV).
- *Technology development*: This is the investment of corporate funds in research and development with a view to developing a new technology.
- *Technology acquisition*: This is the decision to acquire a technology from a technology provider. When this technology is acquired, a key challenge is to transfer it from the seller to the buyer.
- *Technology retirement*: This is the decision to abandon a technology that has reached the end of its commercial life.

TECHNOLOGY TRANSFER AND DIFFUSION

Technology Transfer

Technology transfer is the process of transferring a technology from a provider to a buyer. The 2 by 2 classification of Ernst and Kim (2002) shown in Figure 26 provides an illustration of the different types of technology transfers.

The most traditional form of technology trade is a commodity trade, i.e. the simple commercial trade of machinery. As shown in Figure 26, such a transfer is market mediated (that is, regulated by a sales/purchase contract) and requires little involvement from the technology supplier. Once the production means has changed hands, it becomes the buyer's responsibility to use it adequately. Typically, a contract may require the seller to provide an owner's manual, a repairs' manual, and a list of spare parts. Although a training session and a production launch phase may be included as part of the commercial transaction, eventually the customer will have to operate independently. Consider the example of an automotive manufacturer purchasing a robot, or a hospital using a new X-ray machine. After the initial phase of training, the responsibility to operate,

The Role of Knowledge Supplier

	Active	Passive
Market Mediated	Formal Mechanisms (FDI, FL, turnkey plants, technical consultancies)	Commodity Trade (standard machinery transfer)
Non Market Mediated	Informal Mechanisms (Flagship provides technical Assistance to local suppliers)	Informal Mechanisms (Reverse engineering, observation, literature)

Figure 26   Different types of technology transfer (Reprinted from Research Policy, 3 (8–9), Ernst, D. and Kim, L., 'Global production networks, knowledge diffusions, and local capability formation', p 13, © 2002, with permission from Elsevier.)

maintain, and improve the equipment lies on the buyer's side – a fact which involves risk.

As an alternative to the risk of failure in the commodity-trade technology transfer, buyers can demand more from their suppliers. For example, the buyer of a piece of equipment may purchase additional services such as a three year maintenance plan and a technical service plan, guaranteeing that a technician will be sent to the plant any time there is a problem with the equipment. As an extension of this principle, companies will often elect to purchase 'turnkey' factories rather than taking on the responsibility of managing a large scale project. This means that instead of purchasing independently the various equipment, interfaces, supplies, etc. needed to run a factory, a single contract is signed. A project manager takes full responsibility for the entire project and guarantees that the customer will only have to 'turn the key' to make the factory work.

A proactive role by the knowledge supplier may also occur within an investment relationship rather than within a commercial transaction. In the case of *Foreign Direct Investment* (FDI), a parent company will provide both the funds and the expertise to create a factory in a foreign country.

TECHNOLOGY DIFFUSION

Figure 26 shows that the transfer of technology is not always market mediated. The term *technology diffusion* is used to refer to instances when the transfer of knowledge has a non-commercial nature. A second distinction between technology transfer and technology diffusion is the fact that in a transfer, there are only two parties, whereas diffusion means the communication of knowledge to a potentially very broad audience.

In some cases, the diffusion of a technology may take place without the knowledge supplier being involved, or even without the knowledge supplier being willing to part with the technology. For example, *reverse engineering* is the dismantling of a product by a competitor's engineers in order to discover various ideas and technologies to copy. To avoid the uninvited use of technology by a competitor, using a patent is a useful protection. However, not all ideas and products can be protected by a patent. For example, it is impossible to patent a software program or a service concept.

Although technology diffusion has a dark side – that of a technology leak or technology theft – it can also be seen from a more benevolent angle. For example, knowledge suppliers may offer training, assistance, or even part of a product for free in order to benefit from the mass acceptance of a core technology. For example, part of the success of many internet-based multiplayer role games can be explained by the fact that the technology to develop landscapes and scenarios was made available to programmers for free. To play the game, users needed the core game software (available at a fee) and a variety of free add-ons. The availability of several free add-ons (developed by advanced users) makes buying the core software more attractive.

The extent to which technology development should be made publicly available or should be protected is often the source of heated debates. For example, private companies will always try to keep secret their development project to benefit from first movers' advantages. However, some private firms – such as Microsoft and JVC – have greatly benefited from the broad diffusion of their products (respectively DOS/Windows and the VHS video tape format) as technology standards. University researchers will often have to choose between the commercial exploitation of their patents and the publication of an academic paper.

The apparently contradictory co-existence of technology transfer and technology diffusion can be explained by differentiating *need pull* from *technology push* mechanisms. Need pull means that a technology offers ways to satisfy needs which were previously unmatched, or only partially matched. It means that a cost benefit analysis can be done, and that it will indicate that the benefits of adopting the technology will outweigh its costs. Purchasing an advanced statistical software package is one example of a need pull force: it is only once a company has diagnosed that it needs to use an advanced statistical package that it will consider its purchase. A technology push, on the other hand, refers to a scenario where a company feels itself 'pushed' to adopt a certain technology. For example, many firms in recent years have had to adopt the **ISO 9000** quality standard, although they had not necessarily felt a need for it. Instead, it was their customers who put pressure on them by telling them that they might lose their business if they did not gain an ISO 9000 certification.

Perhaps the most important theory regarding technology diffusion is that of *FDI spillovers*. Spillovers mean the diffusion of skills, knowledge, and competences brought in by a foreign investor beyond the boundaries of their local subsidiaries. For example, manufacturing practices may be passed down the supply chain to the first tier suppliers, who themselves can then pass best practices down to their own suppliers. Another form of spillover occurs when employees from the local subsidiary seek employment in other local firms: when an employee leaves, they take with them all their expertise and knowledge of processes. FDI spillover is one the main reason why many governments highly encourage FDI, and provide incentives for investors (e.g. tax breaks, free land). The extent to which spillover is a real phenomenon is extensively debated in international economics research. Some research studies conclude that FDI spillovers do exist, others argue that FDI spillovers do not exist, and yet other research studies point to *negative* spillovers (i.e. that an FDI generates negative economic/knowledge growth locally).

ABSORPTIVE CAPACITY AND TECHNOLOGY READINESS

A key management issue in technology management is the degree to which a firm has the ability to assimilate new technologies. *Technology readiness* is used to describe a firm's ability to work with a new technology. A number of industries have developed technology readiness audit frameworks. Audits are conducted prior to a technology transfer to identify potential problems as well as any actions that should be implemented prior to the transfer.

Absorptive capacity is a concept formulated by Cohen and Levinthal (1990). The absorptive capacity framework provides clear directions for managers who want to improve their ability to absorb new knowledge and technologies. Cohen and Levinthal show that absorptive capacity is a function of prior existing knowledge. In other words, very experienced firms can find the assimilation of new technologies easy, whereas relatively young firms with a limited knowledge stock can find assimilation to be much more of a challenge.

FURTHER READING

Gaynor, G. (1996) *Handbook of Technology Management*. New York: McGraw-Hill.

REFERENCES

Cohen, W.M. and Levinthal, D., (1990) 'Absorptive capacity: a new perspective on learning and innovation', *Administrative Science Quarterly*, 35(1): 128–143.
Ernst, D. and Kim, L., (2002) 'Global production networks, knowledge diffusion, and local capability formation', *Research Policy*, 31(8/9): 1417.

Flexibility

> *Process flexibility is the capability of a process to handle different types of products with a small, or nil, change-over cost.*

FLEXIBILITY AS A CAPABILITY

In the 1980s, the American car industry suffered from Japanese competition as these started to offer many more model versions than the Americans could. How could the Japanese offer more product variety whilst keeping their prices competitive? They clearly had discovered ways to overcome the cost–flexibility trade-off! Remember that, according to conventional wisdom, manufacturing systems perform well either on cost or on flexibility but not on both these dimensions simultaneously.

There have been several research studies that have shown that the product **process** matrix is overly prescriptive. In a survey of 128 manufacturing plants, Ahmad and Schroeder (2002) found that only 40 per cent of the surveyed firms operated near the diagonal line of the product-process matrix. Their review of similar research surveys also indicated that there was ample empirical evidence showing that the majority of modern firms operate slightly away from the diagonal.

Therefore, evidence supports the idea that managers have found ways to expand the feasible region of the cost–flexibility trade-off. Process flexibility is achieved either through investment in *flexible technologies* or by *innovative management practices*.

Investment in robotics is one example of a flexible technology. A robot is a programmable mechanical device that can be used for simple assembly tasks. Robots are general-purpose devices that can be quickly reprogrammed to perform another task. Accommodating a simple change of specifications in a product's component will therefore be dealt with via a minor change-over cost. Compare the investment in a robotic system with one for a dedicated machine, built solely for the purpose of assembling two components. If the design of one of the components is changed, the dedicated machine is not usable. The machine may have to be rebuilt, or, in the worst case, it may be necessary to scrap it and then purchase a totally new machine.

Set-up time reduction is an example of an innovative management practice supported by technological improvements. In the 1980s, Japanese manufacturers invested considerable R&D time in finding ways of being able to switch from product A to product B on a single machine as quickly as possible. As a result, production lines can be quickly reconverted at a minor cost from the production of one version of a product to another.

FLEXIBILITY AS A PERFORMANCE DIMENSION

It is impossible to provide an exhaustive list of all the technologies and management practices by which managers have invested in process flexibility. Being flexible is a key strategic performance dimension along which a firm can clearly differentiate its offerings. There are four key traditional strategies for competing on flexibility:

- *Product flexibility*: The ability to introduce a new product whilst incurring only a minor reconfiguration of plant and equipment.

flexibility

- *Mix flexibility*: The ability to produce simultaneously two different versions of a product or two different products. Mix flexibility allows firms to achieve *production smoothing*, i.e. to schedule daily production so that it perfectly matches daily demand patterns, which means that finished goods inventories are almost totally eliminated.
- *Volume flexibility*: The ability to process simultaneously on the same production line large and low volume series without any major cost differences.
- *Delivery flexibility*: The ability to change scheduled delivery times when needed without generating delays and extra costs.

Which type of flexibility strategy is more desirable for a firm is a function of the positioning of the firm. For example, service firms with a strategic priority on quality should invest on service flexibility (the ability to customise the service) and on delivery flexibility. Airline companies that serve a broad variety of routes should invest in volume flexibility, i.e. the ability to remain profitable on low traffic and high traffic routes. A company such as Toyota can be famous for its outstanding mix flexibility, which results in its ability to deliver cars when needed with minimum levels of inventory.

INVESTING IN PROCESS FLEXIBILITY

Several research studies in operations management have demonstrated the superiority of investing in process flexibility: process flexibility is generally associated with reduced inventory levels and an intensification of competition between firms (Fine and Freund, 1990). However, despite the desirable features of process flexibility, investing in process flexibility has remained a controversial managerial decision. On the one hand, Kaplan (1986) pointed out that traditional investment appraisal techniques, such as the Net Present Value method (NPV), often systematically assess investment in flexibility as being unprofitable. This limitation of the NPV method can be simply explained: take two investments in plants D and F. D is a dedicated plant whereas F is a flexible plant. Flexibility comes at a cost, so the investment in F is heavier than the investment in D. When the two projects are assessed, analysts estimate what the future sales are likely to be, but their sales forecast is likely to be the same for the two plants. With the same future cash flows but differences in costs, project D will clearly come out ahead of project

F! Does it mean, as Kaplan suggests in his paper, that an investment in flexibility should be 'based on faith alone'?

Investing on the basis of intuition, however, is not without risk. A number of authors have warned about the danger of investing blindly in flexibility. Williams et al. (1987) studied the process strategy of the Austin Rover group in the 1980s. They pointed out that an investment in flexibility can be overly 'romantic', i.e. that managers will often believe an expensive investment in flexibility will solve all their problems automatically (European manufacturing managers have for example been criticised for investing in robotic equipment as a piece of dedicated machinery). One of the key advantages of a robotic system is that it can perform several different tasks and can easily be reprogrammed to perform new tasks as needed: not utilising this capability is an indication of a management problem.

One solution to this investment appraisal challenge is the real options valuations techniques in technology selection. A full explanation of how **real options** valuation addresses the challenge is given elsewhere.

Fine and Freund (1990) suggest that for each factory there is an optimal level of investment in process flexibility given its economic environment. Their contribution is to highlight that the value of an investment in flexibility is a direct function of the degree of demand uncertainty that a firm is facing. Firms with easily predictable, stable demand patterns have no reason to invest in flexibility. On the other hand, firms experiencing highly volatile demand patterns should invest heavily in flexibility.

A final consideration when considering an investment in process flexibility is the degree to which flexibility should be limited or complete. A factory with some limited process flexibility is a factory where products can be processed on at least two process centres, but not on all process centres. In a complete flexibility configuration, any single product can be produced on any single process centre. Research has shown that too often complete flexibility is an unnecessary luxury. To reap the rewards of flexibility, an investment in limited flexibility is often sufficient.

REFERENCES

Ahmad, S. and Schroeder, R. (2002) 'Refining the product-process matrix', *International Journal of Operations and Production Management*, 22(1): 103–124.

Fine, C. and Freund, R. (1990) 'Optimal investment in product-flexible manufacturing capacity', *Management Science*, 36(4): 449–466.

Kaplan, R.S. (1986) 'Must CIM be justified by faith alone?', *Harvard Business Review*, 64(2): 87–97.

Williams, K., Williams, L. and Haslam, C. (1987) *The Breakdown of Austin Rover: A Case-Study in the Failure of Business Strategy and Industrial Policy*. Leamington Spa: Berg.

Real Options

> *A real option is the right, not the obligation, to acquire a real asset (or to lease or make another form of management decision relative to this asset).*

REAL OPTIONS

An option is the right, not the obligation, to do something. Most business transactions are regulated by strict contractual terms. In a sales contract, for example, both parties commit to the exchange of a good or service in exchange of money. A key innovation in modern finance has been the introduction of option contracts written over financial assets. In the system view of operations systems (see **System**), we saw that these are built from resources. These resources are *real* assets rather than financial assets. Some real assets are tangible, as for example inventory and plant and equipment, whereas other real assets are intangible: process capital, human capital, and relational capital. A real option is basically the right, but not the obligation, for an operations manager to purchase or lease an asset. Options are a powerful way of modelling and investigating *managerial flexibility*, that is, the capability of adapting a plan, a process, or a product design as market and technological conditions change.

REAL OPTIONS ILLUSTRATED

Copeland and Keenan (1998) argued that the first account of a real option can be found in the writings of Aristotle. Aristotle described how the sophist philosopher Thales, having divined that an exceptionally good olive harvest would occur in six months' time, paid a small fee to the owners of olive presses for the right to rent olive presses in six months at a price set that day. Thales did not grow olives, and thus he was *speculating* on the quality of the harvest rather than trying to preempt his future needs. When the exceptional olive harvest occurred, Thales sublet his olive pressing right to the olive growers. He was able to do so at a premium fee due to the inevitable market shortage for presses. Thales' profit was the premium fee minus the standard rate agreed six months in advance. Should the exceptional harvest not have occurred, Thales would have only incurred a minor loss, i.e. the original amount paid to book capacity.

REAL OPTIONS AND THE EVALUATION OF INVESTMENTS

Real options are famous for their ability to better assess investments in flexible assets (see **Flexibility** for a discussion of the difficulty of assessing investments in flexibility).

The following example is a simplified presentation of the option to acquire a licence for a new technology as discussed by Bowman and Moskowitz (2001). Assume that a company X is considering the purchase of a licence for a new technology currently being developed by company Y. There is some uncertainty (1) regarding the success of company Y's product development (i.e. what will be the performance of the product embedding this new technology?), and (2) regarding the market potential of this project. The initial cash outlay is £900, which can be decomposed as the purchase of the licence (£100) and an investment in a manufacturing facility to produce the product (£800). For the sake of simplification, there is only one terminal cash flow, two years after the initial investment, which is estimated at £1000. The first year of the project is spent waiting for the results of company Y's development process, and the second year corresponds to the manufacturing investment and product commercialisation by company X.

Assuming a risk free rate of 5 per cent and a risk premium of 5 per cent, this project would traditionally be assessed through the following NPV formula:

$$NPV = \frac{1,000}{(1.1)^2} - 900 = -73$$

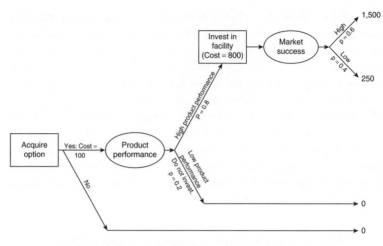

Figure 27   Example of a real option to defer investment

In this case, the project would be rejected as its NPV is negative. This NPV criterion is, however, unnecessarily penalising in this case. Its 'all or nothing' approach does not take into account the fact that managers actually have the option not to invest in the manufacturing facility should the product performance turn out to be low. This is represented in the decision tree shown in Figure 27.

In the above example, the option is the right to exploit a licence for the production and commercialisation of a new product. The underlying asset in this case is the market value of the product being developed. This value is clearly uncertain as it is a function of the product performance and of market success. The option is acquired by purchasing the licence for the product before the end of its development process. Thus, the cost of the option is 100. Should the product development be successful, the exercise price of the option is the further investment needed to buy the underlying asset: in this case, the exercise price is the further investment of 800.

The value of the option can be computed in this simple case as the discounted value of the expected payoffs from owning the underlying asset. In this case, the expected present value of the option can be computed as:

$$EPV_{option} = 0.8 \times \left(0.6 \times \frac{1500}{1.05^2} + 0.4 \times \frac{250}{1.05^2} - \frac{800}{1.05}\right) + 0.2 \times 0 = 116$$

In this case, the value of the option (116) is superior to the cost of the option (100), and the decision should be to purchase the licence. It is common in the literature to define a project's *strategic NPV* as the difference between the value and the cost of the option (16 in this case). By purchasing the licence, the company acquires the right – but not the obligation – to exploit the product commercially in a year's time. Given the current perception of uncertainty (the probabilities in Figure 27), owning this option adds value to the firm.

TYPES OF REAL OPTIONS

The most common types of options are growth, learning, abandonment, and exchange options.

Growth options are the option to expand capacity, to develop a new product, to invest in and enter new markets. The purpose of a growth option is to identify what small 'foothold' investment is needed to acquire the right to exercise that option if future conditions warrant a full competitive deployment.

Learning options are options to extend, defer, wait, or stage an investment. These options are concerned with the initial investment which has to be made whilst waiting for more accurate information about the underlying asset. These are commonly used when organisations are considering risky strategic projects. The development of a complex IT system can be very uncertain, for example, and staging options can be used to decompose the projects into different work packages, each providing their own business benefits. Postponement options are also very important in technology management and research management.

Abandonment options deal with project termination, exiting a market, cancelling an order, shutting down a factory, or abandoning a product line. The value behind an abandonment option is that continuing to invest would be a waste of organisational resources. Should a project or initiative be abandoned, corporate resources can be redeployed elsewhere. Not all projects can be abandoned however, and thus a project that can be abandoned will be more attractive than a project where an exit is impossible.

Exchange options are options to switch inputs (e.g. raw materials or suppliers), processes (using a network of factories to serve a global demand), or outputs (flexible manufacturing systems). Again, the driving idea here is that should market and demand be uncertain and volatile, facilities with switching options will be more competitive than facilities without switching options.

Real options are used in practice in two different ways. A first school of thought – option valuation – requires managers to put a financial value on all the options that they consider. A second school of thought – options thinking – only adopts the philosophy behind real options: in this approach, options are considered and analysed qualitatively at the outset of an investment project.

REAL OPTIONS IN INTERNATIONAL OPERATIONS MANAGEMENT

Large multinationals operate *global production networks* (GPNs). As these multinationals operate in a diversified economic environment, international business researchers have for a long time posited that multinationals will necessarily be more competitive than non-international business firms. A pioneering model was formulated by Kogut (1984) who described the economies of scale, economies of scope, and learning and real options which were experienced exclusively by multinationals and not by domestic producers. The link between multinationality and performance is easily explained from a real options perspective: (1) multinationals experience exclusive opportunities; (2) in response to these opportunities they flexibly modify or reconfigure their assets; and (3) a negative form of volatility is turned into a source of increased profitability. Switching capacity within an international manufacturing network to reduce one's exposure to currency fluctuations is one example of a traditionally adverse form of volatility (exchange rates) being utilised to one's advantage.

REFERENCES

Bowman, E. and Moskowitz, G. (2001) 'Real options analysis and strategic decision making', *Organization Science*, 12(6): 772–777.

Copeland, T.E. and Keenan, P.T. (1998) 'How much is flexibility worth?', *The McKinsey Quarterly*, 2: 38–49.

Kogut, B. (1984) 'Normative observations on the international value-added chain and strategic groups', *Journal of International Business Studies*, 15: 151–167.

key concepts in operations management

Innovation Management

Managing Innovation

> *Innovation management is the set of managerial activities dedicated to the deployment of innovation resources in order to bring new products, services, and processes into the marketplace.*

OVERVIEW OF INNOVATION MANAGEMENT

Perhaps one of the industries where managing innovation is most critical is the pharmaceutical industry. Companies which are unable to formulate new drugs at the same speed as their competitors will be unable to lock in large margins through patent protection, and will then be left with the exploitation of known, and therefore low-margin, drugs.

A common misperception is to equate innovation with design. Whereas design is the final technical specification of a given product or service form and function, innovation is more generally the set of activities through which ideas are elicited, selected, and gradually refined until they feed the design stage. Another key distinction is that innovation deals with *product concepts*, rather than only with the final, clearly specified, product or service. A product concept is an abstract idea of a product in use.

THE SCOPE OF INNOVATION

It is useful to distinguish three basic innovation scopes:

- *Incremental innovation* is used to refer to small improvements brought to an existing product concept. It does not result in a new product but rather in a new derivative version of a product.
- *Next generation innovation* means that major changes are taking place in terms of the product or service architecture. In other words, the product concept has significantly evolved, although it is based on the previous generation of products and the legacy of the old generation is visible in the design. The evolution of mobile phones from 1G, 2G, 2.5G and 3G capabilities is an example of next generation innovation.

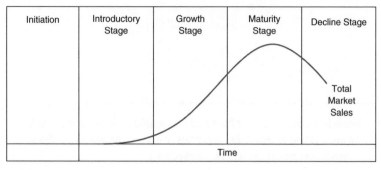

Initiation	Introductory Stage	Growth Stage	Maturity Stage	Decline Stage

Figure 28   Product lifecycle

- *Radical innovation* means that a product concept is totally new and has never been seen or used before. Clearly, it is the most expensive and risky approach to innovation as one cannot capitalise on lessons learnt in previous generations of products.

PRODUCT LIFECYCLE

Figure 28 displays a typical product lifecycle curve. A key issue in innovation management is to estimate accurately:

- The likely duration of the stages of the lifecyle.
- The quantities and cash flows (i.e. revenues and expenses) associated with each stage.
- The possible impact of competitors on the product's lifecycle.

Figure 29 displays the cash flow curves during the product's lifecycle. It exhibits a flat maturity stage lasting nearly two years. The cost curve represents the cash outflows for developing and manufacturing the product. It is at the point where the sales curve intersects the cost curve that the company has cash inflows in excess of its cash outflows for this product. The two curves define a profit area and a loss area. To be a viable product, a product's total profit surface should be less than its loss surface. Also notice in the decline stage the point at which the sales curve intersects the cost curve again: it indicates the point at which the company should retire the product.

PRODUCT PLANNING

Product planning is a set of decisions about when to design, produce, introduce, improve, and retire a product to/from the market. There are

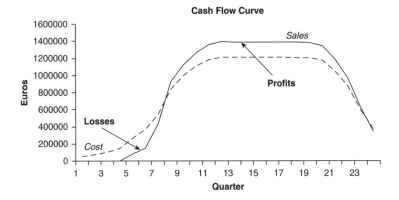

Figure 29   Cash flows during the product lifecycle

two important issues in product planning. The first is to ensure that products are introduced before those of competition in order to capture a large market share. The second issue is to make sure that firms manage a continuous portfolio of new products: as soon as a product enters its decline stage, another product should be entering its maturity phase. Making sure that there is a continuity of products at the maturity stage is important for several marketing (not losing customers who are loyal to the brand), operational (keeping the operations system busy), and financial reasons (keeping a steady stream of cash flows).

INNOVATION PERFORMANCE ASSESSMENT

Ahmed and Zairi (2000) grouped innovation performance measures into three key categories:

- *Process-focused measures* that are primarily concerned with the effectiveness either of the new product or service development process or of the overall innovation process. Examples of such measures are milestones progress ratios (the number of projects which reach their milestone on time), or the age distribution of currently commercialised products (e.g. how many current products are less than three years old?).
- *Product-based measures* that are concerned with the performance of the end product itself. A company which has extremely fast and effective innovation processes will not derive any competitive advantage if its products always perform below the competitors' standards.

Examples of such measures are market share, measures of value and degree of differentiation from the customers' side. Scores achieved in reviews and buying guides are also product-based measures.

- *Business-level measures* attempt to link innovation variables (e.g. new product introduction rate) to overall corporate performance, usually measured in financial terms. The objective of these measures is to remind managers that the innovation is not an end in itself, i.e. that the innovation performance is only a productive target if it results in a corporate-level performance.

ORGANISING FOR INNOVATION

Several research teams have studied the question of the extent to which innovation work control should be formal or not. Kono (1992) reviewed the organisational structures and control systems of 154 Japanese R&D laboratories. His conclusions were that effective innovation was the result of a careful trade-off between control and freedom. In other words, too much control blocks innovation but too much freedom leads to chaos. A survey of 130 US manufacturers conducted in 2002 concluded that formal structures generally had a negative impact on the ability to elicit new ideas (invention speed) and on the ability to bring these new ideas to the market (innovation speed). The findings also showed that invention speed tended to increase organisational stress, whereas innovation speed tended to decrease organisational stress. The conclusion of this study was that informal control should be applied at the invention stage whereas more formal controls should be applied at the innovation stage (Lukas et al., 2002).

CONCURRENT ENGINEERING

Finally, a key issue when organising for innovation is to capitalise on relationships and collaboration. Corporate innovation is above all a collective exercise. The principles of concurrent engineering were formulated in the 1980s in the USA when product manufacturers came to the conclusion that a serious competitive gap existed between themselves and foreign competitors: they suffered from long product cycles, products of low quality which did not address customers' demands well, and products that could not compete on the basis of cost. Manufacturers recognised that the source of the problem was the inability to rely on relationships between functional departments. Concurrent engineering requires a re-organisation and new processes so that the functional barriers to innovation are removed. Initially focused on the design and manufacture interface, concurrent engineering was later extended to include the participation of all stakeholders. Examples of the tools used in concurrent engineering are: team work, creativity techniques, processes eliciting collaboration and participation, and design improvement methods (e.g. value engineering).

FURTHER READING

Prasad, B. (1995) *Concurrent Engineering Fundamentals: Integrated Product and Process Organizations* (Volume I and II). New York: Prentice-Hall.

REFERENCES

Ahmed, P. and Zairi, M. (2000). 'Innovation: a performance measurement perspective', in J. Tidd (ed.), *From Knowledge Management to Strategic Competence*. London: Imperial College Press, pp. 257–294.

Kono, T. (1992) 'Organizational problems of research and development', *International Journal of Technology Management*, 7(1/2/3): 61.

Lukas, B., Menon, A. and Bell, S. (2002) 'Organizing for new product development speed and the implications for organizational stress', *Industrial Marketing Management*, 31: 349–355

New Product Development

129

New product development (NPD) is the set of processes, routines and best practices used by companies to create new product concepts and to transform these concepts into product and process designs. The outcome of NPD is the commercialisation of a product.

NPD PROCESS MODEL

In the pharmaceutical industry, less than 1 per cent of the compounds initially considered as potentially new products will make it to the clinical testing phase (i.e. human testing). Out of all the compounds which go through clinical trials, only 20 per cent will actually reach the market. When bringing a new product into the market becomes that difficult and risky, it is important to control costs and also to manage the efficiency of innovative processes.

Figure 30 presents a popular NPD model which was initially developed in 1968 and revised in 1982 by Booz Allen Hamilton.

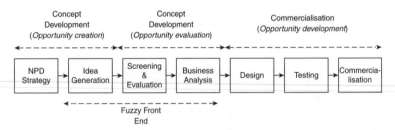

Figure 30   The BAH model of new product development
Note: The BAH model is displayed by the white activity boxes and the thick black dotted lines indicate other activity descriptions labels used by other authors

The process starts with the *NPD strategy*. This strategy is the result of strategic positioning decisions and product planning decisions: it sets the overall long-term objectives and specifies the type of portfolio of products that the firm wants to manage.

Once an NPD strategy is agreed on, the BAH process will include four key phases. The first is the truly creative part of the process where new ideas are elicited and explored. The second is design, i.e. the full physical specification of the product's structure and components. The third is the testing phase, where the designers will verify that their design matches the original specifications which were sought. The final stage is commercialisation.

THE FUZZY FRONT END: NEW CONCEPT DEVELOPMENT

Idea generation is a serious challenge as it requires imagination and creativity. This phase is also commonly referred to as the *fuzzy front end*

(FFE), implying that while it is a necessary step to go through, it is very difficult to manage, plan and control.

It is customary to associate the FFE stage with the design funnel model displayed in Figure 31. This shows that at the idea generation stage several ideas will be formulated and considered for adoption. The less worthy ideas are then gradually eliminated using screening and evaluation, and only the best ideas – from a business standpoint – are eventually retained.

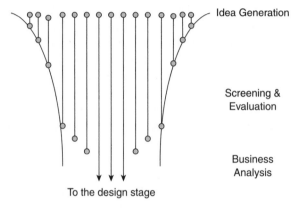

Figure 31   The design funnel

The FFE is not necessarily a stepwise process, as suggested by Figure 30. The authority in the matter – the *Product Development and Management Association* (PDMA) – would argue that the fuzzy front end is a relationship exercise, where a number of creativity and selection techniques are used to agree collectively to a new product concept (Koen, 2002). The participants in the fuzzy front end are numerous: senior management, product development specialists, marketers, etc.

The first set of FFE activities is *idea generation* or *idea enrichment*. For these activities, creativity and imagination matter highly. Examples of the techniques which are relevant here are *brainstorming, benchmarking* (comparing the performance of a product or process with those of competitors), and *reverse engineering* (the dismantling of a competitor's product to learn from their designs).

Idea selection is a set of activities through which several ideas and screened and selected. The PDMA suggests using a *portfolio methodology*, i.e. to combine several potential indicators of worthiness: probability of technical success, commercial success probability, strategic fit, and strategic leverage (i.e. what the potential impact of the new idea is in terms of achieving the long-term strategic goals).

Concept definition activities take place when ideas are documented and proposed for full scale development, but only if there is a valid business case supporting these ideas. At this stage, a final report regarding the expected benefits of the project will be expected.

In the case of technologies for which future applications and markets are very uncertain, some companies use a *Technology Stage Gate* (TSG) process rather than a New Product Development process. An NPD process has for its objectives the commercialisation of a product with a horizon of a few years, or less. A TSG will take the development of a technology through several gates before commercialization would appear on the agenda.

Opportunity identification is the set of activities concerned with the identification of opportunities to pursue. *Market research* is a common source of data for opportunity identification. Examples of other opportunity identification techniques are:

- *Roadmapping*: This is a group exercise where experts discuss future business opportunities and how they think that business conditions will change. The result is a graphical map which pictures the anticipated evolution of a line of business.
- *Competitive intelligence*: This is also known as business intelligence, and is the systematic collection of data about competitors, research and science institutions, technological trends so that a firm is kept up to date with the latest developments in its field of interest.
- *Scenario planning*: This is an exercise where individuals or groups are asked to write a scenario of how a product or a technology will be received or will impact one's business.

Opportunity analysis checks that an idea is worth pursuing. The techniques used in opportunity analysis are primarily concerned with understanding who the customer is, how large the target segment is, and who the competitors are. This will typically be handled by the marketing function.

DESIGN

Design activities are usually based on the following steps (see Cross and Roozenburg, 1993):

- *Clarify and define the task through a set of specifications*

  o A written and/or graphical summary of the specifications from an end user perspective are compiled and agreed to.

- *Determine the key functions of the product and their structures*

  o Determine the functions (e.g. heating, cooling, cutting, grasping, computing) that the product should be able to perform and how each function is inter-connected. This activity is often called functional analysis.

- *Search for solution principles and their combinations*

  o For each function, the designers have to find the best solution from a list of alternatives. The interfaces between the different solutions of the different functions have to be specified.

- *Divide into realisable modules*

  o Each set of connected solutions is regrouped into modules. For example, in the case of a personal computer, the key modules are the motherboard and its components, each peripheral, the communication bus, the internal cards, etc.

- *Develop the layout and key modules*

  o The spatial arrangement and the attachment interfaces of the components within the modules, and between the modules, are defined.

- *Complete overall layout*

  o The overall layout, for example of a computer, is defined. A choice is made between a tower, desktop, or laptop format. Specific sizes and constraints can be taken into account.

- *Prepare the production and operating instructions*

  o This includes producing a list of spare parts, a user's manual, and a maintenance manual.

A design process can be supported by the building of a *product prototype* which will go through a series of tests. These tests can provide useful feedback on improving the quality of the design. When designers are knowledgeable and experienced in an aspect of a design, they can usually forgo the prototyping stage. On the other hand, if they are dealing with new materials or new technologies, a prototype may be a strict requirement to gain some feedback about the properties of the new item.

REFERENCES

Booz Allen Hamilton (1982) *New Products Management for the 1980s*. New York: Booz Allen Hamilton.

Cross, N. and Roozenburg, N. (1993) 'Modelling the design process in engineering and in architecture', *Journal of Engineering Design*, 3 (4): 325–337.

Koen, P. (2002) 'Fuzzy front end: effective methods, tools and techniques', in Belliveau, P., Griffin, A. and Somermeyer S. (eds), *The PDMA Toolbook for New Product Development*. Mount Laurel, NJ: Product Development & Management Association.

New Service Development

> *New Service Development (NSD) is a cycle of activities used by companies to create new services concepts and to iteratively bring these concepts to the marketplace. The outcome of NSD is the full scale commercial provision of a service.*

OVERVIEW OF NEW SERVICE DEVELOPMENT

It was only in the 1990s that operations management researchers turned their attention to new service development. It was customary to believe that service development was the result of 'intuition, flair, and luck' (Menor et al., 2002). Many firms have used new service development models by simply copying or adopting new product development processes such as the BAH model (see **New Product Development**).

This approach was primarily successful in the case of the *production-line approach* to services. This approach, which was first documented by Theodore Levitt (of the Harvard Business School) in the 1970s, meant that a service was designed by using the same principles as those used for a manufacturing facility. The most famous example of this production line approach is the kitchens of fast food restaurants. Instead of a complicated, customisable cooking process, fixed menu items are ordered according to a pre-set process, the order is then transferred to the kitchen and employees will process the food and deposit this in a distribution slide. In a traditional restaurant, the service providers (chefs) will need to know a great deal about cooking. In a fast food restaurant, employees will not need to know anything about cooking: in fact, a knowledge of cooking may be detrimental to their performance as it may give them incentives to deviate from the standard pre-designed cooking processes! Another example of the production line approach to services is telephone banking, or more generally, call centres. The principle of call centres is to apply manufacturing principles (queue management, routing, and process design) to a service which used to be provided by personal advisers.

The production line approach however cannot work for all types of services. It does work well for 'service factories' (see **Process**) but it does not apply to services that fall under the *service-driven service paradigm*. Such services are by definition only obtained through the personal touch and application of skills of individual experts.

NSD PROCESS MODEL

In a review of New Service Development (NSD) models, Johnson et al. (2000) took a critical view of step-wise linear development models. They suggested an alternative model where they eliminated the start-to-finish approach of the NPD process and replaced it with a continuously looping system. This NSD process cycle represents the iterative nature of service designs and shows how development processes can quickly provide new forms of innovative services which are adaptable to a wide range of contexts.

The NSD process cycle includes four key stages. The initiation of a new concept is labelled *design* and corresponds to the fuzzy front end (see **New Product Development**). It is at this stage that innovative service formulas are generated, selected and refined into a full service concept. The following stage is *analysis* where the focus is on specifying a business model and assessing the financial feasibility of the service concept. The following stage, *development*, is the beginning of the execution stage of the cycle where a service concept becomes an actual service. The development phase includes a 'service design and testing' task. Design is used here in the operational sense of the term, and includes all the recruitment, training, facility and process design which are required to launch the service. It may also include a pilot run where the service is tested in the marketplace on a small scale.

While it is relatively easy to separate the product design from the process design in manufacturing operations, this distinction is not so clear cut in the case of services. This is especially true in the case of services which are co-produced with customers: the higher the level of customer interaction, the more difficult it is to rigidly specify how the service encounter is going to take place. It may only be after several iterations of the service provision that clear customer segments can be identified and clear procedures to serve them can be finalised.

The *final launch* is the release of the service at its target operating scale. This is often a delicate step in the life of service development as last minute adjustments may be needed, but also because more and more resources are needed to deliver the service. Whereas it is relatively easy to train and select excellent service workers for a small-scale pilot run, it is more of a challenge to recruit on a large scale and ensure that services are delivered consistently throughout a national network of service delivery points according to the initial specifications.

The NSD process cycle also highlights the role of the enablers of the development process: teams, the organisational context, and tools. Enablers are the elements of a service firm that make it good at innovation, such as hiring the right employees. It is also important to use the appropriate organisational arrangements, and to rely on teams to benefit from the synergistic performance of experts.

REFERENCES

Menor, L., Tatikonda, M. and Sampson, S. (2002) 'New service development: areas for exploitation and exploration', *Journal of Operations Management*, 20: 135–157.

Johnson, S., Menor, L., Roth, A. and Chase, R. (2000) 'A critical evaluation of the new service development process', in J. Fitzsimmons and M. Fitzsimmons (eds) *New Service Development*: London: Sage.

> *A platform is a generic product architecture from which several product versions can be designed and manufactured by combining different components, called modules.*

A recent development of innovation management in terms of product architecture has been the introduction of the product *platform*. Table 4 summarises the differences between traditional design and platform design.

Table 4   Comparison of the traditional design approach with the modern platform approach

	Traditional Approach	Platform Approach
Design of product architecture	Duplicated for each product version	Unique, the platform is designed once
Design of product component	Specific to each product version – if a component changes, the architecture should be redesigned	Components are attached to unique functionalities and have to respect tight interfacing specifications
Organisation of design	Team is responsible for the design of a product version	Team is responsible either for the design of the platform, or components, or a specific version
Process engineering	Each version requires a separate process design	A standard process can be used for all versions

Sanchez (2002) developed the following model of platform design:

- The process begins with a formulation of the value proposition, i.e. the product concept.
- Then each required functionality is attached to specific components.
- A full specification of the interface between each of the components completes the specification of the platform.

platform

The specification of the interfaces between the components is a crucial step of using platforms. This specification includes:

- *Attachment interfaces*: How the different components attach to one another.
- *Spatial interfaces*: In what volume and shape should a component fit.
- *Transfer interfaces*: What the inputs are (information, movement, power, etc.) and the output of each component.
- *Control and communication interfaces*: How the components send signals and information to one another.
- *User interfaces*: What the specification of man–machine interactions is. What types of devices are used for these interactions.
- *Environmental interfaces*: How each component behaves in its environment and is impacted by other components and external factors.

One of the most well-known examples of a product platform is the Swiss army knife: these have a standard architecture and use standard components which can be customised in an almost infinite variety of ways. Other examples of platforms include Swatch watches, Xerox copiers, Hewlett-Packard printers, and the Boeing 747 family of aircraft. In the automotive industry, innovation and design are entirely based on platform technology. Although a large manufacturer may commercialise up to 50 different models of cars, their innovation departments and factories are often based on three or four actual platforms (e.g. the small car platform, the compact car platform, the executive car platform).

Once a company has developed a robust platform, it can then innovate by bringing in new modules to the market. The Sony Walkman was originally designed as a platform in 1979. Since its launch, more than 250 models of the Sony Walkman have been sold. Only 25 per cent of these models were the result of a major innovation, i.e. a re-design of the platform. This means that 75 per cent of the 'new' versions which have been commercialised were a simple combination of different components.

SERVICE AND EXPERIENCE PLATFORMS

Initially developed in the manufacturing sector, it is more difficult to visualise and to specify a service platform.

To a certain extent, Hollywood movies are an example of experience platforms. American comedies, for example, tend to be based on relatively standard scripts. The same goes for action movies, where the timing of the different phases of a movie will be about the same. A car chase scene, for example, is one of the modules filmed every time, which can be inserted within a set movie architecture. When a movie is especially successful and delivers a genuine experience, it is common to release second or even third versions to capitalise on the money-making potential of a good movie platform.

However, the intrinsic difficulty in maintaining consistency is common, and often the daily reality, in the case of services. This can easily be explained by the following two reasons:

- Services are often dependent on service workers for their delivery. Workers have bad days, can be biased, and generally speaking can behave differently on different days. This generates a source of variability which is often difficult to control for.
- Services often involve the customer during the provision stage (co-production), or involve extensive customer contact. If ensuring consistency between the provision of a service by different service workers were a challenge, ensuring consistency of behaviour from the customer side is an even bigger challenge!

REFERENCES

Sanchez, R. (2002) 'Designing strategic flexibility into your product and processes', Perspectives for Managers, IMD, http://www.imd.ch

platform

Process Management

Process Management

> *Process management is the set of management activities by which managers design, monitor, and improve the way in which business operations are conducted.*

OVERVIEW OF PROCESS MANAGEMENT

Process management is the direct consequence of the principle of a vertical division of labour developed by Frederick Taylor in the early twentieth century. The vertical division of labour implies the separation of the individual executing a task from the individual designing the task. Instead, a specialist – a process analyst – is in charge of using a number of techniques to identify the best ways to do things, to document and implement them, and to seek ways of improving them as an organisation evolves.

When applied properly, processes and operating routines result in *process capital*, i.e. a unique source of competitive advantage that companies can tap into to differentiate their provision of products and services to customers.

Process managers should make sure that their decisions are aligned with corporate strategy: this forms the domain of process strategy. To complement process strategy, technology management is primarily concerned with the identification of the promising technologies that a company should develop or acquire. Once a process strategy is agreed upon, managers have to adopt an appropriate process system. If this process is developed internally, it is a *process design* task. If the process is adapted from well known 'off-the-shelf' process systems, then it is a *process selection* task.

Processes are not static resources. As markets, customers, and competition change, firms have to improve their processes continually to make sure that these are adequate and appropriate. *Process analysis* refers to the use of process design techniques to model and analyse existing processes for the sake of finding ways to improve them. If this redesign is radical rather than incremental, it is referred to as *Business Process Re-Engineering*, or BPR.

Finally, one of the difficulties of process management is that processes and operating routines can exhibit independent lives beyond the will of process owners! For example, for the sake of expediency and simplicity, it is often tempting to customise processes without formal documentation and analysis. This means that companies will often end up relying on a few process experts who are the sole recipients of the knowledge of 'how things get done'. Managing *process visibility* means making sure that everybody knows who does what and how.

In organisation theory, it is common to differentiate mechanistic organisations from organic ones. Organic organisations are informal and they rely extensively on collaboration and frequent communications between their members. In contrast, mechanistic organisations are very formal: clear boundaries and responsibility demarcations exist, individuals are assigned to clearly defined tasks. Whereas in organic organisations, co-ordination is achieved through communication and organisational capital, it is achieved through process management in mechanistic organisations.

Therefore, it is worth bearing in mind that the use of process management techniques presents both advantages and disadvantages. If process management is overly used in small and entrepreneurial firms, it may stifle innovation and bring operations to a halt. Alternatively, if it is ignored in a growing firm, it may result in non co-ordinated, erratic operations, which will end in business failure.

PROCESSES AS EVOLUTIONARY ROUTINES

According to the two famous evolutionary economists Nelson and Winter (1982), firms survive and expand through technological competition. Nelson and Winter's idea was to draw a parallel between evolutionary theory in biology and the evolution of firms. Firms compete by reinvesting their earnings in new and more productive technology and equipment. Firms with modern, effective processes survive whereas firms with inadequate, outdated processes go out of business.

Nelson and Winter base their work on the observation that organisational actors tend to be procedural and exert 'bounded' rationality when making decisions. This behaviour is what behavioural scientists call satisfying behaviour. Satisfying behaviour means that individuals will naturally seek to apply the simplest rules, provided that these rules will result in satisfaction. It is only in the case where satisfaction is not achieved that individuals will actively explore better ways of doing things.

Nelson and Winter called processes *'routines'*. Routines, in Nelson and Winter's work, are both a resource (i.e. process capital) and a risk. The essence of the problem of process management, according to Nelson and Winter's theory, is that although at an organisational level survival and competitiveness are the result of process adaptation and innovation, the individuals executing these processes exhibit satisfying behaviour rather than innovative behaviour. In other words, Nelson and Winter thought of organisations as being resistant to change.

The performance of firms and organisations is determined by the routines that they possess and the routines possessed by the other firms and economic units with whom the firms interact. In this way, routines act as a connecting point between the behaviour of the business and the environment of the firm. Routines are the inheritance of the firm's past and they give the underlying basis for predicting future behaviour. Although Nelson and Winter think that firms are resistant to change, they explain that routines can be changed through a hierarchy of routines, in which routines at a higher level will shape the modification of routines at a lower level.

PROCESS ANALYSIS

Process modelling is the foundation tool of process management but also of numerous other operations management techniques. Continuous improvement, six-sigma, and Business Process Reengineering all rely extensively on a preliminary step of process analysis. Irrespective of the reason why a process analysis is initiated, it requires a thorough and systematic modelling of existing processes.

The most general process modelling tool is the *process flowchart*. Graphical conventions vary but the general idea is to represent a process inputs, tasks, sub-processes (rectangles), decisions (lozenges), and outputs on a timeline. An example is shown in Figure 32.

It is beyond the scope of this book to offer a detailed presentation of every single process technique used in operations management. The different graphical conventions used by different techniques result in minor cosmetic distinctions. More important differences are the purpose and scope of the techniques. The purpose of process modelling techniques can be to:

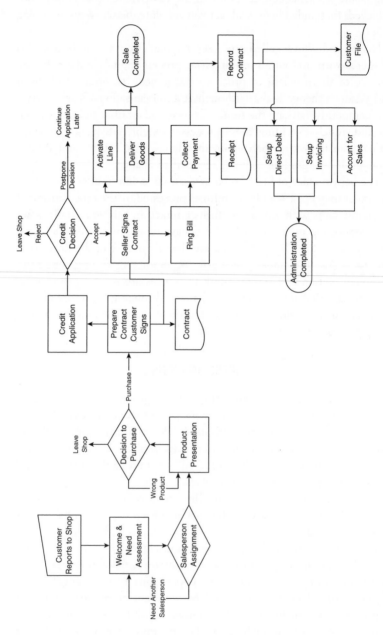

Figure 32   An example of a process flowchart

- *Model a workflow*: Process flowcharts, GANNT charts, and the ASME Mapping Standard.
- *Design an entire system rather an isolated process*: The Structured Analysis Design Technique (SADT, also called IDEF in software engineering), and the Structured System Analysis and Design Method (SSADM).
- *Document organisational interactions within a process*: Role activity diagramming (RAD) or using case scenarios such as those produced with the Unified Modelling Language (UML).

The scope of a modelling technique is also linked to the degree to which a technique is used for all stages of a process design:

- The *conceptual stage* deals with understanding the process at stake, and with providing an overall business model for an activity.
- The *logical stage* deals with documenting the inputs and outputs of each activity, and the inter-relationships between the activities.
- The *physical stage* deals with the selection of components and the description of the final process/system which will be used.

The lack of an international standard in process modelling has always been an issue, and a good review of the numerous attempts at contenders can be found in Ryan et al., 2009. Most standardisation efforts have actually taken place in the IT industry: this is why many modelling techniques (SSADM and UML for example) are better known in information management disciplines than in operations management. An exception is the Business Process Modeling Notation, or BPMN, which is a standard that was specifically designed to represent the business process. Consistently with process flowcharting, BPMN attempts to represent processes through a consistent and relatively small set of graphical symbols. Four categories of symbols are used:

- Flow objects are used to represent key process elements such as events, activities, and gateways.
- Connecting objects link the flow objects together. Examples are sequence flow arrows, message flow arrows, and association arrows.
- 'Swim lanes' are used to represent the fact that different sub-processes are executed by different teams or units. The organisation as a whole is represented as a pool, and each department is a 'swim lane'. For example, Figure 32 could be redrawn by categorising processes in three swim lanes: shop (front office), credit office, and administrative back office.

- Artefacts are the data objects which are being processed, annotations which are used to explain the diagram, or groupings made to clarify organisational responsibilities over processes.

PROCESS IMPROVEMENT

There are several possible higher-level routines used to improve processes, such as BPR and process modelling tools: they are discussed in the following paragraphs. It is important to note, though, that in line with the continuous improvement concept, organisations can improve their processes by permanently seeking to adjust their processes to current business conditions. This idea of small, but ever ongoing, improvement corresponds to the Japanese philosophy of **Kaizen** change.

Much of the operations management literature has promoted 'big' and radical approaches to process management, such as BPR. Although such approaches are needed in some contexts, it is important to remember that *process improvement*, or PI, is an activity in its own right.

Bateman and Rich (2002) documented the problems with PI initiatives in UK companies, and they highlight that a key issue is the sustainability of process improvements. Many improvements are applied locally to a specific cell in the factory but are never passed on to other cells that could benefit from them. Other improvements will generate results initially, but they are eventually abandoned as either a budget or commitment is lacking to keep them alive. Bateman and Rich have formulated a sustainable process improvement framework which illustrates a four-level hierarchy of routines which are involved in process improvement initiatives. The idea is that a local cell improvement may (1) be standardised and applied to several other local cells. In this quest to transfer knowledge, a process engineer may attempt to (2) apply the initial knowledge to a different context. This in turn leads to (3) many other new ideas for local cell improvement, and potentially, to the discovery of new cycles of improvements. Finally, in the process of customising a process improvement to a new context, a process analyst may (4) need to acquire new knowledge and techniques, which could be the starting point of other improvements in specific local areas.

BUSINESS PROCESS RE-ENGINEERING

Business Process Re-engineering (BPR) was introduced in the 1990s by Hammer and Champy with the business bestseller *Reengineering the Corporation*. The extent to which BPR was truly a novelty is a controversial point. First, from a technical standpoint, BPR does not differ from traditional methods of engineering as it has been practised since the 1920s, and as with these methods, BPR heavily uses process modelling and analysis techniques. The distinctive point of BPR, thus, is not the set of techniques that are used, but the managerial approach which is used to apply them. Instead of adopting the careful, incremental, and controlled experimentation approach of continuous improvement, BPR analysts seek the radical redesign of corporate processes. Why such a radical standpoint when quality managements suggest the opposite approach? BPR finds its legitimacy in the idea that after decades of incremental changes, organisational processes can find themselves completely at odds with market demands. In such cases, a more radical 'design optimal processes from scratch' approach can pay off.

With BPR, companies that had been promoting teamwork, empowerment and corporate citizenship for years suddenly started to promote aggressive performance targets (e.g. reduce inventory by half, increase profitability by 150 per cent) and took dramatic action to achieve these targets. BPR programmes in the 1990s became infamous for their more or less systematic association with corporate layoffs, often on a grand scale.

REFERENCES

Bateman, N. and Rich, A. (2002) 'Process improvement programmes: a model for assessing sustainability', *International Journal of Operations and Production Management*, 22 (5): 515–526.

Hammer, M. and Champy, J. (1993) *Reengineering the Corporation*. New York: Harper Collins.

Nelson, R. and Winter, S. (1982) *Evolutionary Theory of Economic Change*. Cambridge, MA: Harvard University Press.

Ryan, K., Ko, S., Lee, S. and Lee, L. (2009) 'Business process management (BPM) standards: a survey', *Business Process Management Journal*, 15 (5): 744–791.

process management

> *Work design is concerned with the analysis of the interactions between worker, task, and the organisational environment.*

HUMAN CAPITAL AND OPERATIONS MANAGEMENT

During the Industrial Revolution, a factory manager's role would have included human resource management. It was only in the 1920s that human resources management (HRM) emerged as a specialised discipline. Although there are different ways to define the boundaries of HRM, it normally deals with the process of recruitment and selection, human resources development (e.g. training), personnel issues (administrative, career management, running of appraisal schemes, etc.), or other support and administrative tasks. In some modern organisations, it is also common that most operations management tasks are located in a specialist 'technical department' (for example, a process engineering department or a production planning unit), whilst the management of the line workers is the responsibility of management. Management, operations management, and human resources management are therefore three different functions that all deal with some aspect of the management of human capital. It is tempting to differentiate these functions by giving textbook definitions, such as: management deals with the direct supervision of workers, human resource management with the administrative management of workers and their development, and operations management with the way things should be done. Although this is a useful description of the working mechanisms of what Mintzberg calls the machine bureaucracy, it is important to bear in mind that different organisational forms exist, and that for each form, different delineations of roles between HRM, management, and operations management will take place. In the professional bureaucracy, for example, the investment in human capital is much higher and professional workers will tend to resent the influence of technical support workers, preferring to work according to their own professional codes.

This means that it is not possible to prescribe a unique or best way to integrate HRM, management, and operations management. In some cases, like small businesses, the three functions may be the work of a single department or of a single individual! Human capital, however remains an essential component of the set of resources behind operations systems. The factory of the future – where only machines perform work and all workers have been eliminated – only exists in a handful of facilities in Japan. In fact, there is evidence that there is no need for further automation in many industrial sectors, as the cost of automation would be too high when compared to human operators. Robots, for example, are nearly always more expensive than a human operator. Robots are used when the working conditions are dangerous (for example, a paint room), when a task is physically hard and cumbersome (for example, assembling a windshield), or when the task requires a very high level of consistency (for example, welding). Thus, apart from rare exceptions, operations managers cannot ignore the human dimension of operational resources.

WORK STUDY

Work study is in many respects the ancestor of operations management. Many regard the pioneering work of Taylor's scientific management methods as the first in operations management. Work study is basically concerned with the analysis of how work is done and of how it should be done. It is therefore a direct application of the principle of the vertical division of labour (see **Operations**). Prior to the work of Taylor, craftsmen were basically responsible for setting their own work methods. Taylor's innovation was to use a scientific method to observe, measure, and document how workers completed a task. Through a comparison of the different methods, Taylor was able to specify a 'best of breed' work method, which should be adopted by all workers in order to increase productivity. The efficiency gains that resulted from his efforts were such that his ideas were quickly adopted. These were influential, for example, in the development of the first assembly lines, such as that designed by Henry Ford to build the first mass-produced car – the Model T.

Throughout the twentieth century, *work study* analysts concentrated on refining the principles of scientific management. Examples of work study projects are:

- Work study can investigate a whole production system. In this case, the purpose is to identify delays, redundant steps, or any form of wasted time. This form of work study is based on drawing blueprints or flow diagrams of processes. It is the ancestor of modern process analysis techniques (see **Process Management**).

- The most well-known application of work study is the analysis of a worker at his or her workstation. Here, the purpose is to formulate the best method of work. Taylor's original method of study was developed by his followers and became known as the field of *motion studies*. In motion studies, analysts study human motion and identify the most efficient. Time and motion studies handbooks contain very large databases indicating how much time it takes to grasp an object depending on the object's weight, how long it takes to move it across a workstation, and so on. Bennett (1986) summarised the different steps to conducting a work study:

  o Select the method to be studied.
  o Record the present method of working. This includes an exercise of work measurement, where workers' performance with the current method is observed.
  o The results are examined and compared to standard motion studies benchmarks. Ideas for improvement are formulated and evaluated, and an improved method is suggested, along with a new target 'standard' time for the task. This may be supported by another measurement study, to validate the different allowances and the standard.
  o The validated method is installed and maintained.

- The design of the workstation is also important, as a workstation should provide a work configuration which is compatible with the recommended method. This is the domain of *ergonomics*. Ergonomics also includes the study of the interactions between man and machine. The objectives of these studies are to utilise as well as possible both humans and machines. An idle machine waiting for an operator to start it and an idle operator looking at a machine are not very productive notions, and a variety of diagramming techniques are used to document existing methods in order to identify directions for improvement.

- Finally, work study can also deal with interactions between workers. Again, a variety of activity charting and diagramming techniques are used to study and formulate improvements to work methods.

WORK DESIGN VS. WORK STUDY

Work design is a more general activity dealing with the definition of roles and boundaries associated with the work assigned to individual workers. Whereas work study has a clear technical focus (e.g. the analysis of motions) and is primarily concerned with performance, work design combines (1) work study (i.e. the analysis of tasks) with (2) the analysis of workers and (3) the analysis of the environment. In this broader perspective, questions such as 'Is the training of workers adequate given their task assignment?' or 'Do societal values correspond to the type of work being performed here?' can be asked. Consistent with the views of socio-technical systems thinking, work design attempts to make sure that workers, tasks, and environment are consistent and *fit* with one another. The car manufacturer Volvo was famous in the 1980s for its efforts to develop production systems and work methods which were consistent with the level of knowledge, motivations and values of its local workforce in Sweden.

Whereas work study remains strongly associated with operations management, work design is considered more of a management problem rather than an operations management problem. This is especially the case for the task of job design, i.e. the specification of the roles and responsibilities of an employee. Parker and Wall (1998) reviewed the history of work design and concluded that Taylor's work was basically the first formalised school of work design. Parker and Wall called it the job simplification school, as its working principle was to decompose jobs into successively finer levels of simple activities and sub-activities. It was only in the 1950s that alternative approaches to work design were formulated.

Leseure and Brookes (2000) proposed a contingent model that described which schools of work design work best as a function of the knowledge context in which work is taking place. Their model is shown in Figure 33. The horizontal axis represents the type of knowledge requirements which are required at work. Some jobs require individuals to come up with new ideas and create new knowledge, whereas others only require workers to re-use known knowledge. Workers, however, rarely work totally autonomously: specialisation patterns require that the different specialists exchange knowledge whilst performing work. This is captured by the vertical scale, which indicates the frequency with which knowledge should be shared at work.

Figure 33 is not a discrete two-by-two classification. Instead it represents a full spectrum of work contexts. The centre arrows indicate that should a work context lie in one of the corners of the space then only one school of work design will work. Imagine that a work context falls in the middle of the space: in that position, all approaches are equally suitable.

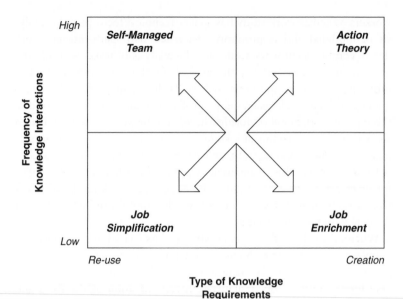

High

Frequency of
Knowledge Interactions

Low

| **Self-Managed Team** | **Action Theory** |
| **Job Simplification** | **Job Enrichment** |

Re-use   Creation

**Type of Knowledge
Requirements**

Figure 33   *A context-based model of work design*

In contexts where jobs do not demand a lot of interaction between workers and where the work is primarily about re-using knowledge (e.g. following process specifications), job simplification will naturally work very well. In this context, Taylor's ideas and the formal methods of work study are perfectly adequate.

On the bottom right-hand side of the diagram, work requires individual specialists to innovate and these individuals can carry out their task relatively autonomously. This is an area where the school of job enrichment works best. Job enrichment encourages managers to design a job and work environment that accommodates individual rather than group needs: keeping individuals happy and motivated is the priority. From an operations management perspective, job enrichment will require adequate processes and expertise in scheduling in order to integrate into a whole the role of the different specialists.

When work only requires knowledge re-use but demands extensive interactions between workers, self-managed teams will provide the best work design approach. The purpose here is to design the perfect job for a group rather than for an individual. It is down to the individuals to self-organise themselves and to perform the group task according to expectations. This approach is commonly used in mass production environments in order to alleviate the negative aspects of too much job simplification: boredom, physical strain, etc. Japanese production teams are one example where teams are responsible for designing and implementing their own job rotation patterns in order to bring in task variety for individuals working on an assembly line.

Finally, the top right corner represents the most demanding work environment: one where individual experts are needed to create new knowledge but cannot do so in isolation. In order to complete their task, they will need frequent and sustained interactions with other experts who are performing differentiated tasks. Parker and Wall (1998) discussed a fourth job design school – action theory – which happened to match this context. The key ideas behind action theory are that when designing jobs whole actions should be allocated to a job and actions should never be broken down. If you are responsible for an action, you should be responsible for its planning, execution, and performance assessment. In other words, action theory deals with jobs where neither the vertical nor the horizontal division of labour will work. In operations management, this is often associated with project management for radical innovation and practices such as concurrent engineering or the use of platforms. Complex co-production service environments and service outsourcing schemes also correspond to this context.

REFERENCES

Bennett, D.J. (1986) *Production Systems Design*. London: Butterworth.
Leseure, M. and Brookes, N. (2000) 'Micro knowledge management: a job design framework', in R. Rajkumar (ed.), *Industrial Knowledge Management: A Micro Level Approach*. London: Springer-Verlag, pp. 163-178.
Parker S. and Wall, T. (1998) *Job and Work Design*. London: Sage.

Learning Curves

Learning curves are a set of mathematical models that capture the time reduction incurred when completing a task repetitively and as a worker's experience increases.

LEARNING SPECIALISED WORK

In a 1987 landmark experiment, Roger Holtback, the president of Volvo Cars, manually assembled an entire car from scratch in a new factory in Sweden. It is reported that Holtback did manage to start the car and drive it off the factory floor, but that the car was not defect free! This experiment goes counter to the principle of a division of labour. In a modern automotive assembly factory, an assembly line worker would be assigned a single task, e.g. fitting brake drum assembly.

This intense specialisation has two rationales:

1 If a worker handles several tasks, he permanently wastes time switching from one task to another. In the case of Roger Holtback assembling an entire car by himself, a great deal of time would have been spent looking for parts and tools and moving around the car.
2 It is likely that Roger Holtback's second car would have had fewer defects and been assembled faster. His fifth car might have actually been defect free, and it may have required only a fraction of the time required to assemble the first car. This is because of individual learning. *Individual learning is easier on simpler tasks.*

In 1935, industrial engineers in the US aerospace industry discovered that the rate of learning when completing a new task was a fairly identical process across several operators. They also discovered that the rate of learning could be modelled, and measured, mathematically: thus the concept of a *learning curve* was born.

LEARNING CURVES

The individual learning of operational tasks has been studied extensively and is modelled by learning curves. The general idea of a learning curve is that the time (and thus the cost) of completing a task will reduce as the volume produced increases.

The general formula of a learning curve is shown in the equation below:

$$T_i = T_1 i^n$$

where:

- i is the unit number
- T_i is the time required to complete unit number i (T_1 for the first unit).
- $n = \log b / \log 2$, b is called the learning percentage.

By convention, the learning percentage is defined as the reduction in time achieved when the output is doubled.

For example, consider the case of brake drum assembly. T_1 is 10 minutes, and b is 70%. With these data, we can compute the time it would take a worker to perform the second assembly of a brake drum:

$$T_2 = T_1 2^{\log 0.7/\log 2} = 10(2)^{-0.515} = \frac{10}{1.4290} = 7.00 mn$$

You may point out that we could have computed T_2 as $0.7 \times T_1$, which would have been a bit more simple! The advantage of the first equation is that it allows you to compute T_3, T_7, and T_{25} without computing the intermediate values.

Figure 34 displays the assembly completion time as more and more units are produced.

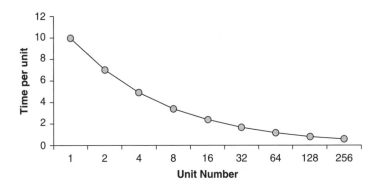

Figure 34   Example of a 70% learning curve

It suggests that at the 256th assembly, only 0.58 minutes are required. This is clearly an issue, as it is unlikely that the best assembly line workers would assemble a brake drum in less than two minutes. In a highly repetitive work context, where tasks are repeated several hundred times in one day, learning curves will only model the period of learning: learning ends when the task is completed so quickly that there is no more room for learning or improvement. This idea is captured in this equation:

$$T_i = T_0 + T_{Max} i^n$$

where:

- T_0 is asymptote (the minimum possible time in which the task can be completed).
- T_{Max} is the difference between T_1 and T_0, and represents the maximum possible time reduction.

USING LEARNING CURVES IN PRACTICE

In practice, learning curves are used in a great variety of contexts for the sake of costing and budgeting:

- In non-repetitive job environments to estimate the time and cost of a small batch of identical jobs. For example, in precision machining, an order of five parts should be based on a cheaper average price than an order of two parts.
- In repetitive job environments to plan for output during the first month of production and for the maximum achievable output once the learning phase is finished.
- In repetitive job environments to select workers with better learning skills and to plan for training activities.

In these situations, the problem for operations managers is to estimate what the learning rates are. A general rule of thumb is the learning rate (i.e. the learning coefficient b) will range from 70 per cent to 95 per cent. Low learning coefficients tend to prevail in work environments where the manual labour content is high, whereas high coefficients are associated with work environments with a low labour content and high automation. Industry-specific learning coefficients can also be used.

In order to assess a learning coefficient, it is easier to plot values on a graph with logarithmic scales, where the learning curve will appear as a straight line with a slope of b, rather than as a curvilinear function.

LEARNING CURVES FOR VARIABLE TASKS

Although learning curves are traditionally associated with highly repetitive tasks, they can also be used (with more caution) in contexts where the tasks are more variable. This is, for example, the case for service operations which demand a high level of customer contact and therefore where the provision of the service may vary greatly from one customer to another. For example, learning curves have been an increasingly important budgeting tool in the medical sector.

The difficulties in applying the learning curves concept to this sector are:

- Situations where high failure rates prevail in the early stage of implementation. High failure rates mean that management could come to the conclusion that the process is not viable and should be abandoned. By monitoring the learning rate, it is possible to estimate if the process, once matured, will be satisfactory or not.
- Situations where the context of the task is so variable that it is difficult to observe, in practice, if there has been any learning. This is the case for most surgical procedures where the health, medical history and age of the patient can have a dramatic impact on the time spent completeing the surgery.
- Situations where a reduction in processing times is associated with a decline in the quality of the surgery. It is important to differentiate expediting from learning!

Smith and Larson (1989) used learning curves to model the effect of learning on cost in the case of heart transplantation and showed how learning could make the case for a surgical procedure which was initially perceived to be too risky.

Ernst et al. (2003) used learning curves to model learning effects in knee replacement surgery. Their empirical data not only confirmed the existence of learning curves and showed that an experienced surgeon completed a surgery on average 84 per cent quicker than a non-expert, but also showed that a reduction in surgery time was not associated with a higher failure rate or a lower quality medical service.

EXPERIENCE CURVES

Experience curves are *organisational*, rather than individual, learning curves. Individual learning curves, investments in technology and productivity improvement, the adoption of best practices and the experience in a craft that results from repeated practice all contribute to the experience effect. The equation for an experience curve is the same as for a learning curve. Chambers and Johnston (2000) used learning curves to model the experience effect in British Airways from 1974 to 1993. Their analysis showed that British Airways had known two phases in its history where it achieved experience curves: the first during an integration phase (British Airways was created after the merger of two companies) and the second after the privatisation of the company. The phase during which the company was preparing itself for privatisation was, however, associated with an increase in unit costs and thus no experience effects seemed to have been achieved in this interim period.

REFERENCES

Chambers, S. and Johnston, R. (2000) 'Experience curves in services: macro and micro level approaches', *International Journal of Operations and Production Management*, 20 (7): 842–859.

Ernst, C., Ersnt, G. and Szczesny, A. (2003) 'Does learning matter for knee replacement surgeries? Data evidence from a German hospital', *Financial Accountability & Management*, 19 (4): 375–396.

Smith, D. and Larson, J. (1989) 'The impact of learning on cost: the case of heart transplantation', *Hospital and Service Administration*, 34 (1): 85–97.

Outsourcing

Outsourcing decisions are concerned with whether or not to retain in house some operations. The alternative is to subcontract these operations and to manage the business relationship with the supplier so that performance is improved.

OUTSOURCING ACTIVITIES

Should a firm try to own and control all aspects of a production value chain, or should it attempt to concentrate on one specific task within this value chain? *Vertical integration* refers to the extent to which a firm participates in all the transformation stages of a product. For example, a firm which involves itself with the extraction of raw materials, primary transformation, manufacturing, distribution and commercialisation is completely vertically integrated. Historically, manufacturing firms have been heavily vertically integrated and have gone through a phase of gradually outsourcing, i.e. of divesting peripheral activities, in order to focus on their core competences. Also note that in recent years, the trend to vertically disintegrate operations has also been implemented in conjunction with *horizontal integration*, i.e. with the tendency to enrich a core product provision with related products and services. The servitisation of manufacturing firms is a prime example.

Outsourcing is not only a manufacturing phenomenon as service organisations have traditionally also been very vertically integrated. Consider for example the management of the operations of a hotel: this can include facility management, reservation and billing services, cleaning services, catering, inventory management, and may even be the management of a vegetable garden supplying the kitchen. Similarly to manufacturing firms, service firms have actively sought to divest what they consider to be non-core activities. *Business process outsourcing* is the systematic study of the business processes within a service firm in order to decide if these business processes should be kept in-house or externalised. As a result many service firms have outsourced some of their business processes, such a customer service, billing services, payment collection, call centres, etc. Business process outsourcing has been very intense in some service areas, as for example in the case of information technology (IT) outsourcing. Whereas some companies will only outsource specific IT processes, as for example in the development of custom software, others will outsource the daily monitoring and the operation of their computer networks, while others will outsource all IT processes, inclusive of the definition, validation and implementation of their IT strategy.

The outsourcing of manufacturing and services has also been associated with companies seeking to relocate labour intensive operations systems in those parts of the world where labour is cheap. International outsourcing is a rich field of research in international operations management. *Offshoring* is the term used to denote that this is taking place at an international scale. Many emergent economies, such as those of India and China, have experienced significant economic growth as a result of receiving offshoring investments.

The widespread popularity of outsourcing and offshoring is not without creating operations management problems when it comes to delivery dependability, quality, or other performance dimensions. Such concerns are addressed through **supply chain** management techniques.

It is also noteworthy that the general trend to outsource does not mean that vertical integration is never a sound business strategy. For example, many primary sector firms (mines, farms) have improved their profitability by moving up the value chain and investing in facilities transforming raw materials. Similarly, Leseure et al. (2009) explain the growth of the Mauritius offshore textile sector and the relative demise of the Moroccan offshore textile sector by the fact that the former, and not the later, invested in vertical integration.

DECISION VARIABLES

There are several variables in the decision of whether to vertically integrate operations or not:

- *Cost efficiency*: Firms that are vertically integrated often find that they can purchase some of the products made in house at a cheaper price from an external supplier. If a firm cannot find ways of decreasing its internal production costs, it should consider outsourcing. Alternatively, a product made in house can be cheaper if the production facility is relocated to a low labour cost country.
- *Control and dependence*: Although relying on external suppliers can provide a cost advantage, it also creates a dependence link. For example, if a supplier delivers products late, this will have a negative impact on customer operations.
- *Capital rationing*: Although internally controlling every single aspect of the value chain may be seductive, the limited corporate funds available for investment may prevent a full vertical integration.
- *Value of downward/upward process*: Firms will sometimes observe that they are operating at a low value added echelon of the value chain. When they do so, they will often attempt to expand their operations upward or downward in order to operate in those echelons with higher margins. For example, opening a farm shop is one attempt to capture higher retail margins through a vertical integration strategy.
- *Existence of a supply base*: Companies operating in transition or emerging economies will often face the problem of not being able to find any reliable suppliers. In this case, they will have no other option than to vertically integrate, i.e. to create an internal department that can feed and support their core operations.
- *International issues*: When a firm is considering the decision to offshore, it will also have to consider a number of factors in addition to

cost and dependence issues. Examples here are cultural difference and their impact on operations, exchange rate volatility, tax regimes, etc.

DECISION-MAKING FRAMEWORKS

There are three key schools of thought when it comes to making decisions about the degree of vertical integration of a firm: (1) make or buy models, (2) transaction cost economics, and (3) core competency thinking.

Accountants have for a long time developed '*make or buy*' decision models. Make or buy decision frameworks are the result of the permanent quest by managers and cost accountants to try to reduce costs. For example, should a cheese producer manufacture the boxes in which its products are sold or should it purchase these from an outside supplier? The decision has two parameters: the performance of the supplier and the company's internal performance. Although modern make or buy decisions models incorporate dimensions such as leadtime and quality, make or buy models were initially developed with a sole focus on costs.

Outsourcing, however, does not come free in terms of management effort. This fact is the key tenet of *transaction cost theory*. The economist Oliver Williamson (1975) formulated this theory in order to stress that firms have several alternative mechanisms to co-ordinate operations. His starting point was that according to the theory, firms should specialise in one activity only in order to take advantage of economies of scale: in other words, according to the theory investment in capital intensity makes sense, whereas investment in vertical integration, or more generally distinct activities, does not. Williamson observed that in practice firms did carry a portfolio of activities which were co-ordinated through various means. Firms could first co-ordinate operations internally, through hierarchical forces. Alternatively, they could rely on the market and the price mechanism to acquire supplies: by paying the right price, a firm can make sure that it will be delivered a supply of the right quality when needed. If a supplier becomes too greedy, the firm can exert its purchasing power by switching to another more competitive supplier. Finally, firms could enter partnerships, alliances, or other trust-based business arrangements where co-ordination between a buyer and a supplier is achieved through a hybrid combination of hierarchy and market forces.

Williamson's model posits that the decision to internalise or outsource the production of a product depends on three characteristics of the product being traded. Asset specificity is the degree to which the product is a simple commodity or a product whose demand and characteristics are very unique to the firm. Non-specific assets can be outsourced whereas highly specific assets should be internalised, especially if their acquisition will involve high transaction costs. The frequency with which an asset is being traded is also a parameter of the decision. If an asset is traded frequently, its sourcing becomes a routine matter and all the problems encountered during the first deliveries are eventually solved. Conversely, if the purchase of the asset is a one-off order, a lot of management effort will be required to make sure that the product is delivered to specification: in this case, in house production is worth considering. Finally, transaction uncertainty deals with the extent to which the quality of the asset (e.g. its feasibility) is considered risky. If a transaction is certain (i.e. if it is clear that no risks are being taken) outsourcing is fine. On the other hand, if feasibility problems, potential delays and issues of quality are likely to have a high impact on the seller's operations then it is better to arrange for the production of the asset internally.

In transaction cost theory, the objective of the decision whether or not to outsource is to minimise transaction costs. Although management will do its best to control transaction costs, the actual outcome of the decision remains unpredictable because of:

- *Bounded rationality*: Managers will make decisions on the basis of the information they have, i.e. they will make rational decisions that are bounded by the quality of the data that they have based their decision upon.
- *Opportunism*: External parties may seize opportunities in ways that will be detrimental to the firm. For example, a supplier may knowingly delay a delivery to give priority to another customer.

Finally, the last decision-making framework for outsourcing decisions is the core competencies view (Prahalad and Hamel, 1990). With the core competencies view, the focus of the decision moves away from cost to strategic considerations. If managers can ascertain that an activity is part of the core competencies of a firm, then the activity should remain internalised. Conversely, if an activity can only be described as a support function, a 'necessary evil', then managers should endeavour to externalise it. In the core competencies view, costs are a short-term expression of the strategy execution: what matters is not what the activity costs the firm today, but what it will cost in the long term, once its execution has been honed to perfection.

REFERENCES

Leseure M., Hurreeram, D. and Bennett, D.J. (2009) 'Playing catch-up with China: challenges and strategies for smaller developing countries', *Technology Analysis and Strategic Management*, 21 (5): 617–637.

Prahalad, C. and Hamel, G. (1990) 'The core competence of the corporation', *Harvard Business Review*, July–August: 79–91.

Williamson, O. (1975) *Markets and Hierarchies*. New York: Free.

outsourcing

Quality

> *Quality is an operations system's performance dimension: it is, at a minimum, the ability of a system to deliver a product or service that matches the customer's specifications.*

QUALITY IN HISTORY

There is no general agreement about the historical origin of mankind's concern with quality. Some consider the guilds and master craftsmen of Europe's Middle Ages as the first 'organised' forms of quality management, although there is ample historical evidence that quality mattered in older civilisations. The history of quality is in fact a complicated one: whereas logic would suggest a sustained interest in the search for quality by all civilisations and epochs, the Industrial Revolution and the two World Wars led to an 'accident of history', a two hundred year-long era where maintaining quality became a delicate matter for organisations.

What we know is that at the end of the Second World War, industrial companies did not shy away from the fact that quality was a secondary concern. In its own history, the Toyota Motor Corporation acknowledges that the quality of its trucks was so poor that the show vehicles would often break down on their way to car exhibitions. In the 1950s, Citroen was also well aware of the problems and breakdowns that plagued its newly released models. In a post-war reconstruction economy supply can undershoot demand and, thus, customers cannot afford to be too 'picky'.

This state of affairs changed in the late 1970s when US manufacturers found themselves at a growing competitive disadvantage when their products were compared to Japanese imports. Europe should have suffered the same fate, but the shock of competition on quality was attenuated by protectionist policies. In the USA this quality challenge led to a response, which has often been called the *'quality revolution'*. This response resulted in the development, growth and adoption of quality management practices.

In the industrialised world, the days of thinking of quality as a marginal and secondary concern are long gone. Quality is recognised in most contexts as a key competitive dimension and organisations need the capability to manage their performance along this dimension. However there are still economies today where, due to various reasons (shortage of goods, lack of knowledge, thriving opportunism, etc.), the quality revolution has not taken place yet.

DEFINING QUALITY

It was in the middle 1980s, in the midst of the competitive battle between Japanese and US manufacturers, that Garvin (1984) wrote his seminal paper on defining what product quality is. In this paper, he describes five ways of defining quality:

- *Transcendental quality* has its roots in philosophy and can be equated with the philosophical debate about beauty. Quality describes a condition of innate excellence associated with a product or act, and we recognise it when we see it.
- *Product-based definitions* have an economics root: it is because of the mix of ingredients or the possession of certain attributes that a product is perceived as being of good quality. High quality comes at a high cost.
- *User-based definitions* enrich the economics view with the marketing preoccupation with the needs of the user. In this definition, it is the user's requirements and the satisfaction of these requirements that result in a perception of quality. This view is represented by Juran and Gryna's (1988) definition: 'quality is fitness for use'. In this outlook, there is no need to exceed customers' expectations.
- *Value-based definitions* suggest that the perception of quality is akin to a value judgment: for example, the performance of a product is acceptable given the low cost of the product.
- *Manufacturing-based definitions* describe quality from the viewpoint of the industrial producer: this describes to which extent a product matches the design specifications. It is often called *conformance quality*.

SERVICE QUALITY

In the case of services, Parasuraman, et al. (1988) developed the SERVQUAL model and propose the following ten dimensions to measure service quality: tangibles, service reliability, responsiveness, assurance, empathy, availability, professionalism, timeliness, completeness, and pleasantness. Despite a strong initial interest in SERVQUAL, it is today recognised as being overly complex, statistically unreliable, and subject to conceptual controversies (Buttle, 1996). Although some improved formulations have been produced (e.g. the RATER model by the same authors), there are a great number of other service quality frameworks:

- The SERVPERF model criticised the SERVQUAL conceptual definition of service quality as the difference between expectations and performance, and suggested that service quality should be measured directly as the perceived performance by the customer.
- Transaction analysis is an alternative approach arguing that service quality perception is the aggregate of many 'unit' perceptions incurred within a service exchange: for example, a customer may rate a hotel service poorly despite an excellent dinner only because the reception staff were unfriendly. This approach often starts with the modelling of the *customer journey*, i.e. the list of all transactions incurred by the customer.
- A number of service quality frameworks use direct observation (rather than customer surveys). Audits and mystery shoppers are examples of some techniques used.
- The critical incident technique focuses on critical service encounters, i.e. the pivotal transactions or exchanges that condition the overall perception of service quality.
- Finally, the latest measurement framework is the commercial NetPromoter package where consultants argue that overall service quality can be captured using a single question: would customers recommend the service to others? Questionnaires are administered to customers who are then classified on the basis of their responses. Some customers, called promoters, will tend to recommend the service to others and bring in new customers, and the firm should do everything to keep these customers happy. Other customers, called detractors, will do the opposite. These should be managed differently and the firm should make efforts to transform them into promoters, or else discourage custom.

REFERENCES

Buttle, F. (1996) SERVQUAL: review, critique, research agenda, *European Journal of Marketing*, 30(1): 8–31.

Garvin, D. (1984) What does product quality really means?, *Sloan Management Review*, 26(1): 25–43.

Juran, J. and Gryna, F. (1988) *Quality Control handbook*, 4th edn. New York: McGraw-Hill.

Parasuraman, A., Zeithaml, V. and Berry, L. (1988) Servqual: A multiple-item scale for measuring perceptions of service quality, *Journal of Retailing*, 64(1): 12–40.

Quality Management

> **Quality management is the set of managerial actions taken to ensure that operations systems perform adequately on the quality performance dimension.**

THE HISTORICAL EVOLUTION OF QUALITY MANAGEMENT PROCESSES

In business history, the first efforts to manage quality have always been associated with *inspection*. In order to make sure that customers would not be sold defective products, quality inspectors used to inspect products at the end of assembly lines. Should a product be found to be faulty, it could either be scraped or reworked. In either case important costs are incurred by an organisation.

Inspection is the ancestor of modern *quality control*. Quality control is the set of activities by which a company makes sure that its products are fault-proof and match customers' needs. Quality control means that all production is checked against certain standards before being released to customers. If standards are not matched a number of corrective actions can be implemented.

Inspection, though, is not the only way to implement quality control. Early on, manufacturers realised that 100 per cent inspection does not guarantee 100 per cent quality, as human errors are unavoidable in repetitive inspection tasks. This led to experimenting with the idea of asking workers to self-check the quality of their own work. These experiments paved the way from moving away from a mentality of relying on inspection and toward a mentality of 'doing things right the first time'.

Furthermore, in the old days of inspection-driven quality management, the focus was on detecting and fixing a quality failure, but not on questioning why the failure happened in the first place. It became clear that quality control was only one step in a quality management programme, a step which fed other quality management processes: *quality assurance*, *quality improvement* and *quality planning*.

- *Quality assurance* is based on the premise that a faulty product is the result of a faulty process. If engineers can fix the process and ensure that the process only produces good quality parts, then there is no need for inspection any longer (see **Statistical Process Control**).
- Quality control and quality assurance both feed a *quality improvement process*. Quality control and quality assurance help to flag up outstanding quality issues in product and process design respectively. The issues are addressed by improving either the product and process designs. Quality improvement is often described as a permanent and iterative process rather than as a one-off exercise (see **Kaizen**).
- *Quality planning* is a necessity with the abandonment of passive quality management practices (i.e., dependence on inspection). The adoption of quality assurance requires a much more pro-active stance on the question of quality within a company. Managing quality will consume resources, hence the need for planning. The purpose of quality planning is to formalise what the standards of the companies are and to set forth a co-ordinated plan for the simultaneous implementation of quality control, assurance and improvement.

TOOLS OF QUALITY MANAGEMENT

Quality management as inspection was a simple process. Modern quality management, as a practice, is complex and relies on a rich battery of analytical tools. The 'quality toolbox' is composed of:

- *Scatter diagrams* display two variables in an X-Y system of coordinates in order to discover potential relationships. For example, a scatter graph could be used to display the number of paint defects on a car as a function of paint density.
- *Pareto diagrams* display on a vertical scale the frequency of occurrence of a set of problems ranked in decreasing order on the horizontal axis. Their purpose is to manage efficiently by revealing Pareto or 80–20 distribution patterns. The principle is that if management concentrates on the 20 per cent most frequent problems, the number of customer complaints (or the cost of poor quality) may decrease by 80 per cent.
- *Histograms* graphically display the distribution over a period of time of a quality dimension (number of defect, weight of a product, etc.). They are similar to Pareto diagrams but the distribution may not exhibit Pareto properties. Instead, they simply display the degree of variability exhibited by a productive process.

- *Check sheets* or *check lists* are forms containing a specification of a list of quality defects that can occur. They are used to make sure that self-inspection is done, but also to feed data into quality control systems.
- *Run charts* or *control charts* display the characteristics of a product (dimension, weight, number of defects, etc.) over time. These are use to study the evolution of quality defects and to alert management when defect rates suddenly pick up.
- *Cause and effect diagrams* are a fishbone-like diagram where the head of the fish represents a specific issue with a product or service. A branching structure ending at the root of the diagram is used to indicate all the possible causes of the problem.
- *Acceptance sampling* is a set of statistical procedures using the properties of statistical distributions to reduce the size of the samples required to validate the quality of a large number of products. For example, with acceptance sampling, a batch of 10,000 parts could be validated as being of good quality through the random inspection of 100 parts from the batch. Acceptance sampling is not fool-proof however. It is only within a pre-specified confidence, say 95 per cent, that the 100 parts will validate the quality of the 10,000 parts. This means that there is still a 5 per cent risk that the sample was unrepresentative, and that the 10,000 parts do not match the requirements set by the customer. Although still widely used today (it does reduce the cost of inspection), acceptance sampling has been abandoned by all companies embarking on quality assurance programmes (see **Statistical Process Control**).
- *Quality circles* are work teams focusing on discovering quality issues and generating ideas for quality improvements. Pioneered in Japan, quality circles are famous for breaking down hierarchical barriers, as they require managers, foremen and line employees to work collaboratively on quality issues.
- *Quality training* is the systematic training of all personnel, regardless of their rank and authority, in the basic methods and tools of quality management.
- *The Taguchi loss function* is concerned with the costs of under-engineering or over-engineering products. As such, it is a useful design improvement tool that guides design engineers to design products that deliver exactly what customers want.

KEY PEOPLE IN QUALITY MANAGEMENT

The development of quality management ideas originated in the 1930s in US research laboratories. It was not until the late 1940s that these tools became widely used. The interest in quality management peaked in Japan in the 1950s and 1960s. The first conference on quality control was held in Tokyo in 1969. Although most of the consultants initially involved with quality were American, it was only much later that their ideas and writings became popular in the West. Key contributors in the development of quality management are:

- Walter Shewart, a statistician at Bell Labs in the USA in the 1920s and 1930s. His work resulted in the development of **statistical process control**, and he is seen by many as the true pioneer of modern quality management.
- W. Edwards Deming, a professor of statistics who adopted Shewart's ideas and synthesised them in an integrated management framework, **Total Quality Management** (TQM).
- Joseph Juran formulated the notion of quality as being 'fitness for use' and developed the cost of quality management tool (see **Total Quality Management**).
- Armand Feigenbaum was famous for popularising the idea of quality control as being 'total', i.e. everybody's responsibility within the company. He was also a proponent of the use of cost of quality reports.
- Philip Crosby is famous for his book entitled *Quality is Free* in which he explains that investments in quality management will always repay themselves. He is also the person who introduced the concept of zero defects as a guiding goal in quality management in order to highlight the importance of doings things right the first time.
- Kaoru Ishikawa is also credited as the first person to insist on the fact that quality is total, and that all employees should be involved through quality circles. His best-known contribution is the development of cause and effect diagrams.
- Genichi Taguchi specialised in product design quality and is well known for the formulation of the Taguchi loss function, a cost specification which penalises strong over and under achievement of customers' specifications.

REFERENCES

Juran, J. and Gryna, F. (1988) *Quality Control Handbook* (4th edition). New York: McGraw-Hill.

Statistical Process Control

> *Statistical process control is a quality management approach rooted in statistical analysis by which quality is achieved by making sure that processes are designed to produce goods or services that are within specifications, thereby eliminating the need for inspection.*

PRINCIPLE

Statistical Process Control (SPC) was developed as a quality assurance rather than a quality control method. In **Quality Management**, we saw that a quality control method consists of inspecting a good and accepting or rejecting it on the basis of some specifications. In contrast, SPC is used to validate the quality of the *process* which is used to manufacture this good. If the process is found to be '*in control*', then we have a guarantee that (nearly) all the goods produced are of good quality. In such a case, the need for quality control, i.e. inspection, has been eliminated.

CUSTOMER TOLERANCES

Consider a factory manufacturing fasteners, for example bolts and nuts. An M10 bolt, for example, means a bolt with a thread diameter of 10 millimetres (mm). In practice, when these bolts are machined, they do not all have a precise diameter of 10.000 mm. Some will come out at 9.990, others at 10.023, etc. The degree of precision required for a thread's diameter is a function of the use that you, as a customer, will make out of the M10 bolt. Should you require these bolts for the assembly of sub-system that will be embarked on a satellite system, you are likely to want a bolt and nut assembly with a very tight and mechanically-resistant fit. This is achieved by machining the diameter of both the thread and the bolt to very strict tolerances. Although it is possible, it will be very expensive as you will need high precision equipment.

Figure 35 illustrates the concept of customer tolerances. If X represents the diameter of the thread, Figure 35 shows that bolt A satisfies

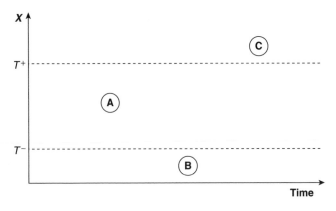

Figure 35   The concept of customer tolerances

the customer requirements. Bolt B, however, is outside of the acceptable specifications: its diameter is below the lowest function tolerance. It is likely that bolt B will not 'grip' or may get jammed in an M10 nut. Similarly, bolt C will not fit with an M10 nut as its diameter is too wide.

PROCESS CAPABILITIES

The key principle of SPC is, given tolerances T^+ and T^-, to assess the capability of the processes and machines to produce products that respect these tolerances. In order to assess the capability of processes, we produce a batch of bolts and measure the diameter of each bolt. We can then graph the distribution of diameters. In most cases, the distribution of a measured variable matches the normal distribution. Figure 36 shows two examples.

In the left-hand side diagram, a manager should detect that the process variability (measured by the width of the distribution) is much greater than what the customer would be willing to accept. Remember that the surface under the normal distribution represents all possible occurrences or 100 per cent of outcomes. Thus, the portion of the normal distribution situated outside of the T^+ and T^- band is a measure of the percentage of defective parts that will be produced by this process. Roughly estimated, it appears that there is a 40 per cent probability that the process would produce a C-type bolt, and a 5 per cent probability that a B-type bolt would be produced. Overall, a 45 per cent defective rate!

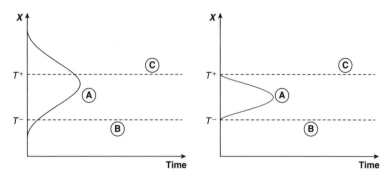

Figure 36   Process capability illustrated

Under a quality assurance approach, this is unacceptable. Thus, in the left-hand side diagram, the conclusion of a quality manager would be that production should cease. Process engineers would be brought to the rescue and asked to redesign the process so that the variability and the average of the process would be improved to better match the customer tolerances. This has been achieved in the right-hand side diagram. In this case, the probability that a B- or a C-type bolt will be produced is so small that it can be considered to be zero. In other words, with such a process, all the parts produced will match the customer tolerances.

SPC AND DEFECTIVE RATES

It is worth remembering that the normal distribution never actually intersects with the zero-axis: for example, in the right-hand side chart of Figure 36, the distribution does not end at T^-. Instead it runs infinitely close to the vertical axis. This means that there is still a (low) probability that a defective part will be produced.

When do we tell designers to stop improving the process? Should we stop at the case shown in the right-hand side graph? Or do we want to improve the process further? Under the normal curve sits a surface of 100 per cent of all outcomes. Instead of talking in the percentage of outcomes, statisticians prefer to measure variability in standard deviations. Remember that the standard variation is a measure of dispersion: a distribution with a high standard deviation will be broad whereas a distribution with a low standard deviation will be very narrow. A typical SPC specification is to ask that six times the standard variation (σ) of natural variability of the process should fit within customer tolerances. Why *six* standard deviations? It is just a standard statistical benchmark that corresponds to a surface below the normal curve of 99.73 per cent. In other words, if process engineers make sure that natural process variations of 6σ fit within tolerances (the case illustrated in the right-hand side chart of Figure 36), then the maximum defective rate of parts will be 0.27 per cent. If, as a quality manager, you consider that a 0.27 per cent defective rate is unacceptable, then you need to continue improving the process, for example by moving to 8σ.

MEASURING PROCESS CAPABILITY

An alternative measure of the ability of a process to match customer tolerances is to compute a process capability index. Although several formulations exist, the most simple is the C_p index, which is computed as:

$$C_p = \frac{T^+ - T^-}{6\sigma}$$

Figure 37 below illustrates different levels of process requirements and the resulting different defective rates.

IMPLEMENTING SPC

Once the process has been improved to achieve the desired level of capability, it can be used in production. Provided that nothing 'abnormal' happens to the process, nearly all the parts manufactured will match customer tolerances. An abnormal variation is caused by any incident which results in a variation of output which was not modelled when process engineers designed the process. For example, a cutting tool may wear out or break. Dust or debris may have accumulated in a machine. The challenge for an operations manager then is to detect when such abnormal variations are happening. When they do, production should be stopped. The machine should be repaired and production resumed only when it has been established that the process is on course again.

Checking that a process is under control is done through the use of *SPC charts*. Their working principle is to collect short, frequent samples (for example four parts every hour) and to graph statistics about the samples. The sample values are compared to an upper-control limit (UCL) and a lower control limit (LCL). Figure 38 provides an example of such a control chart. In the first part of the graph, the process is in control: thus, the operations manager can be confident that no defective parts – or very few – are being produced. Towards the end of the chart in Figure 38, a worrying downward trend is appearing. Although the lower control limit has not yet been reached, it is likely that the machine would have to be stopped and checked as early as the third point in the run-down series.

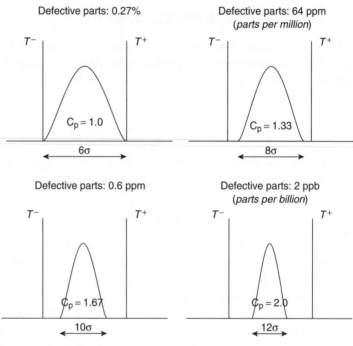

Figure 37   Process capability

WHEN CAN SPC BE USED?

With the example of a bolt's diameter, the presentation of SPC has focused on controlling for a customer specification that can be measured. Figure 38, for example, is one example of an X-bar chart, i.e. a chart based on average sample values. Another control tool is an R-chart, which controls for the range of values within a sample.

SPC can also be used to control for processes where outcomes are counted rather than measured. Examples are p-charts and c-charts:

- *P-charts* are used to control for the proportion of nonconforming units and are based on the binomial distribution. This would, for example, be used to control the percentage of faulty letters sent by a customer service department.
- *C-charts* are used when controlling for the number of non-conformities per units, e.g. the number of paint defects on a car. C-charts are based on the Poisson distribution.

In addition to a variety of different charting tools, SPC charts can be multivariate, i.e. used to observe process conformance on several dimensions.

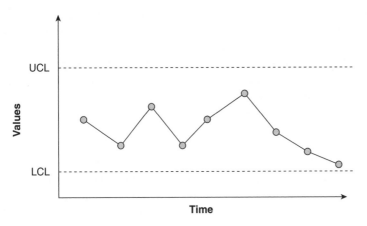

Figure 38   Example of an SPC chart

IMPLEMENTING SPC

Antony and Taner (2003) listed the following factors to explain the difficulty of implementing SPC:

- A lack of commitment and involvement by top management.
- A lack of training and education in SPC.
- A failure to interpret control charts and take any necessary actions.

- A lack of knowledge of which product characteristics or process parameters to measure and monitor within a process.
- Invalid and incapable measurement systems in the workplace.

Antony and Taner insisted that the successful implementation of SPC in a company needs to integrate statistical, engineering, management and team working issues. They proposed a framework (see References) to guide companies through this process.

SPC IN THE SERVICE SECTOR

SPC procedures were designed in the manufacturing sector and questions have always been raised regarding their applicability to service operations. Roes and Dorr (1997) highlighted three key challenges when applying SPC in a service context:

- Unlike manufacturing settings, the customer is often directly involved in the process and thus is a source of variability which has to be taken into account during the process design.
- The application of the SPC approach will inevitably require considerable service reworking and process redesign: this is difficult, expensive, and requires a strong management commitment.
- There are measurement challenges in the service industry, especially in front-office operations.

Despite these hurdles, there are many examples of how service organisations have implemented SPC. Jones and Dent (1994) showed how the hospitality group Forte Plc initiated reflection around the use of SPC in the hospitality sector by running a trial implementation of this in its corporate cafeteria, where control charts were prepared for food variety, the temperature of food items and hygiene.

McCarthy and Wasusri (2002) provided an interesting literature review about the application of SPC in non-standard settings. This includes:

- *Engineering, industrial, and environment applications*: Monitoring the quality of water, hygiene in food manufacture, setting up preventive maintenance plans, etc.
- *Healthcare*: Monitoring the performance of an HIV test, monitoring customer satisfaction in a major hospital, etc.

- *General service sector*: Software defect detection process, monitoring crime rates, performance of invoicing process, etc.
- *Forecasting*: Monitoring forecast performance, selecting appropriate forecasting methods, etc.

REFERENCES

Antony, J. and Taner, T. (2003). 'A conceptual framework for the effective implementation of statistical process control', *Business Process Management Journal*, 9 (4): 473–489.

Jones, P. and Dent, M. (1994). 'Lessons in consistency: statistical process control in Forte plc', *TQM Magazine*, 6 (1): 8–3.

McCarthy, B. and Wasusri, T. (2002) 'A review of non-standard applications of statistical process control (SPC) charts', *International Journal of Quality and Reliability Management*, 19 (3): 295–320.

Roes, K. and Dorr, D. (1997) 'Implementing statistic process control in services processes', *International Journal of Quality Science*, 2 (3): 149–166.

ISO 9000

> **ISO 9000 is a family of quality standards that were initially concerned with the documentation pertaining to an organisation's quality system.**

STANDARDS

Standards are specifications of the performance and connection interfaces (e.g., required voltage or air pressure) of products. Standards are essential to make sure that products work together. For example, the signal from your DVD player must be readable by your television. Beyond this issue of compatibility between products, 'standards' are also more controversially seen by some analysts as *hidden trade barriers*. It is important to appreciate that differences in specification (different electricity specifications, the use of white or yellow light in cars, different accounting standards, etc.) result in extra costs for manufacturers and service firms.

One of the earliest industrial standards was the system of parts tolerancing. When a company buys a mechanical part – say with a diameter of 50 mm – it never receives a part with an actual diameter of 50.000 mm. Instead, the received part could be 49.950, 50.025, and so on. In some cases the part will function within its intended final assembly, but in other cases any deviation from the specification will be such that fitting (an extra cost) will be necessary. Industrial engineers developed a system of communicating their functional expectations: for instance, an order would be placed for a part with a diameter of 50.000 mm, +/-0.05 mm. Any dimension within this range means that refitting costs are avoided.

Standards, however, will only work if they are shared within and across industries. It is with this in mind that most industrial nations have created their own standardisation agencies. Examples are British Standards (BS) norms, the French AFNOR norms, and the German DIN norms. The International Standard Organisation (ISO), based in Switzerland, was created to formulate standards at an international level. One of the ISO's most famous standards, ISO 9000, deals with quality.

QUALITY STANDARDS AND QUALITY MANAGEMENT SYSTEMS STANDARDS

Quality standards are the components of quality management systems. If unconstrained, most companies would develop self-tailored quality management systems that would match their commercial context. This poses a problem when companies work with one another, as their quality policies and practices may not be aligned. A quality standard is a specification of how a company should manage quality. The objective of following a standard is to align the quality practices of companies, for example in buyer–seller relationships. The benefits incurred by a company with state-of-the-art quality practices would be of little value if the purchased parts inserted in their products are defective. To the end customer experiencing a product failure the fact that the failure originates with a second-level supplier rather than with the seller does not matter!

Some standards, such as parts tolerances, deal with quality control, i.e. the final functional specifications of the product being produced. Other standards deal with environmental issues, as for example the Euro emission standards that regulate the emissions from nitrogen oxide, hydrocarbons, carbon monoxide and particulate matter from motor vehicles.

The ISO 9000 family of standards, however, is a standard about quality management systems. As such, it is a *quality assurance* tool rather than a quality control tool. It is important to differentiate such a quality assurance standard, which lays down the quality systems that a company should adopt from an 'output' standard which deals with some aspect of the performance of a product. Contrary to a common misperception, ISO 9000 says nothing about the actual performance of the product or service being provided. It is theoretically possible, and practically a common occurrence, that a company with an ISO 9000 compliant quality management system can deliver a defective product to a customer.

To explain this point, it is useful to look at the content of ISO 9000. The first part stipulates that management responsibility toward quality is important. This implies that the organisation should produce documentation demonstrating how management responsibility is implied in quality matters. For example, policies may have to be amended so that quality exceptions are systematically reported to management, or so that management are systematically trained about quality management. Another requirement of ISO 9000 is to require traceability: should a defective product occur, is it possible to retrieve the date and time of production, the operators involved, and the machine used? Again, suitable policies and record systems will have to be set down and maintained. Finally, an important aspect of ISO 9000 is that an adequate documentation system should be used to support the quality management system. For example, a requirement is that a company should have a quality manual. The standard also specifies what should be included in this quality manual. It also requires that this manual be available to all employees.

ISO 9000 CERTIFICATION

The adoption of ISO 9000 is a voluntary exercise, i.e. there are no legal obligations to do so. A team of consultants will visit an organisation and audit their quality systems to check that the system conforms to the standards in all respects. Certification is an expensive process but it will result in the company publishing and advertising the fact that it is certified. There is nothing stopping a company from following ISO 9000 specifications for its own benefit and not seeking certification. This form of 'self-certification', however, carries much less weight than that done by official auditors. Many large and powerful industrial buyers require that their supplier be ISO 9000 certified. In this case, certification becomes a business necessity rather than an option.

Sampaio et al. (2009) conducted an extensive literature review of the research literature on ISO 9000 certification. They showed that while European in origin ISO 9000 is now a truly global quality certification, with 897,866 active certificates in 170 countries by December 2006. The leading country is China, followed by Italy, Japan, Spain, the UK and the USA.

Surveys about the motivations and benefits of ISO 9000 certification reveal that these can be decomposed as either internal or external. Internal motivation is a genuine need to implement a quality management system, in which case the benefits are usually measured through quality metrics (e.g. a decrease in defective rates). External motivations include complying to customer pressure or the desire to use ISO 9000 as a marketing tool. For example, in their survey of the UK construction sector, Hughes et al. (2000) found that 84 per cent of respondents sought certification because of client pressure.

There is evidence in the literature that the perceived benefits of ISO 9000 certification will tend to decrease over time (Sampaio et al., 2009). One possible explanation for this, initially formulated by Juran, is that going through certification is a challenge for those companies that are starting to implement a quality initiative. They will learn a lot through the certification exercise, and as result, will experience immediate benefits. More quality-mature companies, however, will have little if anything to learn from the exercise. As a result, the certification process is only an add-on cost – a marketing necessity for the quality-savvy firm.

Typical drawbacks and barriers to ISO 9000 implementation are a lack of management commitment; high implementation and maintenance costs (especially for small businesses); different interpretations of standards across auditors; and not taking into account specific industrial contexts.

Overall, ISO 9000 certification tends to be associated with higher organisational performance. Only a few research studies have questioned this impact on performance. The few that have have usually explained that suppliers 'forced' into seeking certification do not experience the same benefits as those in firms seeking certification for internal reasons. The literature, however, is much less unanimous when studying the link between ISO 9000 certification and financial performance, with some studies concluding that there is indeed such a link and others concluding that there is not.

Finally, a number of research studies have explored the relationship between ISO 9000 certification and the adoption of quality management as a best practice. Sampaio et al. (2009) categorised the literature in three groups:

- Some researchers will recommend ISO 9000 as a first step; once certification is achieved firms should consider increasing their investment in quality management by considering quality excellence or TQM frameworks.
- Some researchers will consider the two as independent and complementary tools for quality management. What ISO 9000 contributes to is not easily done through TQM, and vice versa. In this perspective, both initiatives can be pursued at the same time.
- Other authors do not see any relationship between the two. Some research has shown that firms having adopted TQM and ISO 9000 together do not perform better than firms having solely adopted TQM. Other research studies conclude that the best quality improvement strategy is to implement TQM without ISO 9000.

REFERENCES

Hughes, T., Williams, T. and Ryall, P. (2000) 'It's not what you achieve it is the way you achieve it', *Total Quality Management*, 11 (3): 329–340.

Sampaio, P., Saraiva, P. and Guimaraez Rodrigues, A. (2009). 'ISO 9001 certification research: questions, answers and approaches', *International Journal of Quality and Reliability Management*, 26 (1): 38–58.

six sigma

187

> *Six sigma is a quality management approach that places heightened managerial attention on customer satisfaction and on seeking business process improvements.*

THE ORIGIN AND DEVELOPMENT OF SIX SIGMA

Six sigma was developed at Motorola in 1986 on the back of several years of using various quality management frameworks which were then popular: total quality control, zero defects, the Taguchi method, etc. Today, proponents of six sigma describe it as a *business improvement strategy* rather than as a quality management methodology. As discussed in the following sections, the relationship of six sigma to the quality movement is debatable, and not surprisingly a lot of the tools and techniques used by six-sigma specialists are those of quality management. There are however two specific tools which are its trademarks: the DMAIC process model and the six sigma training programme.

THE SIX SIGMA PROCESS STEP MODEL

Although specific to six sigma, the DMAIC improvement cycle model is not without a similarity to the Deming PDCA cycle for improvement (see **Kaizen**). The DMAIC cycle defines the backbone of a six sigma improvement programme and should be used for all interventions.

- Define (D): This is the stage where managers must identify, evaluate and select potential improvement projects. The emphasis is on identifying those projects with a proven impact on customer satisfaction and profitability.
- Measure (M): At this stage, managers must collect data about existing processes and operations. The purpose is to document quantitatively the problem which should be addressed.
- Analyse (A): Through a variety of graphical tools and process modelling techniques, individuals must analyse the process behaviour and identify the root causes of any problems revealed at the measurement stage.
- Improve (I): This is where managers must intervene and redesign the process to overcome the issues which have been measured and analysed.
- Control (C): Thanks to the performance measures identified at the M-stage, a plan for control is now prepared in order to verify whether or not the performance has been improved, during and after the improvement process.

This process step model is sometimes also abbreviated to DMADV (Define, Measure, Analyse, Design, and Verify), or as DFSS (Design For Six Sigma).

THE SIX SIGMA TRAINING PROGRAMME

Six sigma as a management method has retained the 'quality for all' theme of total quality management. As such, it has grown over the years into a structured system for encouraging participation by requiring that a specified number of employees (as a percentage of the total head-count) should be certified as six sigma specialists. The first training session, usually completed in one intensive week, leads to the six sigma green belt and covers the DMAIC process model in depth along with the tools to be used at each stage. The follow-on training, requiring more time and the completion of a successful six sigma improvement project, ends with the black belt certification.

The consulting world has been keen to offer certification training programmes and the result today is a rather confusing situation where several institutions are providing competing certification programmes. For example, some will offer a white belt programme for employees of small businesses (Kumar et al., 2008). Others will offer a yellow belt certification where statistical tools are not covered. Yellow belts are sold as relevant either for individuals who will assist with a green or black belt project, or for individuals working in the service sector where there may not be a requirement for the complex statistical analysis of data which is common in manufacturing settings.

SIX SIGMA IN RELATION TO OTHER QUALITY TOOLS

How different is six sigma from continuous improvement (see **Kaizen**) or from **Total Quality Management**? This question has been debated extensively in the quality management literature.

Many have criticised six sigma for being a management fad. A management fad is a management practice which is in fashion at a specific point in time. Typically, hundreds of companies will adopt fads and invest large amount of resources towards their implementation only to give them up mid-project to redirect corporate resources toward the next new fashion. Senapati (2004) is one of these critics who have argued that 'sick' sigma is a management fashion with no differentiating features from Statistical Process Control, Continuous Improvement and Total Quality Management.

A number of six sigma experts have reviewed the critical literature and identified the seven most common myths about six sigma (Kumar et al., 2008):

- Six sigma is the flavour of the month.
- Six sigma is all about statistics.
- Six sigma is only about manufacturing companies.
- Six sigma works only in large organisations.
- Six sigma is the same as Total Quality Management.
- Six sigma requires a strong infrastructure and massive training.
- Six sigma is not cost effective.

SIX SIGMA AS A MANAGEMENT INTERVENTION TOOL: EXPERT'S OPINION

In their (2008) paper Kumar, Anthony, Madu, Montgomery, and Park, all respected experts in the six sigma field, proceeded to demystify the myths listed above.

Fads come and go. The authors pointed out that six sigma has now been around for more than two decades, that it is well established in some companies, and that an entire industry (specialised press, conferences, consultants, etc.) exists around it. Six sigma does appear to be more pervasive than a fad.

Kumar and his colleagues recognised that six sigma has a strong statistical basis. It is however more general than statistical techniques: it adopts their overall philosophy, their emphasis on process capability and process design, but it does not necessarily require statistical computations.

It is especially in the service sector that statistical tools do not always apply. The authors provide a number of examples of the successful implementation of six sigma, for example in the banking and health sectors. Similarly, there are plenty of examples of small businesses that have successfully adopted it. This is important in supply chain environments, where small businesses have to align their process capabilities with the rest of their supply chain.

When discussing why six sigma is different from TQM, three key differentiating features are listed:

- It is results oriented.
- Its DMAIC process model links all tools and techniques sequentially.
- It creates a powerful infrastructure for training champions.

The first point remains moot: the cost of quality approach (see **Total Quality Management**) is just as concerned about the bottom line as six sigma claims to be. The second point is a genuine difference. The training framework of six sigma is also genuinely unique.

It is so unique that it turns out to be one of the aspects of six sigma which is most often criticised. Kumar et al. (2008) recognise that some six sigma consultants have over-exaggerated the need for trained specialists.

Finally, Kumar and his colleagues point to numerous case studies of companies whose success and increased profitability are primarily linked to the adoption of this sigma approach. Kumar et al. (2008) therefore provide a strong case for defending six sigma as a genuine management intervention tool. The question of differentiating six sigma from TQM remains a controversial point. A simple distinction may be that TQM is an unstructured set of tools which emerged from the quality movement in Japan in the 1980s. Six sigma, although based on the same tools, is a Western-based approach from birth and development. Thus, both it and TQM may only differ in terms of the cultural context in which they are applied. It may be that six sigma is well suited to the cultural definition of work in the Occidental world.

REFERENCES

Kumar, M., Anthony, J., Madu, C., Montgomery, D. and Park, S. (2008) 'Common myths of six sigma demystified', *International Journal of Quality and Reliability Management*, 25 (8): 878–895.

Senapati, N. (2004). 'Six sigma: myths and realities', *International Journal of Quality and reliability Management*, 21 (6): 683–690.

Kaizen

> *The principle of Kaizen, or continuous improvement, is to seek the improvement of operations systems through small incremental changes rather than through one-off radical change initiatives.*

THE KAIZEN PRINCIPLE

Kaizen is a Japanese world meaning 'continuous improvement'. The concept of Kaizen, however, is more general, and includes the philosophy and approach used when implementing an improvement. In other words, when operations managers talk about Kaizen they are referring to a particular method of working. Today, the concept is strongly associated with the quality movement and is often perceived to be a Japanese management approach. This could be a gross simplification, as Imai (1986) has shown how Kaizen is actually the result of a customisation within the Japanese work context of quality management ideas brought to Japan by US consultants after World War II. Bessant et al. (2001) point out that the concept also has roots in other fields such as sociotechnical system theory and the human relations movement.

Is Kaizen a new concept? The following quote from the French classical writer Boileau, expressed in his treatise in the seventeenth century about writing poetry, would suggest that it is not:

> Before writing, learn to think
> As what is well understood is easily described,
> And words to say it come naturally.
> Proceed with a slow haste, and without losing courage,
> Twenty times revisit your work,
> Improve it incessantly, and improve it again,
> Add a few things, and erase often.
> (Boileau, *L'Art Poétique* (1674) author's translation)

The Kaizen concept incorporates three key principles in one work method:

- *Commitment and Persistence*: Improvement will not be achieved if there is not a clear and strong motivation to seek and implement improvement, and if this effort is not sustained in the long run. The approach is a philosophy which should be adopted at work.

- *Small and incremental processes*: The Kaizen approach is against radical change and its key methodology is to proceed by frequent, small, but controlled attempts at improving practice.
- *Participative*: In an organisational context the adoption of the philosophy by one employee alone would be pointless. Thus it is important that all employees and departments within an organisation adopt and practise the Kaizen work method.

THE DEMING WHEEL

The incremental work method at the heart of the continuous improvement work philosophy is modelled through the Deming Wheel. Initially developed by the American statistician Walter Shewart, it was adapted and promoted by Edwards Deming. Figure 39 displays the Deming Wheel, which is also called the Plan, Do, Study, Act (PDSA) cycle.

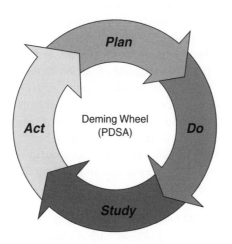

Figure 39   The Deming Wheel

When a problem has been identified the approach suggested by the Deming Wheel is:

- To plan for changes, discuss alternatives and make choices.
- To execute the plan, usually through small, controlled steering, staying clear of radical, one-off change initiatives.

- To study the results: Once the plan has been executed, collect the data and any observations. Check that its execution went well. What has been learnt?
- Take action to improve or standardise the process.

It is important to note that the improvement approach is based on a permanent cycle, so that a given process may be revisited and analysed numerous times before it becomes standardised.

THE IMPLEMENTATION OF CONTINUOUS IMPROVEMENT

In their survey of the adoption of continuous improvement by Australian manufacturing firms, Terziovski and Sohal (2000) reported that:

- The motivation to adopt the methodology can be linked to seeking improved quality conformance, increased productivity, reduced costs and improvements in delivery reliability.
- Respondents prefer to use basic problem-solving tools, checklists, and the seven quality tools in conjunction with continuous improvement. More advanced problem-solving techniques such as failure mode and effect analysis (FMEA) and quality function deployment (QFD) were not popular. Other 'soft' options, which rely on the behavioural people and teams concepts, were also avoided by respondents.
- The majority of respondents had introduced continuous improvement to at least part of their organisations, but half of the respondents had limited this adoption to their manufacturing departments, which goes counter to the participative, organisation-wide approach suggested by theory.

Bessant et al. (2001) reported that many organisations had experienced disappointments and failures with continuous improvement programmes. They explained the disappointing results by the fact that too much of the implementation literature focused on the technical aspects (for example, adoption of the seven quality tools) and not on behavioural issues. They also criticised the literature for treating companies as having adopted or not having adopted the methodology. Due to its long-term and pervasive nature, continuous improvement is a methodology that will take time to become fully integrated in everyday work practices. To address these shortcomings, Bessant et al. developed, on the basis of case studies, a maturity model of the implementation of continuous improvement.

A MATURITY MODEL FOR THE IMPLEMENTATION OF CONTINUOUS IMPROVEMENT

Bessant et al.'s (2001) approach consisted of studying a large database of cases of the typical process routines within firms at different stages of their adoption of continuous improvement. The result was a 5-level maturity model.

- *Level 1: Pre-Continuous Improvement Stage*
  There is an interest in the concept of continuous improvement, but no formalised or organised approach within the company. There are occasional improvement efforts and 'pockets' of continuous improvement practice, but these are isolated and unstructured.
- *Level 2: Structured Continuous Improvement*
  The firm makes a formal commitment to adopting continuous improvement. A system, recognising and encouraging the practice, is put in place. Training is made available to employees. The purpose is to diffuse good practices across the organisation. The method is not used systematically however.
- *Level 3: Goal Oriented Continuous Improvement*
  Structuring the approach (see Level 2) continues, but with the addition of linking this to the attainment of strategic goals. Continuous improvement activities become part of the main business activities and are used increasingly for cross-organisational problem solving.
- *Level 4: Proactive Continuous Improvement*
  Continuous improvement becomes a natural way of working. Individuals and departments naturally use the approach to address problems without waiting to be asked to do so. This goes hand in hand with a corporate will to devolve autonomy and to ask each employee to be in charge of the improvement of their own process. There is a lot of experimentation and searches for better processes.
- *Level 5: Full Capability*
  The process has been fully adopted and is in widespread enthusiastic use within the organisation. Thanks to the use of continuous improvement, the organisation exhibits all the characteristics of a good 'learning organisation'. It is able to respond flexibly to problems by seeking small but controlled improvements to processes.

REFERENCES

Bessant, J., Caffyn, S. and Gallagher, M. (2001) 'An evolutionary model of continuous improvement behaviour', *Technovation*, 21: 67–77.

Imai, M. (1986) *Kaizen: The Key to Japan's Competitive Success*. New York: McGraw-Hill.

Terziovski, M. and Sohal, A. (2000) 'The adoption of continuous improvement and innovation strategies in Australian manufacturing firms', *Technovation*, 20: 539–550.

Inventory

Inventory

> **Inventory refers to the stock of various items which is kept on site or in a facility in anticipation of a future use.**

Manufacturing inventory has traditionally been described within three categories:

- *Raw Materials Inventory*: Sheets of metal, wood panels, etc. that are purchased for the purpose of using them in the manufacture of a product.
- *Work in Process Inventory*: Partially completed products which are located on the shopfloor and which are not ready for sale.
- *Finished Goods Inventory*: Goods which are finished and ready for sale, but which have not yet been purchased by final customers. This also includes goods purchased for resale, as for example in the case of a supermarket.

Factories often involve many additional types of inventory: spare parts, supplies, indirect materials, tools and fixtures, etc. Pipeline inventory is composed of units that have left a production facility and are in the process of being distributed to the end customer.

Service organisations can also require extensive inventory keeping. Large hotels for example have to hold a large variety of items in stock such as food, beverages, cleaning chemicals, office stationeries, office sundries, emergency items, china, glass, cutlery, linens, etc. The diverse nature of inventory can make inventory management (see **Inventory Systems**) a complicated task. Inventory complexity is often measured by the number of *Stock Keeping Units* (SKUs) associated with an organisation.

In accounting terminology, inventory is an asset, i.e. a resource from which future economic benefits can be derived. Operations managers are directly involved with the management of inventory in order to increase the profitability and effectiveness of an organisation. The reasons why inventory is a resource, (i.e. the positive motives for holding inventory) are:

- *To meet anticipated demand*, i.e. to deliver goods when the customer has requested them. For example, a car dealership will have a car delivered to their site and will keep it for the customer until the agreed delivery date.
- *To protect against stock-outs*, i.e. to meet unanticipated demand. Stock-outs have negative business consequences as they represent a frustration to customers, lost sales, and potentially lost customers who will turn to the competition for their supply.
- *To hedge against price increases*, or to take advantage of quantity discounts, i.e. a heavy industrial user of crude oil will stock up on oil when market prices are low and refrain from purchasing when market prices are high.
- *To smooth production requirements*, i.e. some goods are highly seasonal and put unmanageable loads on manufacturing systems. By producing goods to stock in advance, the production load can be levelled out.
- *To more efficiently absorb the fixed costs of ordering or producing*, i.e. placing an order which is large enough to fill a delivery truck.
- *To de-couple operations*, i.e. this means breaking down two sequentially dependent operations into two loosely-coupled operations. For example, work in process inventory between successive manufacturing steps (buffer stock) permits operations to continue at each workstation independent of what is happening at other workstations (e.g. a breakdown).

Inventory has, however, been a controversial resource in operations management, as it often turns out to be an operational liability. First, holding and managing inventory has a cost. The cost of holding inventory includes the cost of warehouses, their staff and equipment, and also the cost of administrative processes used to monitor inventory levels (administrative salaries, IT systems, etc.). For example, the Ford Motor Company estimated in 1992 that its cost of holding inventory was 26 per cent of the inventory value. Similarly, Barlow (1997) estimated that the cost of holding inventory in a large London hotel is 26.73 per cent of the inventory's worth.

A second cost aspect of inventory is that organisational funds need to be invested in inventory holdings. A closely associated concept is the *inventory cycle*, i.e. the period of time between acquiring a unit of inventory and selling it. High inventory levels and long inventory cycles consume organisational funds. Accountants describe this phenomenon as creating a 'need in working capital', as capital (i.e. long-term funds) is used to finance a short-term working asset. As inventory can tie in significant amounts of monies, specific financial ratios are used to monitor inventory levels. The most commonly used is the inventory turnover ratio, obtained by dividing the cost of goods sold by the average inventory for a given accounting period. A high turnover indicates short inventory cycles and, generally, a good management of inventory. A low turnover ratio suggests long inventory cycles and the potential existence of excess inventory. (**Inventory Systems** describes the different types of inventory management systems used by operations managers to reduce inventory levels and inventory cycles.) A third type of cost is wasted resources through *excess inventory*. Excess inventory is inventory which is either unutilised, turns over too slowly, or becomes obsolete and cannot be sold.

It is important to note that each industry comes with its own specificities and difficulties in terms of inventory management. Consider the following examples:

- In the automotive industry, manufacturers have by law to maintain a stock of spare parts for all models commercialised in the last ten years. Spare part inventories are expensive and complex to manage.
- In the fashion apparel industry, items are difficult to sell once they are out of fashion. This is dealt with in two ways: by adjusting demand through 'discount' seasons and by adjusting the supply with quick response initiatives (see **Responsiveness**).
- In supermarkets and grocery stores, the management of inventory of fresh products (fish and meat counters, fruit and vegetables) is complicated by the fact that inventory is perishable. Excess inventory should be avoided at all costs.

Japanese companies were the first to realise that funds tied in excess inventories were hurting their firms' profitability. They developed **Just-in-Time (JIT)** inventory management systems which allow firms to run their operations with as little inventory as possible, as parts are delivered in the right quantities, at the right time, to the right place. In Japanese management rhetoric, it is not unusual to describe inventory as an 'evil', i.e. as a financial liability rather than an asset. For example, even the decoupling function of inventory is criticised in Japanese management thinking: the need to decouple operations rather than maintain a steady uninterrupted product flow is seen as an indication of a poorly designed production process. Thus, Japanese engineers would recommend redesigning the process so that buffer inventory between workstations is completely eliminated.

Just-in-Time inventory management seeks whenever possible to reduce inventory. This is not to say that an operations system should run with zero inventory, as such a system could be prone to operational disasters (shortages stopping production, inability to address a small increase in demand, etc.). Although zero-inventory 'preachers' exist, it is good to remember that some degree of inventory helps to run smooth and efficient operations, and that 'zero-inventory operations' are more a theoretical abstraction than a desirable pursuit.

REFERENCE

Barlow, G. (1997) 'Inventory: asset or liability?', *International Journal of Hospitality Management*, 16 (1): 11–22.

Inventory Systems

> *Inventory management systems are sets of policies, processes, and controls that monitor levels of inventory within an organisation and determine how much inventory a firm should order and when.*

INVENTORY MANAGEMENT SYSTEMS

An inventory management system is the result of a number of decisions, as shown in Figure 40. Each decisional parameter (in rounded rectangles) and decision (rectangles) is discussed in the following sections. The decision objective is to target a specified level of inventory management performance. Examples of possible performance targets are:

- To avoid excess inventory, specified as a maximum stock level, or as a percentage of sales.
- To avoid low inventory levels and especially stockouts. Policies that specify minimum inventory levels are often known as *service level specifications*.

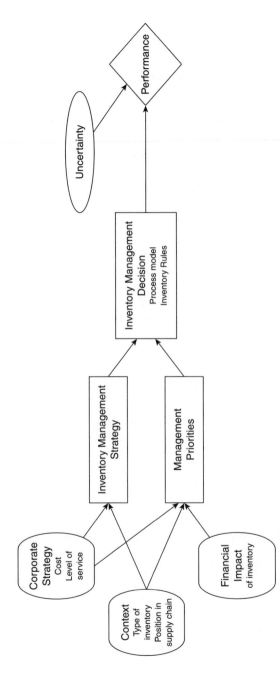

Figure 40   A decision model of inventory management

- To demonstrate excellent inventory management in financial terms (see **Inventory**).

DECREASING INVENTORY

There has been so much written on just-in-time inventory systems and zero-inventory policies that this has resulted in the popular perception that operations managers should permanently work on decreasing inventory in order to increase the financial performance of the firm.

Inventory is both an asset and a liability. Too much inventory is a financial burden whilst not enough inventory may result in a service level failure. Neither scenario is desirable. As suggested in Figure 40, the corporate strategy of a firm is likely to include a trade-off between a cost performance target (minimising the cost of carrying inventory) and a service level performance target (guaranteeing that stock-outs will never happen). Thus, each firm will have its own *optimal inventory level* as a result of setting its strategic objectives.

Rajagopalan and Malhotra (2001) conducted an empirical study in order to assess whether or not US inventory levels have changed significantly during the 1961 to 1994 period. Their findings were that:

- Material and work-in-process inventories decreased in the majority of industrial sectors and showed greater improvement in about half the sectors after 1980.
- Finished goods inventories decreased in some industry sectors and increased in a few others but did not show a significant trend in more than half of the sectors.
- Manufacturing inventory ratios (DSO) decreased from 1961 to 1994 at all three stages – materials, WIP, finished goods.

DEPENDENT *VS.* INDEPENDENT DEMAND ITEMS

Operations managers have always made a distinction between *independent demand items* and *dependent demand items*. Independent demand items are finished goods that are stocked for sale or resale when demand is uncertain. Uncertainty means that demand is either unknown or partially known, but is in any case volatile. As the demand for independent demand items is uncertain, it needs to be estimated (see **Forecasting**).

Dependent items are used *in* finished goods, and therefore their demand is known. For example, if a company decides that it should manufacture 10,000 cars next month, it is easy to deduct how many wheels (a dependent item) should be in inventory.

In this concept, the focus is on the management of independent demand items. (The management of dependent demand items is discussed in **MRP.**)

MANAGEMENT PRIORITIES

Large organisations have to manage very large numbers of stock keeping units (SKU). Not all SKUs are equally important though. Operations managers use the *ABC classification* technique to classify SKUs in terms of financial priority. Operations managers look at the pound-usage distribution of each SKU and allocate each SKU to an inventory class:

- *Class A*: Includes the few items which account for most of the pound-usage. Therefore they require maximum control and have priority over other classes. According to the law of Pareto, class A will typically include 20 per cent of the headcount of SKUs. These 20 per cent, however, represent about 80 per cent of the total investment in inventory.
- *Class B*: These are the middle-of-the-road items which require a normal amount of control. Represented here are the next 20 per cent of items which account for 10 per cent of the total pound-usage.
- *Class C*: These are the majority of SKUs (the remaining 60 per cent), but their cumulative pound-usage is so low (10 per cent as an aggregate) that a minimum amount of control can be exerted.

Note that there is no general agreement on what percentages are used to divide the sets of SKUs into three classes. The law of Pareto is the driving principle behind the classification, but different companies will exhibit different pound-usage distribution. Buxey (2006) reported for example that the UK newsagent chain, WH Smith, uses an ABC system structured as follows:

- *Class A includes 1 per cent of lines, 30 per cent of sales.* Class A is divided into bestsellers and high value items. Separate inventory management rules are used for each.
- *Class B includes 14 per cent of lines and represent 50 per cent of sales.* These are divided into sub-classes and each sub-class is controlled through specific inventory management rules.

- *Class C includes 85 per cent of lines and represents only 20 per cent of sales.* Books are included in this category. Other issues than pound usage are taken into account when managing this class of inventory, as for example, the optimisation of truck loads.

INVENTORY MANAGEMENT STRATEGY

Context in inventory management refers to the type of inventory that has to be managed and to the position of the firm in a supply chain. Context combined with the strategic performance dimensions form the starting point of defining an inventory management strategy. The purpose of this strategy is to specify how inventory management targets will be reached. For example, a firm may for the sake of cost control set a policy stating that expensive spare parts will be ordered only if needed. This strategy may have radical consequences in terms of performance should fulfilment be slow.

Walin et al. (2006) documented through case studies the strategic inventory management choices that managers can make in the case of goods purchased for resale. Table 5 shows the different strategic choices. Decisions are made about who should own the inventory and where the inventory is to be located. Each strategy comes with its benefits and disadvantages and each suggests different inventory management rules.

Table 5   Inventory strategies for goods purchased for resale

Inventory Strategy	Who owns the inventory?	Where is the inventory located?
Inventory speculation	Buyer	Buyer
Inventory postponement	Supplier	Supplier
Inventory consignment	Supplier	Buyer
Reverse inventory consignment	Buyer	Supplier

INVENTORY MANAGEMENT DECISIONS

Once the priorities and strategies for managing inventory have been defined, operations managers have to design the systems by which inventory will be managed in order to attain pre-set performance targets. A considerable amount of research has been conducted in operations research in order to define optimal inventory policies in a variety of contexts.

Inventory policies are essentially concerned with two decisions:

- When a buyer purchases SKUs from a supplier, which quantity should be ordered?
- When, or how often, should ordering take place?

The mathematical complexity of finding an answer to both of these questions simultaneously is such that operations managers have relied on a work-around solution. This consists of looking at the general inventory context and priority of the management task in order to find an easy answer to one of the two questions. Once this is done, it is then easier to find an optimal, or exact, answer to the second question. This approach is the basis of the distinction between *p-systems* and *q-systems*.

P-systems, or periodic inventory systems, are inventory rules for which the frequency of ordering has been set. For example, deliveries are expected on the first day of each month. The question then becomes 'how much should I order each month?'

Q-systems adopt the opposite approach. They set the quantity Q which will be ordered each time, and then proceed to determine what the optimal time is to place the next order.

Through multiple case studies analysis, Buxey (2006) proposed guidelines prescribing when one system is preferable over another. Q-systems should be used when it is possible to obtain quantity discounts, when fixed capacity constraints limit how much can be ordered, when items are expensive or critical, and when demand is either low or erratic. In contrast, p-systems should be used when SKUs are difficult to count (e.g. sugar in a coffee shop), when the firm wants to avoid expensive record keeping, when items are cheap, when delivery is associated with routine visits from the supplier, when it pays to rely on regular transport or for stable demand items.

INVENTORY POLICY: UNDERPINNING ISSUES

There are four key factors to consider when designing an inventory policy:

- *Demand conditions*: Is the demand known or unknown? Is it variable or not? Demand conditions can be analysed by studying past demand patterns. *Deterministic* inventory models are based on constant demand.

Stochastic inventory models take into account the fact that demand is volatile and follows a probability distribution. Volatility is usually measured through the standard deviation of the demand distribution. Standard inventory models are based on very specific assumptions regarding the volatility and distribution of demand. These assumptions have to be verified in practice before applying an inventory policy. If the demand is not stationary (i.e. a constant average over time), forecasting techniques are used to estimate future demand patterns. These demand patterns are then fed into inventory models. Other dimensions that should be taken into account are: low versus high demand, seasonal versus non-seasonal demand, etc.

- *Performance specifications*: Inventory policies are designed to attain certain objectives. We have already defined at the beginning of this concept the different performance targets that can be adopted.
- *Business considerations*: There are a number of business issues that will have an impact on inventory policies. Inflation, for example, can have an impact on the desirability of holding inventory as the value of items deteriorates quickly with time. Many suppliers will offer quantity discounts for large orders or incentives if orders are placed on a given day. Suppliers may also from time to time offer exceptional selling terms, and a company might decide to overlook its regular inventory policy to take advantage of these exceptional terms.
- *Perishability of items*: Whilst some items can be kept in stock indefinitely, others items such as food or newspapers will have a very limited shelf life. Inventory decisions for perishable items are known as the *newsvendor problem*.

An *inventory review* takes place when a company makes a headcount of its inventory position for one or several items. Large supermarkets, for example, used to close for a day at the end of the fiscal year for the sake of auditing inventory so that accurate figures could be used for financial reporting purposes. As discussed previously, there are two types of inventory policies – p-systems and q-systems. The distinction between the two types of systems is based on how often a company's inventory position is assessed. An inventory position (IP) is assessed as:

IP = Items currently on hand + items on order (not received yet) – backlog

Rao (2003) further divides inventory policies into three classes, based on the frequency of reviews:

- The q-system (Q,r) policy is based on *continuous* review systems because they keep track of their inventory positions on a real time basis. Although expensive from an accounting point of view, (Q,r) systems result in lower average inventory levels. Orders (for Q units) are only placed when the inventory drops below a certain trigger: the re-order point (r).
- (T,R) policies are based on p-systems where the inventory position is only assessed at the end of every period T. If required, an order is placed to bring the inventory position back to a desired level R.
- (S,s) policies are an hybrid between the above two policies, but still constitute a p-sytem. Time is decomposed into discrete chunks. At the end of each time chunk, the inventory position is assessed. If it is below s, then an order or S-IP is placed in order to bring the inventory level back to S.

(T,R) INVENTORY POLICIES

(T,R) inventory policies are commonly used in practice because of the convenience of placing orders at set dates. For example, if a firm buys multiple items from a supplier, placing multiple orders at each end of periods T may result in benefiting from quantity discounts or economies in transportation costs, as full rather than partial truck loads are used. Thus, in day-to-day inventory management, the period T is often set by convenience. Rao (2003) demonstrated analytically that the optimal cost for a (T,R) policy is insensitive to the choice of T: what matters, instead, is that for a chosen T, the right (optimal) R is used. Thus, the key question is to identify R given T and the demand characteristics. A (T,R) policy will however result in higher inventory-related costs than a (Q,r) policy. It is only in cases where a genuine business reason exists for placing orders periodically (discounts, transportation savings) that a (T,R) policy is relevant.

In the most simple case, R can be computed as:

$$R = \bar{d} \times (T+L)$$

Here T is the review period and L the leadtime between placing an order and receiving delivery. $\bar{d}$ is the average demand per unit of time.

If IP is the inventory position at time T, then the order placed will be:

$$Q = R - IP$$

Note that this basic formula guarantees that stockouts will not happen only if L is certain and if d, (the demand per unit of time) is constant: $(d = \bar{d})$ In the more general case where the demand is volatile (and where d is not equal to $\bar{d}$), R can be computed as:

$$R = \bar{d} \times (T + L) + SS$$

SS is a safety stock computed to take into account expected demand variations during the review and fulfilment period. Computing the safety stock can only be done when more information is available about the distribution of d over time. In the case where d is normally distributed, the formula for R becomes:

$$R = \bar{d} \times (T + L) + z \times \sigma_d \times \sqrt{(T + L)}$$

Where σ_d is the standard deviation of d. z is a z-score obtained from a normal distribution table and is a function of the specified service level. Given a certain specification of service level, for example a guarantee of no stockout with a 95 per cent confidence, a z-score is identified and used to compute the safety stock. The higher the service level, the higher the required safety stock.

(S,s) INVENTORY POLICIES

Similar to the (T,R) inventory policies, the periodicity with which inventory is reviewed in an (S,s) system is a function of business convenience and past practice. It is through experience that many companies will have discovered and fine-tuned their review periods.

The difference with the (T,R) policy is that inventory will be replenished only if the inventory position falls below a certain reorder point s. If demand is deterministic $(d = \bar{d})$ than s could be simply set at 0, and S would be computed as the expected demand during the review and fulfillment period. The strength of the (S,s) model is to cope with unusual demand conditions. Sani and Kingsman (1997) discussed the virtues of the (S,s) policy when companies are faced with low and intermittent demand. This is the case, for example, for spare parts inventory. Stocking spare parts is expensive and stockists would typically prefer to stock as few parts as possible. Due to different references and uses, demand for spare parts is typically low, although it can experience sudden peaks. Sani and Kingsman's (1997) review of the literature shows that most (S,s) models are based on heuristics, i.e. rules derived from practical insight or from experience. In their paper, they compare theoretical heuristics with heuristics developed by practitioners, and conclude that:

- Simple rules derived from experience by practitioners tend to be the best in terms of service level but they come at high inventory costs.
- Theoretical (S,s) rules perform best in terms of minimising inventory costs.

A variation on (S,s) policies is to add in the possibility of *emergency orders*. Emergency orders can be placed at any point in time. Emergency orders are associated with a shorter lead time but with a higher cost of ordering.

(Q,r) INVENTORY SYSTEMS

Inventory Cycle and Re-Order Point

In practice, a company could select a subjective order quantity Q. Imagine for example a company with a restriction on its ability to store a bulky item beyond Q = 100 units, that consequently decides that it will only place orders of 100 units.

The inventory cycle time is the time between two orders of quantity Q. Assuming that the demand rate is d, the inventory cycle time is given by the ratio of Q to the demand rate, Q/d. The reorder point r is given by the time required to receive delivery after an order for Q is placed. If L is the lead time, then the reorder point is given by: $r = L^*d$. Figure 41 represents the inventory position of a company over time.

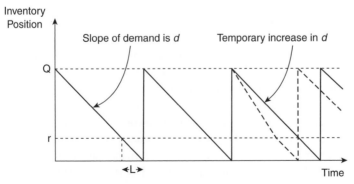

Figure 41   Inventory cycle under constant demand conditions

The economics of (Q,r) systems

The popularity of (Q,r) systems is due to the fact that based on the inventory cycle shown in Figure 41, it is relatively simple to compute an *optimal* reorder level Q so that the cost of inventory is minimised. The cost of inventory is defined as the sum of several components:

- *The cost of carrying inventory*: This includes the rent or depreciation expenses on warehouses, the cost of inventory management systems and personnel, insurance on inventory, etc. It is assumed to be a linear function of inventory size, and is measured through h, the cost of holding one unit of inventory over one unit of time.
- *The cost of placing orders*: There is a fixed cost s incurred every time a firm places an order with a supplier: s includes accounting and purchasing personnel and systems costs.
- *The cost of inventory*: In the most basic (Q,r) model, the price of items is assumed to be constant.

The *Economic Order Quantity* (EOQ) is obtained by expressing the total cost of inventory analytically, and taking the derivative over Q. By setting this derivative function at zero, one can deduct the optimal quantity Q = EOQ for which the total cost function is minimised. What the EOQ formula captures is that there is a trade-off between inventory level and order quantity. Placing small, frequent orders allows a firm to reduce its cost of holding inventory, but the administrative cost is high. Conversely, placing large and infrequent orders will save on administrative expenses but will incur additional carrying costs. The EOQ, given by the formula shown below, is the optimal trade-off:

$$EOQ = \sqrt{\frac{2 \times s \times d}{h}}$$

Although there is some debate regarding the origin of the economic order quantity formula (see Roach, 2005), Harris (in the 1910s) and Wilson (1934) were the two main contributors.

The popularity of the model can first be explained by its simplicity, which makes it very easy to implement in companies. The second explanation is the relative robustness of the model. For example, one of the assumptions of the model is that the demand rate d is constant, as shown in the left-hand side of Figure 41. If it is not, the inventory cycle will automatically become shorter as the reorder point r is reached faster: this automatic adjustment is illustrated in the right-hand side of Figure 41 with the dashed inventory cycle. Note that in the temporary increase in demand example in Figure 41, the assumption was made that demand returns to d during the leadtime L. If this were not the case, then a stockout would occur. To avoid such a scenario, the EOQ model is often associated with a safety stock. With an EOQ model, a safety stock is computed as a probabilistic level of demand during L. If the demand follows a certain distribution, as for example normally distributed demand, then statistical tables can be used to determine the required safety stock to guarantee no stockouts with a certain level of confidence.

EXTENSIONS AND LIMITATIONS OF EOQ MODELS

The basic EOQ model is popular in theory and practice due to its simplicity and robustness. It is important to stress that the formula shown in the previous section is derived under a rather exhaustive list of assumptions: d is constant, s is not a function of Q, the price of items is not a function of Q, the leadtime L is constant, etc. As EOQ computations are based on these strict assumptions, a common mistake is to apply them to contexts where the assumptions are not met. Erel (1992), for example, shows that the EOQ model can lead to expensive and sub-optimal solutions when the price of inventory items is changing in an erratic fashion.

The operational research literature is so rich in papers extending the basic EOQ model to more general contexts that it is impossible to list them here. EOQ models with quantity discounts (where the price of items declines with the quantity order) and EOQ with non-instant replenishments are some of the most well-known extensions of the basic model.

Zangwill (1987) highlighted that the EOQ model is based on an implicit underlying philosophy that rests upon the production of batches. This can be contrasted with zero inventory policies where large batches are avoided by reducing set up costs s. Through a mathematical analysis, Zangwill showed how most commonly held properties of the EOQ model do not hold in more general contexts.

THE NEWSVENDOR MODEL

The newsvendor model is a specific category of inventory models used in contexts when the stocked items have a limited useful life. This may be because they are perishable items (e.g., food items) or because their utility quickly decreases (e.g. a daily newspaper). The model is concerned with two cost elements:

- The cost of shortage, C_s, is the cost associated with not holding enough of an item on a given day. It is usually defined as an opportunity cost (lost sales, lost margin, or lost customers).
- The cost of excess inventory, C_e, is the cost of having bought too much inventory and being left with unsold items at the end of a trading day. It is the cost of the initial purchase plus any disposal costs, if applicable. If the items can be salvaged, then the salvage revenue is deducted from the initial cost of purchase.

In the case of perishable items, there is clearly a trade-off between holding too little or too much inventory, and the purpose of the newsvendor problem is to maximise profitability by finding an optimal trade-off, defined as a *critical fractile*. The critical fractile C is the proportion of demand that the vendor should seek to satisfy. If the vendor stocks below this critical fractile, then the cost of this shortage rises quickly. Conversely, if the vendor stocks above the critical level C a shortage will be avoided, but the vendor will be exposed to the increasing cost of unsold inventories. C is also sometimes called the service level, as it represents the percentage of expected demand that the vendor is planning to serve.

C is given by:

$$C = \frac{C_s}{C_s + C_e}$$

Suppose that the above formula yields a critical fractile of 80 per cent. This means that the vendor will only stock 80 per cent of the expected *average* demand. Note that the cost of excess inventory plays a key role in increasing the denominator value. This is why in industries such as newspaper and magazine retailing it has become common practice to offer buy-back agreements to retailers. The idea of buy-back agreements is that publishers prefer retailers to offer high level of stocks in order to capture every possible sale. By offering to buy back, usually at a discounted price, any unsold items, publishers decrease C_e, and therefore increase of retailers willingness to stock more items.

It is also noteworthy that the newsvendor model is based on an assumption of risk neutrality. Wang and Webster (2009) point out that research in economics, organisational behaviour, and finance shows that risk neutrality is not necessarily representative of the behaviour of managers. They also propose a loss-averse newsvendor model. Their model show that a loss-averse vendor will order less items than a risk neutral vendor when C_s is low, and more than a risk neutral vendor when C_s is high.

REFERENCES

Buxey, G. (2006) 'Reconstructing inventory management theory', *International Journal of Operations and Production Management*, 26 (9): 996–1012.

Erel, E. (1992) 'The effect of continuous price change in the EOQ', *Omega*, 20 (4): 523–527.

Rao, U. (2003) 'Properties of the periodic review (R,T) inventory control policy for stationary, stochastic demand', *Manufacturing and Service Operations Management*, 5 (1): 37–53.

Rajagopalan, S. and Malhotra, A. (2001) 'Have US manufacturing inventories really decreased? An empirical study', *Manufacturing and Services Operations Management*, 3 (1): 14–24.

Roach, B. (2005) 'Origin of the economic order quantity formula: transcription or transformation?', *Management Decision*, 43 (9): 1262–1268.

Sani, B. and Kingsman, B. (1997) 'Selecting the best periodic inventory control and demand forecasting methods for low demand items', *Journal of the Operational Research Society*, 48: 700–713.

Wallin, C., Rungtusanathan, J. and Rabinovich, E. (2006) 'What is the right inventory management approach for a purchased item?', *International Journal of Operations and Production Management*, 26 (1): 50–68.

Wang, C. and Webster, S. (2009). 'The loss-averse newsvendor problem', *Omega*, 37 (1): 93–105.

Wilson, R.H. (1934) 'A scientific routine for stock control', *Harvard Business Review*, 13: 116–128.

Zangwill, W. (1987) 'From EOQ towards ZI', *Management Science*, 33 (10): 1209–1223.

inventory systems

Material Requirements Planning (MRP)

> **MRP is the process through which operations managers plan for purchase and work orders in order to feed a factory with parts and materials to attain the production objectives set down in the master production plan.**

PRODUCT BREAKDOWN STRUCTURE

The product breakdown structure is a specification of the different parts and components used to assemble a finished product. Figure 42 shows an example of a product breakdown structure for a cold frame used by gardeners. A product breakdown structure is usually based on a hierarchical structure. For example, in Figure 42 the finished product exists at level 0. The cold frame is the result of the assembly of three level 1 components: one frame, two hinges, and one top assembly. A level 1 component can be further decomposed into a level 2 list, and so on. In the case of complex products, such as a car, a product breakdown structure will have many hierarchical levels. Note that for the sake of simplification, minor items (wood glue, wood screws, and nails) were excluded from the specification. In a real industrial application, these would be included.

The *bill of materials* is a technical document often produced in conjunction with the product breakdown structure. It is simply a list of all the parts, materials, and components used in the manufacturing or assembly of a product.

Given a production plan for the level 0 independent item, when should the various level 1, 2, etc. items be bought? Answering this question, i.e. planning for dependent demand items inventory, is the purpose of Material Requirements Planning, or MRP.

MATERIAL REQUIREMENTS PLANNING

MRP is the process by which operations managers plan for purchase and work orders in order to feed a factory with parts and materials to attain the production objectives set down in the master production plan.

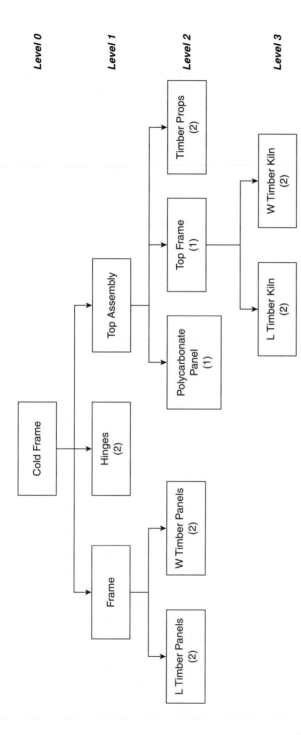

Figure 42   A product breakdown structure for a cold frame

The inputs of MRP are:

- *The master production schedule*: This contains information about when level 0 items should be completed. For example: 50 cold frames should be completed on Day 30.
- *Current inventory positions*: For example there may be five cold frames in inventory today (Day 10).
- *The product breakdown structure*: This indicates which parts and components are required to produce a cold frame. Lead time information will be included in the product breakdown structure. Lead time includes assembly time information (e.g. it takes 0.5 hours to assemble a cold frame from level 1 components) and purchasing time information (e.g. it takes two weeks to place an order for and receive a delivery of polycarbonate panels).

The outputs of MRP are *order releases*, i.e. the official release of a production instruction in the factories. Examples of instructions are:

- *Purchase orders*: A production planner releases an instruction to purchase items from a supplier.
- *Work orders*: A production planner releases an instruction to start working internally on production.
- *Rescheduling notice*: In the instance when a new order for cold frames has been accepted, it may be necessary to re-shuffle prior production plans. This means that past purchases and work orders will have to be amended.

The computational task of MRP is, simply put, to deduct required orders from the master production schedule. For example: we need 50 finished cold frames by Day 30. We have five in inventory today, so we should produce 45. To assemble 45 frames, we need $0.5 \times 45 = 22.5$ hours. If we work eight hours per day, then assembly will require $22.5/8 = 2.8$ days, or three days. Thus, we should release a work order for 45 frames for Day 28. Full-time work on the frames will then be completed at the end of Day 30, i.e. when it was initially requested.

Will 90 hinges be available to start production on Day 28? Will 45 top assemblies and 45 frames be available? If the answer to these questions is no, we need to release adequate work orders (top assembly and frame) and purchase orders (hinges). In other words, starting from the top level, MRP planners will work down the product breakdown structure and make decisions so that all materials are ordered, received, and assembled in order to finish production when it was specified.

MRP computations can quickly become complex. Consider the following examples:

- Assume that we are now on Day 22. A new order for five frames for Day 25 is received. Given the short lead time, the easiest solution is to sell the five cold frames currently on hand. This means however that all previously released work and purchase orders will have to be amended in order to produce five additional frames.
- Typically, a cold frame manufacturer will sell from a catalogue of at least 20 different frame models, all using some common parts but also some specific ones. Orders are received daily with different customer requirements. Conflicts between different orders will quickly emerge, and rules for prioritising orders will be needed.

Complexity is an important dimension to consider in an MRP system. Cooper and Zmud (1989) conducted a telephone survey in order to understand why so many MRP implementation projects failed to deliver the expected benefits. Their survey results show that although companies with complex production processes are more keen and willing to adopt MRP, they are often unable to use MRP at its fullest.

Complexity is also the reason why companies seldom use manual MRP systems and instead use computer-based MRP systems. The systems are programmed on the basis of advanced MRP scheduling rules, and often offer the user the possibility to customise these rules. Mabert (2007) reviewed the historical development of MRP and showed that the formulation and design of MRP methods was not an instant matter, and that information technology has played a key role in enabling the development of modern MRP systems.

MRP II, OR CLOSED-LOOP MRP

Contrary to expectations, MRP II does not stand for materials requirements planning, but for *Manufacturing Resources Planning*. One of the limitations of MRP systems is that they make an infinite capacity assumption. In the example used in the previous section, we decided to release a work order on Day 28. However, we did not check whether or not a worker was available to be assigned to this work order on days 28, 29, and 30. An infinite capacity assumption implies that we must base our plan on the fact that workers, machines, or any other resource used in manufacturing can be added on at will. This clearly does not work in real life, as factories will have *capacity constraints*.

MRPII systems keep track of the usage of manufacturing resources per working day. Assuming that all workers are all busy on days 29 and 30, an MRPII system will release a work order for Day 26, so that the order for cold frames will be completed on days 26, 27, and 28 when enough workers are available.

The idea behind MRPII – to keep tabs on the availability and utilisation of resources – proved to be a powerful management tool, and it eventually led to the development of *Enterprise Resource Planning* systems, or *ERP*. ERPs basically extend the principles of MRPII to the whole firm. (ERPs are discussed in more detail in **Integration**.)

REFERENCES

Cooper, R. and Zmud, R. (1989) 'Material requirement planning system infusion', *Omega*, 17 (1): 471–481.

Mabert, V. (2007) 'The early road to material requirements planning', *Journal of Operations Management*, 25: 346–356.

Just-in-Time

> *Just-in-Time inventory management consists of sourcing materials and parts at the right time, in the right place, and in the right quantity. Its purpose is to eliminate any form of unnecessary inventory in order to achieve a continuous flow of production state.*

THEORY OF SWIFT, EVEN FLOW

According to Schmenner and Swink (1998), the theory of swift, even flow holds that the more swift and even the flow of materials through a process, the more productive that process will be. This theory corresponds to a number of laws:

Law of variability: 'The greater the random variability, either demanded of the process or inherent of the process itself or in the items processed, the less productive the process is'.

Law of bottleneck: 'An operation's productivity is improved by eliminating or by better managing its bottlenecks'.

Law of scientific method: 'The productivity of labour can be augmented in most instances by applying methods such as those identified by the scientific management movement'.

Law of quality: 'Productivity can frequently be improved as quality is improved and as waste declines, either by changes in product design, or by changes in materials or processing. Various techniques of the quality movement can be responsible for these improvements'.

Law of factory focus: 'Factories that focus on a limited set of tasks will be more productive than similar factories with a broader array of tasks'.

(Schmenner and Swink, 1998: 101–2).

JUST IN TIME SYSTEMS

Just-in-Time production (JIT) is perhaps the most well-known operations management practice, and its diffusion has spread well beyond operations management circles. The basic idea behind JIT is to design operations systems so that materials, parts, components, and labour are available at the right place, in the right quantity, and at the right time. It could be argued that such a definition could be used to define pretty much any form of production schedule! For example, many have seen Henry Ford as a genuine pioneer of JIT when he designed and operated the first assembly line at Le Rouge's industrial complex in the 1910s.

There is more to JIT than the above definition however. JIT, as a form of production *system*, was born in Japan out of management concerns for the lack of flow in factories. Process engineers were working hard to design a shopfloor where products would flow easily from start to finish. In practice, though, managers experienced discrete rather than continuous flow, volatile rather than even flow, and sluggish rather than swift flow. JIT, therefore, is an example of how production managers have translated the theory of swift, even flows into a work reality.

The starting point of developing the JIT approach was to look at the hurdles of achieving flow in the factory. Reda (1987) provided an early and structured account of the elements of a JIT system. A JIT production system is composed of a production method, an information system, and a defect-free approach to production.

PRODUCTION METHOD

The objective of JIT is to achieve a swift, even flow of product. This is feasible, as Henry Ford demonstrated in the 1910s, when a unique version of a product is being processed. If a unique product is being produced, all machines, workstations and tasks are dedicated to the production of this product. But what happens in the more common case when different versions of a product, or even of different products, are manufactured in the same facility? Product variations will wreak havoc on a facility, as different process times and changeover times are incurred.

It is important at this stage to distinguish make to stock from make to order production systems. In a make to stock system, production managers will produce according to a production plan which is itself based on a forecast of demand. This later approach to production is call '*push production*' because an organisation basically pushes products through the factory and onto the market.

Push production systems have a number of shortcomings. Take the example of an assembly line with a cycle time of three minutes and let us assume that a batch of ten 'special' products has been pushed onto production. If these special products require five minutes of work on some but not all workstations, this will result in the standard three-minute workstations pushing products too quickly onto the slow workstations. Beyond the five-minute bottlenecks, downstream three-minute workstations are then partially idle as they are not being fed fast enough. In other words, the flow has now been disrupted. One of the key innovations behind JIT was to question the entire approach to production: given the complex processes used to manufacture a variety of variable products, is push production a sensible approach? The product–process matrix (see **Process**) shows us that this is not the case. High-scale continuous production is only possible in the case of a completely standardised product. In the case of customised products, we should use make to order types of production processes, but unfortunately these processes are not easily scalable. Behind these processes, though, is the idea that *variety should be handled as one-of-a-kind production*. Would it possible to design a production system able to cope with large-scale demand *and* a one-of-a-kind production system? The answer was the formulation of a new approach to production planning: *pull production*.

Instead of trying to push as many products onto the market as possible, push production starts with the question 'What does the market want today?' This specification could be based on a mix of confirmed orders and forecasted assumptions. This demand is divided into small batches which are then pulled from the factory rather than pushed through it. This is achieved by recognising that:

- Each workstation should have the same cycle time, regardless of the product configuration.
- Potential differences in requirements between product configurations are handled through flexible workers and equipments.
- Set-up and changeover times should be as short as possible so that only small lots are being produced.

INFORMATION SYSTEMS

Unlike push production, pull production does not work in a vacuum. In a push system, work orders are released but it is never clear when products will be finished as this is a function of queues and patterns of utilisations at the different workstations. In a pull system production steps have to be perfectly synchronised and this is why an information system is necessary.

Take the example of an assembly line making products (AB_1C_1D) and (AB_2C_3D) (the second product is produced by assembling element B_2 into base A at workstation 1, then by adding element C_3 at workstation 2, and element D at workstation 3). Production starts at the end of the assembly line where the worker at workstation 3 is told to produce one unit of (AB_2C_3D). Here is what then happens:

1 The worker receives a production order (information) to produce AB_2C_3D.
2 The worker sends a production request (information) to workstation 2 asking for a unit of (AB_2C_3) and a withdrawal request (information) to the inventory room for a unit of D.
3 All other workstations exchange similar instructions. At the beginning of the line, a worker releases a unit of A from the stock.
4 A completed unit of (AB_2C_3) arrives at work station 3 (maybe with a document containing the initial request). A unit of D arrives from the stock room at the same time (again, with an attached document). The worker removes the 'request' documents, assembles

(AB_2C_3D), attaches the initial request document received in step 1 to this, and sends it to the end of the assembly line.

Aside from the process design challenges discussed in the previous section, a key challenge in implementing a pull production system is to implement such an overarching information system. Workers at workstations need to pass down requests as needed so that the flow can be maintained. Japanese factories addressed this challenge through the introduction of '*kanbans*', small cardboard cards which are exchanged between the workstations. Different requests (withdrawal, production, etc.) are based on different kanban designs. Many modern organisations have now replaced kanbans with bar-coded cards or 'electronic' kanbans.

DEFECT-FREE PRODUCTION

What happens on an assembly line if a tool breaks or if a product is found to be defective? In a push system, upstream workstations may continue to produce and a large queue of partially completed products might quickly build up in front of the problem workstation. Downstream workstations may also continue to work if they have a queue or inventory buffer stock of products waiting to be processed. In a pull production system, a stopped workstation does not feed downstream stations with products and upstream stations with kanbans: thus, the entire line comes to a stop. The conclusion is that such problems should not occur! This is why the development of JIT took place in conjunction with teamwork and quality control. Defect-free production is the only way to derive the benefits from a pull production system.

JIT IN PRACTICE

Running defect free production, team-based flexible workers and an information system such as kanbans is not a simple affair. Push production systems are in fact much easier to implement, and also much more insensitive to small errors and perturbations. JIT production systems are widely recognised for their positive impact on performance (measured by productivity or in financial terms) and also for the fact that they constitute high stress work environments both for managers and workers. JIT systems are essentially a work environment with 'no safety net'. McLachlin (1997) used case study research to look at the conditions under which a JIT management initiative could be successful. He concluded that management's visible commitment, employees' training and the promotion of teamwork and employee responsibility are necessary conditions for the implementation of JIT. In a similar vein, Selto et al. (1995) have shown that a lack of fit between the worker empowerment required by JIT systems and an existing authoritarian management culture explains poor implementation performance.

REFERENCES

McLachlin, R. (1997) 'Management initiatives and just-in-time manufacturing', *Journal of Operations Management*, 15: 271–292.

Reda, H.M. (1987) 'A review of kanban, the Japanese just-in-time production system', *Engineering Management International*, 4: 143–150.

Schmenner, R. and Swink, M. (1998) 'On theory in operations management', *Journal of Operations Management*, 17: 97–113.

Selto, F.H., Renner, C.J. and Young, S.M. (1995). 'Assessing the organisational fit of a just-in-time manufacturing system: testing selection, integration and system models of contingency theory', *Accounting, Organizations and Society*, 20(7/8): 665–684.

just-in-time

Planning and Control

> *Forecasting is the organisational exercise conducted to estimate future demand and initiate all planning tasks.*

THE NEED FOR FORECASTING

The task of planning is relatively straightforward in a stable or repetitive environment. It becomes more of a challenge in an environment of uncertainty. Compare, for example, a hotel planning its staffing levels for different seasons after having operated for five years and the task of planning staffing levels for a brand new hotel. In the first case, there is uncertainty but information about past demand can be used to remove some of this uncertainty. In the second case, there is simply no readily available information.

In the two examples above, any information about demand (past or future) is useful. For example, past high demand during the Easter season implies that the plan should recommend a high staff level then. Information is an asset to an organisation, and as such, it should be managed.

For any organisation, 'reliable' information about the future is a source of competitive advantage. Forecasting is the organisational process by which planners elicit information about future demand, use past demand information, and adopt techniques to supplement the intuitive feelings of managers and decision makers. The output of this process is a forecast, i.e. a specification of expected future demand. Forecasts are paramount to the task of planning, as they constitute the starting point for planning processes: it is from a forecast that decisions such as capacity planning, aggregate production planning, and scheduling can be initiated.

FORECASTING AS AN ORGANISATIONAL PROCESS

Forecasting is both an organisational and a technical process. Although operations managers should have a good mastery of the technical side of the process, mastering the organisational side is equally important. Davis and Mentzer (2007) have developed a framework, shown in Figure 43, that describes the organisational issues in forecasting. The framework stresses that:

- *Forecasting should be implemented as an official and legitimate process*: Davis and Mentzer talk of the forecasting 'climate'. Top management refusing to use forecasts, organisational members considering forecasts as inaccurate and useless, and forecasting work not being rewarded are all examples of situations where a negative climate would grow, a state of affairs which would eventually result in forecasting failing to achieve its purpose.
- *As stressed in the opening section, forecasting does not take place in a vacuum*: It is virtually impossible to prepare a forecast when one has no information about market characteristics and past demand. This is why the ability of the firm to manage information is a critical element of the forecasting capability of an organisation.
- *Forecasting is not only an issue in operations management*: Marketing, finance, and human resources will also prepare plans under uncertain conditions, and thus, all parties will need a forecast to initiate their decision making. Moreover, all functions depend on one another to prepare their plans. Human resources will need an operations plan to anticipate staffing needs. Operations will need to align their activity forecast with that of marketing. Forecasting does not 'belong' to a business function: instead it is a cross-functional process and thus it needs to be managed as such in order to be effective.
- *Climate, informational and organisational capabilities together lead to sales forecasting performance*: Note that 'performance' here does not only mean accuracy. Although accuracy is clearly an important dimension of performance, other measures are also relevant here. For example, the satisfaction of all the forecast's stakeholders and the ability of the forecast to indicate a future change in trends are possible dimensions of sales forecasting performance.
- *Forecasting performance leads to business performance*: It is through better forecasts and plans that a firm will achieve superior levels of performance measured in financial or quality terms.
- *Failures to achieve either forecasting performance or business performance can be analysed and used to improve both the climate and capabilities.*

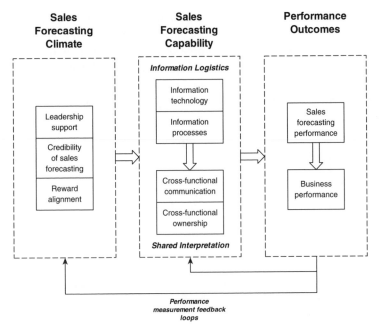

Sales Forecasting Climate

Sales Forecasting Capability

Performance Outcomes

Information Logistics

Information technology

Information processes

Leadership support

Credibility of sales forecasting

Reward alignment

Sales forecasting performance

Cross-functional communication

Cross-functional ownership

Business performance

Shared Interpretation

Performance measurement feedback loops

Figure 43   The Sales Forecasting Management Framework (Reprinted from International Journal of Forecasting, 23 (3), Davis, D. and Mentzer, J., 'Organizational factors in sales forecasting management', p. 21, © 2007, with permission from Elsevier)

FORECASTING AS A TECHNICAL PROCESS

There are three key categories of forecasting techniques: qualitative, time series models, and causal models.

Qualitative forecasting techniques are used when quantitative techniques cannot be used. This is usually the case when there are no available data regarding a phenomenon or when the phenomenon to be forecasted is either distant (the long-term future) or complex (forecasting customers' preference for technologies which have not been developed yet). As data are missing, qualitative forecasting data must rely on expert judgment or opinions. A popular method for qualitative forecasting is the *Delphi method*, where a facilitator will conduct a written survey of a field by contacting experts. Predictions are then fine-tuned through a successive consultation of the experts on the basis of a document synthesised by the facilitator.

Time series methods are quantitative methods that are based on the assumption *that the past contains all the information needed to forecast the future*. Figure 44 gives one example of a time series: it is basically a series of values (here, sales figures) displayed on a graph with time as the x-axis. Time series methods are used to forecast future sales using only the information contained within the graph.

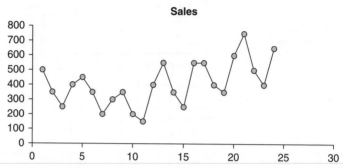

Figure 44 A time series

Look carefully at Figure 44 and you should see some clear patterns:

- From period 10 onwards, there is a clear growth trend in the sales figure. This trend can be modelled mathematically.
- Sales in quarter 1 are always very strong. Sales then dip in quarter 2 and reach a year-low in quarter 3, before rising again in the last quarter. This is called seasonality and once again this can be modelled mathematically.

The most basic form of time series forecasting is based on *moving averages*. Imagine for example that to forecast sales in period 26 in Figure 44 we use a four month moving average. The forecast for period 26 is obtained by adding sales from periods 22, 23, 24, and 25 and dividing the total by four. What about forecasting period 27? Once the sales from period 26 are known, a new average based on the values for periods 23, 24, 25, and 26 can be computed, hence the concept of a 'moving' average.

A strength of moving averages is that they smooth the data. This is illustrated in Figure 45 where a two-month moving average is compared to a 12-month moving average: the two-month moving average follows the original demand curve closely, whereas the 12-month moving average shows a very smoothed out curve where the monthly fluctuations have been removed. When forecasting a very volatile time series, this *smoothing effect* is a desirable property as it removes unpredictable fluctuations. Too much smoothing is not desirable, however, as some important variations will also be removed. The degree of smoothing is controlled by the age of the data: the older the data (e.g. 12 months) the stronger the smoothing effect.

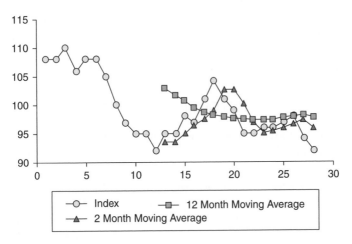

Figure 45   Smoothing effect

One of the limitations of moving averages is that all the data used are given the same weight. In practice, forecasters prefer to give more weight to recent data and less weight to older data. This is achieved through the technique of *exponential smoothing*. Exponential smoothing is a popular forecasting technique, especially in inventory management. (A full review of the state of the art of the theory and use of exponential smoothing can be found in Gardner, 2006.)

Causal forecasting models attempt to link the dependent variable (e.g. sales) to a known and measurable variable. In other words, analysts are trying to discover a cause and effect relationship between two variables. Imagine, for example, a UK-based caravan park trying to decide if during the winter months it would be worth investing in additional caravans or if the current capacity should be maintained. By consulting economic databases, the manager may discover that occupancy at the site correlates well with disposable income. By using a published forecast of disposable income, the manager is then able to forecast if demand on the site will increase. The manager may also discover that the euro/pound exchange rate has on impact on demand: when the pound is low in value, continental holidays are expensive and more holiday makers then choose to stay within the UK. The key technique for building these models is *regression analysis*. More information about regression analysis can be found in all business statistics and research method textbooks.

In their review of forecasting textbooks published in the last twenty-five years, Cox and Loomis (2006) highlighted that one of the modern trends is to combine methods. For example, one can combine the use of time series methods and regression analysis. Combining methods makes sense when trying to capture the benefits of each method, or when different methods bring different perspectives to the data.

FORECASTING IN PRACTICE

The degree of technical sophistication of forecasting techniques is such that it is easy to start to believe that business forecasts are always reliable. In practice, business forecasts are reliable only to the extent that environmental conditions are relatively static. For example, many of the growth forecasts prepared in 2007 by business probably had to be revised in 2008 and then again in 2009 when world economies experienced the 'credit crunch' recession. Forecasts always change as more information becomes available. Forecasts tend to be very inaccurate in the long term (for which little information is available) and tend to be more accurate in the short term (where more and more detailed information becomes available). Research also shows that forecasts for group statistics tend to be more accurate than forecasts for individuals: this reinforces the importance of the organisational side of the forecasting process.

So should managers be concerned with inaccurate forecasts? As discussed above, there are situations (high uncertainty, long term) where forecast accuracy is impossible to achieve. In these situations, it is important to appreciate that *learning, not predicting*, is the real objective of the forecasting process. In situations of high uncertainty, what is important is learning why the expert opinions were wrong, so that a similar error can be avoided in a similar context in the future.

Forecasting is used in practice to different ends:

- Short-term forecasting:

    o Is common in operational functions. Examples of its use are planning and scheduling, manufacturing operations, purchasing, and staffing. Quantitative techniques are mostly used, especially in time series methods.

- Long-term forecasting:

  o Examples are planning for capital investment, facility layout, job shop design, etc. Although causal models are predominantly used, subjective and qualitative considerations also play an important role.

REFERENCES

Cox, J. and Loomis, D. (2006) 'Improving forecasting through textbooks – a 25 year review', *International Journal of Forecasting*, 22: 617–624.

Davis, D. and Mentzer, J. (2007) 'Organisational factors in sales forecasting management', *International Journal of Forecasting*, 23: 475–495.

Gardner, E. (2006) 'Exponential smoothing: the state of the art – part II', *International Journal of Forecasting*, 22: 637–666.

Aggregate Production Planning

> *Aggregate production planning is a tactical task with the objective of coming up with a medium-term (6 to 24 months) game plan to use an operations system's capacity to match demand.*

AGGREGATE PRODUCTION PLANNING: PURPOSE

When making **capacity** decisions, decision makers will set a desired level of activity for a facility. This decision is made because the experts estimate that this level will correspond to the average demand that the facility will experience in the future. Figure 46 shows that even in a case where that estimate was correct as an *average*, real demand will fluctuate. In the first few months in Figure 46, demand exceeds capacity. It then drops below capacity to peak up again above capacity on the right-hand side of the graph. *Aggregate Production Planning*, or APP, is the set of techniques used by an operations manager to come up with a medium-term (6 to 24 months) tactic to use the existing capacity to match demand.

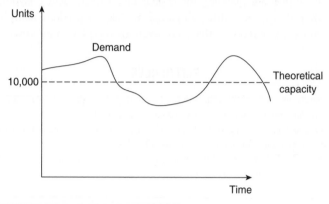

Figure 46   The purpose of aggregate production planning

Note that the need for aggregate production planning stems from:

- *Demand volatility*: This can include seasonality (e.g. higher sales during Christmas) or economic cycles (economic growth or recessions). Cycles and seasonal fluctuations can be forecasted, and thus addressed through aggregate production planning. Random fluctuations of demand cannot be forecasted in advance, and thus will be dealt with later on by scheduling rather than aggregate production planning.
- *Inappropriate capacity*: Imagine in Figure 46 an average demand of 15,000 units. APP can be used to try to adjust the capacity upward, but it would be cheaper to invest in expanding the capacity in the long run, provided that demand will remain at 15,000 units for the foreseeable future. If experts predict that the demand will eventually return to an average of 10,000 units, then APP remains the best approach to cope with the current demand peak.

KEY TACTICS FOR MATCHING DEMAND WITH SUPPLY

Although the theoretical capacity of a facility is set (e.g. at 10,000 units/months), there are various ways by which managers can match demand with supply in the medium term. The marketing function can try to affect demand. For example, by using a price discount campaign, marketing can increase the demand for a product when it is forecasted that a facility will have excess capacity.

Similarly, the operations function can affect supply in one, or several, of the following ways:

- *Inventory*: Finished goods can be produced in advance during periods of low activity, when capacity is available. In periods of high demand, sales are fulfilled both through production and inventory.
- *Number of employees*: In the case of labour-intensive processes, the factory capacity can simply be adjusted by hiring or firing workers. In cases where shortages are unacceptable, a (costly) strategy consists of making sure that a facility is always staffed for peak demand.
- *Working hours*: Employees can be invited to work overtime. Overtime is more expensive than regular working hours and is often subject to legal restrictions. Therefore, it is a punctual rather than a sustained source of capacity increase. Undertime is also possible, for example by inviting employees to take holidays early or unpaid leave. Employees, however, are usually willing to volunteer for overtime (as an extra source of income) and much more reluctant to volunteer for undertime. An alternative to undertime is to ask employees to perform other tasks (such as maintenance, filing, sorting, updating documentation, etc.) during periods of low demand.
- *Contingent workers*: During periods of peak demand, part-time or casual workers can be used to increase capacity. This works well in labour intensive processes where training requirements are low: if the task requires extensive training, bringing in contingent workers becomes a costly exercise.
- *Subcontracting*: Capacity subcontracting means outsourcing a firm's workload to another firm, which will typically be a competitor. Subcontracting is normally costly but is also an easily scalable strategy.
- *Backorders*: A backorder is an order received today that will be fulfilled in the future. In other words, customers know that they are on a waiting list. Using backorders greatly simplifies aggregate production planning (as actual rather than forecasted demand can be used to prepare the plan), but it should be used with caution as customers may prefer faster deliveries. Backordering is a common strategy for luxury goods (e.g. sports cars) where customers are happy to wait for a very specific product.

AGGREGATE PRODUCTION PLANNING: SUMMARY SPECIFICATIONS

The purpose of aggregate planning is – given a demand forecast, policies, objectives and constraints – to prepare a game plan to adjust a firm's capacity so that supply matches expected demand (this is shown in Figure 47). The decisions made will include the number of workers to use (per unit of time), decisions on whether to use inventory or not, overtime, subcontracting, and backorders.

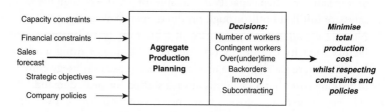

Figure 47   Summary specifications of aggregate production planning

METHODS USED TO SOLVE APP PROBLEMS

A traditional distinction in operations management is made between pure strategies and mixed strategies for solving an aggregate production planning problem.

A *pure strategy* attempts to solve the problem though the use of a single decision variable. There are two standard pure strategies. *Chase demand* means changing the number of workers monthly (or weekly) so that the production capacity exactly matches the demand requirements. The advantage of chase strategy is that expensive capacity adjustments (such as inventory or subcontracting) are not used. The disadvantage is that the company is constantly hiring and firing employees as demand fluctuates: this has a cost in terms of administration (recruitment, training, etc.) and also in terms of productivity (low worker morale). The arch rival of chase demand is a *level production* strategy, where only inventory is used to absorb fluctuations in demand rates. To implement a level production strategy, managers will start by estimating the yearly demand. From the yearly demand, managers then compute an average monthly demand and staff their factory accordingly. The number of units produced per month is constant, and the number of employees is also constant. Demand peaks are anticipated by stocking an adequate number of units that will have been produced in prior lower demand periods.

A *mixed strategy*, in contrast, is one where the decision makers will consider all possible decision variables. By an astute use of overtime, subcontracting, part-time workers and inventory, managers can formulate a game plan with a lower total cost than a pure strategy.

Comparing two pure strategies is a relatively simple matter: it requires listing all the cost data and sales forecast in a spreadsheet model and comparing whether the chase or the production level strategy will cost less. With a mixed strategy, solving a problem is much more complicated because of a high number of combinations between all the decision variables. The *trial and error method* consists of using a spreadsheet model to try out different ideas and then finding one low cost production plan: it is an intuitive, manual method. Another approach when solving a mixed strategy problem is to use analytical techniques. In a review of the theoretical literature about APP, Nam and Logendran (1992) identified nine analytical approaches which were decomposed into optimal methods (giving the best solution to the problem) and near-optimal approaches (giving one good solution to the problem). *Linear programming* is one of most popularly used optimisation methods. Although analytical methods are, technically speaking, the best methods, there are reasons why the trial and error method is commonly used in practice. First, formulating a detailed analytical model is time consuming and costly. An experienced operations manager can often find an equally suitable solution much more quickly through a manual and intuitive procedure. Second, company policies or labour regulations often heavily constrain the setting of feasible solutions. Hiring and firing, for example, may not be an option in many North European countries. Once this variable is fixed (the constant number of workers), the problem becomes much easier to solve manually.

APP IN PRACTICE

A number of postal surveys were conducted in the late 1980s regarding industrial practices about aggregate production planning. Their findings were that APP is often done intuitively rather than via the application of the APP models described in textbooks; constraints such as human resources, marketing and companies policies were more important in practice than in theoretical illustrations; practitioners often lacked the information required to use APP models; and practitioners were not necessarily trained to use mathematical APP models.

Buxey (2003) revisited the theory–practice gap by utilising multiple case studies of Australian companies. His conclusion was that aggregate production planning was a chimera! According to his observations, companies did not prepare aggregate production plans: instead firms adopted a preferred strategy (i.e. chase demand) and went directly to the formulation of a master production schedule. It is important to moderate Buxey's findings by pointing out that all his case studies deal with firms exposed to seasonal demand variations. Seasonality can be a very predictable fluctuation, in which case there is no need to re-prepare APP plans over and over again. In industries where cyclical fluctuations are more prevalent, APP would remain an important stage in the process of hierarchical planning for production. Taking a radically different position than Buxey are Singhal and Singhal (2007) who reviewed the work based on the pioneering APP model of Holt, Modigliani, Muth, and Simon in the 1950s. They concluded that APP had played a central role in the renaissance and evolution of operations management.

REFERENCES

Buxey, G. (2003) 'Strategy not tactics drives aggregate planning', *International Journal of Production Economics*, 85: 331–346.

Nam, S. and Logendran, R. (1992) 'Aggregate production planning – a survey of models and methologies', *European Journal of Operational Research*, 61: 255–272.

Singhal, J. and Singhal, K. (2007) 'Holt, Modigliani, Muth, and Simon's work and its role in the renaissance and evolution of operations management', *Journal of Operations Management*, 25: 300–309.

Scheduling

Scheduling is the short-term planning stage concerned with the preparation of detailed production plans, which will include the allocation of work to different work centres (assignment) and the sequencing of different jobs through these work centres.

SCHEDULING IN CONTEXT

Planning for operations is a context-dependent problem. Industries which are capital intensive need to assess their investment needs a long time in advance, as financing, building, and launching facilities into production can take up to several years. The oil industry, for example, cannot open a new oil well overnight. Installation of new capacity requires an initial exploration phase, the building of facilities, and the installation of an adequate logistics network (e.g. a pipeline). This will require a minimum of five years from the start to achieving commercial exploitation. In these industries, organisations will rely on a strong distinction between hierarchical planning levels: a lot of work is needed to produce long- and middle-term plans. However, once these plans are implemented, the short term is an easy matter. Oil extraction, mining and paper mills are examples of such process industries. Once a process facility has been built, the process – and therefore its schedule – are set. For many process industries scheduling simply means setting the pace of production so that output matches current demand levels. In other industries – as for example in mining – scheduling means the combination of inputs used to produce an output. For example, phosphate mines extract phosphate ore from different areas, each with its own quality and concentration. The daily production problem is to determine which quantities from different areas should be mixed together in order to obtain a pre-specified commercial grade of the final product. These problems are often solved with linear programming models.

In other industries – which are either labour-intensive or characterised by a high level of customisation – long-term planning requires considerably less effort as the capacity is easily adjusted in the medium or short-run. Short-term planning, however, becomes a key issue as the true competitiveness of a firm will reveal itself in their ability to schedule operations as needed. In this concept, we discuss two examples of industries where scheduling is important: scheduling for batch operations and scheduling for service operations.

SCHEDULING BATCH OR JOB SHOP OPERATIONS

Although scheduling job shop and batch production systems has always been the traditional scheduling problem studied in manufacturing management, the problem is also relevant to the scheduling of operations for professional services (e.g. a doctor's practice) and service shops (e.g. an auto repair shop).

The key characteristic of these systems is the high degree of customisation between jobs. Each job will have different requirements and different resource consumption profiles. For example, in a precision machining shop, some orders will require the intensive use of an expensive state-of-the-art high precision grinding machine whereas other orders will require the use of standard drilling machines. Similarly, patients reporting to a health centre will require different tests, equipment and specialists.

Scheduling for job shops involves four key tasks:

- *Routing*: What is the general process sequence that the product or customer will follow having entered the facility? In the manufacturing case, process engineers produce, for each job order, a job sheet indicating the different activities to be performed and their order.
- *Assignment, or 'loading'*: This is about deciding which resource (a worker or piece of equipment) should be used to process a specific job. For example, which jobs should be sent to drilling machine 1 and which to drilling machine 2? Which patient should be sent to which doctor?
- *Sequencing*: This is about deciding, once jobs arrive at a resource, the sequence in which they should be processed. For example, medical services systematically use the first-in first-out sequencing rule as it is viewed as being a fair practice by customers.
- *Monitoring*: This is about keeping tabs on the execution of the schedule. If unforeseen delays are occurring, managerial intervention and 'rescheduling' will be required.

How each of these activities is done depends on the context of operations and the objectives adopted by the organisation. Typical examples of objectives used in scheduling are meeting customers' due dates, minimising response times, minimising time in the system, maximising machine or labour utilisation, etc.

Some activities particularly lend themselves to mathematical modelling and have been the subject of a lot of operational research. For example, assignment problems are often solved by a linear programming application called the 'Hungarian method'. Other activities, however, are so complex, that operations managers and planners will rely on heuristics rather than on optimisation algorithms. Take sequencing for example: it is usually done by using a number of rules, such as first-come first-served or 'shorter processing time' first. Sequencing rules are easy to use in the case of an *n* jobs, one machine problem. For example, if the objective is to minimise late jobs on a single machine, a good heuristics is to sequence jobs by their earliest due date. In the case of scheduling *n* jobs through two machines the heuristics known as 'Johnson's rule' works well.

The more general case of scheduling *n* jobs through *m* machines is what is called an np-hard problem in mathematics – a class of problem for which there is no known optimisation method. Take for example the case of trying to schedule ten jobs going through ten machines: there are theoretically $4*10^{65}$ possible schedules! In practice, operation researchers will use heuristics, simulation methods, or search methods to identify acceptable schedules for these complex problems.

SCHEDULING SERVICE OPERATIONS

Scheduling mass services

In the case of mass services, such as fast food restaurants or call centres, the problem of scheduling is about making sure that the output potential of the service system matches demand patterns. Demand at a fast food restaurant varies during the day, and it would be a poor decision to have a fully staffed restaurant at 10:30 and a minimum staffing level at 13:00! On top of demand, other considerations such as the maximum number of hours of work or personal preferences for work hours can also be taken into account. A basic schedule can be prepared by studying the typical pattern of demand during the day and trying to match this pattern with an adequate staffing level in 'time blocks' or 'shifts'.

Scheduling the service factory: airline scheduling

Unlike process industries, service factories form a specific class of scheduling problems. We will illustrate this class of problem with airline scheduling.

The purpose of airline scheduling is to define the timetable for an airline. Airline scheduling typically starts 9 to 12 months before the anticipated execution of the schedule. The capability to prepare a profitable schedule is universally recognised in the airline industry as a key source of competitive advantage. In the 1970s there was a general belief that, although complicated, airline schedules could be solved through using advanced operational research techniques, and especially those techniques developed in the subfield of operational research known as *transportation science*. However, in 1985 Etschmaier and Mathaisel surveyed the literature and the practice of airline scheduling. Contrary to the general belief that the main hurdle to the mathematical optimisation of airline schedules was the lack of computing power, Etschmaier and Mathaisel's conclusion was that due to their inherent complexity airline scheduling problems could not be solved mathematically for two reasons. The first reason was that optimising airline scheduling amounted to optimising a whole airline's operations system, which was a very large and complex problem. The second reason was that there were many objectives and constraints which were difficult to quantify and thus to include in an optimisation model.

Although they recognised that the role of transportation science models was important, Etschmaier and Mathaisel revealed that airline companies dealt with their scheduling problems through a *structured process*. The first step was *schedule development*. The objective at this stage was not necessarily to construct the best possible schedule, but to build one feasible schedule which seemed satisfactory. Schedule development can be broken down into two phases:

- Schedule development begins with *frequency decisions*, i.e. how often should flights be offered on a route?
- The second phase is to develop the first draft *timetable*, i.e. determining the departure and arrival times.

Once a first timetable is designed, planners will proceed to the *fleet assignment step*. The purpose of fleet assignment is to decide which aircraft will fly which routes. This is generally solved through operational research techniques.

Aircraft rotation is the final step: its purpose is to determine – given the assignment decisions made – how often aircrafts can stop at a maintenance station and whether or not their flight patterns are efficient. If an aircraft is found to be travelling excessively whilst empty, then changes may be brought to the timetable or the fleet assignment decisions.

Aircraft rotation varies depending on the type of schedule being developed. Wells and Wensveen (2004) distinguished four key types of airline schedule:

- *Skip-Stop scheduling* means that circular routes are used by aircrafts. For example, an aircraft can be used on the route Edinburgh–Birmingham–Exeter–Edinburgh. Depending on the time of year and expected demand patterns, some intermediate cities can be skipped.

- *Local service scheduling* is used for feeder flights, i.e. small regional jets that feed a major airport. Local service scheduling means that the aircraft stops at all the airports on the way to the main airport.
- *Hub and spoke scheduling* is applied when an airline route network is based on the hub and spoke design. It is by far the most common type of schedule used nowadays. The key objective of the schedule is to place leverage on the connectivity of the hub by offering convenient connections. In a hub and spoke system, the objective is to permit maximum *traffic flow*.
- *Non-stop scheduling* means that aircraft will only fly directly between two cities and never stop in an intermediate city. When purchasing a ticket, a customer will only have a point to point service guarantee. In comparison, a customer using a hub and spoke system has a guarantee of connections from any city to another city served by the airline.

Once the first schedule, complete with assignment and rotation plans, is finalised, it is circulated to all airline departments for the purpose of *schedule evaluation*. The purpose of this step is to verify the quality of the schedule against the experience of all the operations departments.

REFERENCES

Etschmaier, M. and Mathaisel, D. (1985) 'Airline scheduling: an overview', *Transportation Science*, 19(2): 127–138.
Wells, A. and Wensveen, J. (2004) *Air Transportation: A Management Perspective* (5th edition). London: Thomson.

Project Planning

> *Project planning is the specific set of processes and tools used to plan for production within project organisations. It is about specifying which activities should be performed and in which sequence. The outcome is an estimate of the likely project completion date.*

PROJECTS AS A PROCESS CHOICE

Projects, as processes, are suitable for operations characterised by a low volume and high variety. For example, the construction industry uses project processes to build houses. Although a project may involve building several houses, each house will be slightly different, with different locations, different foundations, and, potentially, different finishing options. Another example is the delivery of consultancy projects. Although a firm may specialise in a certain areas (e.g. tax accounting), the delivery of that service to a customer (e.g. tax advice) will vary with each customer's actual requirements.

It is important to distinguish the subject of project planning from project management. Project planning, as a topic, is concerned solely with how to plan operations in a project context. Project management is a more holistic concern with every aspect of managing a project, such as managing project human resources, sharing knowledge and best practices across project teams, controlling for quality, etc. (Discussing project management is beyond the scope of this text, and readers interested in knowing more are referred to Turner, 2000, and Meredith and Mantel, 2003.)

The unique or non-repetitive nature of projects has a serious impact on planning activities as it implies that project planning has to be done entirely for each project. Contrast for example the case of planning for a fast food restaurant. Many decisions about how the work should be conducted will already be embedded in systems and organisational procedures. The sequence of serving a fast food customer is defined by the company's process standards. In repetitive production environments, short-term planning basically equates to staffing (how many staff should be working at what time of the day) and planning material flows. Projects – being different from work done previously – are such that planning work cannot fully rely on previous projects. In the case of house building projects, it is clear that there will be an element of commonality if the houses being built are of similar designs, and in such cases, a planner will be able to use a 'project template'. Yet, these templates will have to be customised to the specific characteristics of each house. In the case of a radically new project, often called a 'one-off project', then the project planning will pretty much start from scratch.

KEY PROJECT PLANNING CONCEPTS AND TOOLS

Project network

A project network is a graphical representation of the pattern of dependencies between the different tasks making up a project. Tasks are formulated by the project planner by decomposing high-level activities into more and more detailed work specifications. The objective of the project network is to provide an overall picture of the inter-relationships between tasks, and therefore, an overall picture of the inherent complexity in a project.

Two graphical conventions exist to represent a project network. In the Activity-on-Arrow convention, the arrows represent the work to be done and the nodes between the arrows represent start and finish points. Conversely, in the Activity-on-Node convention, nodes represents the work to be done whereas arrows only represent the existence of a dependency between two activities. These graphical conventions are illustrated by a simple network in Figure 48.

Gannt Charts

Gannt charts are named after Henri Gannt (1861–1919), a mechanical engineer and management consultant. They provide a visual display of the activities – and the sequence between activities – within a project. The Gannt chart is a cornerstone of modern management, and it is used both to communicate a plan graphically and to monitor executions (tracking Gannt charts). The popularity of Gannt charts is explained by their intuitive nature and by the fact that they can be produced easily with project software, such as Microsoft Project. Figure 49 shows an example of a Gannt chart.

Critical Path Method (CPM)

One of the reasons for drawing a project network or a Gannt chart is to estimate the duration of a project. CPM is a project duration estimation method which was developed in the 1950s by American consultants involved with the management of very large projects. To estimate the duration of a project it is necessary to identify the project's *critical path*. The critical path is the longest path from start to finish within the project's network (for example, there are four paths in the project network shown in Figure 48).

A simple method to finding a critical path is to measure the length of every single path (the total duration of all the activities on that path). This works well for simple projects but is not practical for large projects. For large project networks, CPM uses the method of *early and late times* in order to discover which path is the critical one. In essence, this method measures the extent to which there is slack or float to perform

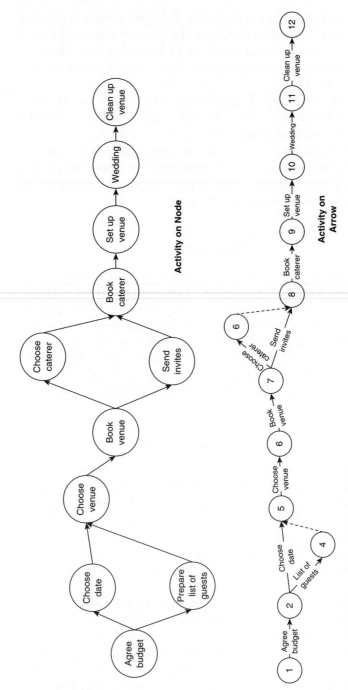

Figure 48   Planning a wedding: examples of project networks

an activity. If an activity has slack (e.g. it can start at a certain point in time plus or minus two days without affecting the project's completion time), it is not on the critical path. If any activity has no slack, it means that delaying this activity would delay the project – and thus, it is a critical activity. The duration of a project is the sum of the durations of all the activities on the critical path. CPM is used by computer packages to automatically identify the critical path.

The critical path has important management applications: a project manager should pay particular attention to the critical activities, and make sure that no delays are taking place there. If a project cannot be completed for a given target date, *project crashing* is a technique used to inject more resources into critical activities to reduce their duration, and therefore to reduce the overall project duration.

PROJECT EVALUATION AND REVIEW TECHNIQUE

CPM was developed using the assumption that the time estimates for the task would be deterministic, i.e. not subject to fluctuations. In reality, a planner may over- or under-estimate the actual completion time of an activity. Moreover, a given task may take more or less time depending on the external conditions (e.g. weather, quality of materials). The Project Evaluation and Review Technique (PERT) was designed to take into account the fact that there is uncertainty attached to time estimates. With PERT, the project planner provides a most likely time estimate for each activity, along with a pessimistic time estimate and an optimistic time estimate. Through the use of statistical procedures, PERT allows a project planner to:

- Assess, given uncertainty, a most likely 'average' completion time for the project.
- Assess the variability of this completion time by computing the project variance.
- Assess the probability that the project could be finished by a given target date.

project planning

249

FURTHER READING

Meredith, J. and Mantel, S. (2003) *Project Management: A Managerial Approach* (5th edition). New York: Wiley.

Turner, J. (2000) *Gower Handbook of Project Management*. Aldershot: Gower.

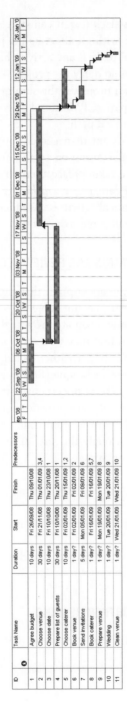

Figure 49 Gannt chart

Waiting Line Management

> *Waiting line management deals with understanding and modelling queues, and with taking managerial actions to reduce waiting time for customers.*

QUEUES AND WAITING LINES

Waiting lines, also called queues, are a universal issue in operations management as they can be observed both in manufacturing and service settings. It is useful to differentiate external waiting lines from internal waiting lines. An external waiting line builds up at the point of entry to an operations system. Once within a system, a product or customer will proceed through different processes or steps, and may on occasion have to wait before entering a workstation: this is an internal queue. The existence of internal queues and therefore their management is directly related to the design and use of production facilities. This means that to avoid internal queues managers should either redesign their facilities or change the way in which they utilise them: this is done through **scheduling** and especially the theory of constraints (see **Throughput**). The focus of this concept is to discuss the management of external queues.

The idea that customers will have to wait before receiving a service is inherently a poor business idea. Customers will see no value in waiting and will often find the experience frustrating and annoying. They will also resent the fact that they are paying for a service and have to wait. There are a number of management techniques that can be used either to avoid the build-up of queues or to make the experience less frustrating for customers. In order to discuss these techniques, it is necessary to define the typical 'anatomy' of waiting lines.

A first key characteristic is the arrival process. Queues are often described by the distribution of arrivals. The simplest case is that of constant arrivals, i.e. exactly the same number of customers arrives per unit of time. In practice, arrival rates will often fluctuate according to known stochastic distribution functions. In the case of stochastic arrival, the arrival rate is usually summarised through the distribution's average, λ (in arrivals/unit of time).

A queuing issue is balking: once a customer arrives at a facility and sees a long queue, they abandon seeking the service. Although some may return later, many will actually seek an alternative service elsewhere. From a business perspective this is very undesirable and therefore managers will invest in solutions to avoid the formation of queues. In other cases, organisations may have a finite capacity and may deny a customer the possibility of joining a queue. This is the case with call centres that can only accept so many incoming calls at any one time.

The second issue is queue discipline, i.e. the order in which customers will be processed. The most standard queue discipline universally judged to be fair is the first-come first-served sequence. There are alternatives though: for example, a *triage* procedure can be used to direct customers to different queues on the basis of the severity or intensity of their needs. Triage is a common procedure in medical services such as accident and emergency departments. To a large extent, queue discipline is related to the queue configuration on arrival: is there only one queue, or several different parallel queues? Is the queuing process structured, such as for example by the use of a 'take a number' facility? Is there a triage configuration, as for example an express or 'baskets only' checkout in a supermarket? Research has shown that multiple queues actually result in longer average waiting times for each customer when compared to a single queue system.

At the end of a queue, customers will reach the different 'servers' where they will receive a service. Again, some service processes exhibit constant service times, whereas others exhibit volatility. In the latter and more realistic case, service time is measured by the average process time μ (in customers served per unit of time; note that $1/\mu$ measures the average time required to provide the service). Once the service is completed, the customer leaves the system.

Although systems can be redesigned to avoid queues, this is not always possible. Consider the following example: λ (arrival) = ten customers/hour and μ = five customers/hour. In this case, service provision would be disastrous as not only would customers always run into a queue, but also this queue would be building up as the trading day goes on. This would result in some customers being sent away and denied service after they had queued!

Assume now that λ (arrival) = six customers/hour and μ (process) = seven customers/hour. You may conclude that this is a great configuration as no queue could build up. Remember however that λ and μ are averages: in real life, λ could be six, five, and then eight customers/hours in three successive periods, while μ could be five, five, and six in the same three periods. In this case, a queue would be observed throughout the three periods. It is important to always remember than even when the capacity to process (μ) is higher than the arrival rate (λ), queues can still build up.

THE PSYCHOLOGY OF WAITING

Research has shown that customers will go through a variety of emotions and feelings whilst waiting. Thus while there are a variety of technical answers to queuing, one should bear in mind that managing waiting lines will affect the perception customers have of a service.

Before discussing the different aspects of the psychology of waiting, it is important to note that there are some serious cultural issues at stake. For example, it is normal to find a queue of more than two hours in Moroccan banks on the first trading day of the month. This is explained by the fact that a large portion of the working population do not have bank accounts and are paid by cheque by their employers. These workers have to go to the issuing bank to cash in their payroll cheque. They all do so on the same day because they are all paid at the same time. While in many countries bank managers would open extra counters to process the sudden surge in demand, this is not a universal rule. The fact that a long queue is taking place may not be a major issue in cultures where time is perceived differently. Similarly, some cultures will tolerate individuals jumping queues on the basis of their class, gender, or sheer cheek! In some cultures, queues are looked upon benevolently by officials who are expecting bribes to help customers through queues. Yet in other cultures queues have been used as rationing devices, i.e. as a way to restrict consumption, and this was the case for example in the Soviet Union.

For the Occidental world context, Maister (1988) has documented that:

- Customer perception is the basis for customer satisfaction, and satisfaction is attained if perception matches the prior expectations of the customer (Maister's first law of service).
- Perception is not always accurate: Unoccupied waiting always appears longer than waiting when customers are asked to complete a task; the other queue always seems to move faster; an unexplained wait appears longer; an unfair wait appears longer; waiting by yourself makes it appear longer than if you were waiting with a friend.

- It is difficult to turn a dissatisfied customer into a satisfied one (Maister's second law).

Assuming that the capacity, queue configuration and queue discipline cannot be improved, understanding the psychology of waiting is useful to help managers formulate potential actions so that customer perception is not too negative. Examples of such actions are:

- *Communicating frequently with the customer:* For example, electronic visual display systems can indicate how long it will take before the service provision can begin.
- *Welcoming the customer:* This gives the impression that the service has begun and that somebody is aware, and cares, about the fact that a customer is waiting.
- *Occupying the customer:* Occupied time goes faster, so asking customers to fill in a form or to consult documentation will reduce the risk of a negative perception of the service.
- *Monitoring and policing the queue:* This demonstrates the service provider's commitment to offering a fair and efficient treatment to all customers.
- *Segmenting queues:* This offers fast lanes for preferred or premium customers.

MATHEMATICAL MODELS OF WAITING LINES

There is a long and well-established research tradition about waiting lines in operational research. The most important relationship is Little's flow equation which links the average amount of time that a unit spends in a system (W) with the average number of units (L) in the system. Little's flow equation states that $L = \lambda W$.

For different scenarios, analytical formulas have been developed to help managers estimate queuing systems' parameters. A formula exists for example to compute the probability (P_w) that an arriving unit must wait for service and the average time (W_q) that a unit spends in the queue. A presentation of all the formulas is beyond the scope of this text, but it is worth knowing the general classification system used to direct analysts to the right formulas.

Queues are classified according to an A/B/s scheme: *A* describes the arrival distribution, *B* the service distribution, and *s* the number of servers. For example, the most traditional model is the M/M/1 model, where both the arrival and service processes are Markov processes (the Poisson and the exponential distribution respectively) and only one server is used. Let us suppose that a bank manager has observed historical data about arrival and service rates, mapped them onto Markov processes and found that W_q = ten minutes, i.e. that an arriving customer will wait on average for ten minutes. The manager could use the same data and compute W_q for an M/M/2 system. If the result is W_q = 1 minutes, this result could be used by the manager to justify an investment in the second server.

Analytical formulas exist for most standard queuing problems, but for the most general cases (e.g. G/G/5, a queuing problem with two general distributions and five servers), methods such as simulations are used to study queue behaviour.

FURTHER READING

Gross, D., Shortle, J. Thompson, J. and Harris, C.M. (2008) *Fundamentals of Queuing Theory* (4th edition). New York: WileyBlackwell.

REFERENCES

Maister, D.H. (1988) 'The psychology of waiting lines', *Managing Services: Marketing, Operations and Human Resource*. New York: Prentice-Hall.

Reverse Logistics

Reverse logistics is the discipline concerned with the logistical planning of the management of returned goods, either because they have reached the end of their lifecycle or because they need to be recycled.

Logistics is the discipline dealing with the flow of products along supply chains and distribution channels. It deals with issues such as inventory management, transportation systems, and warehouse management. Although it is clearly related to many operations management concepts (e.g., supply chain management, the dependability of delivery and scheduling), it is a separate field of study. In most general logistical problems, logistical systems are designed to deliver goods on time at a minimum cost when multiple suppliers (sources) and multiple customers (destinations) exist. Traditional logistics are based on the assumption that products follow a 'cradle to grave' lifecycle. In other words, it is assumed that the lifecycle of a product starts when materials are extracted and finishes when the product is being disposed of in incinerators or landfill sites.

Reverse logistics was initially used to describe the management of the flow of defective products being returned to their manufacturers. For example, a customer having bought a defective fridge may return the fridge to the retailer. This retailer will then ship the product back to the manufacturer. Historically, business organisations have been very good at logistics but very poor at reverse logistics. Typically, reverse logistics involves low volumes, special cases, and is not considered to be a major strategic area by companies. Delays are incurred both during transportation and when waiting for processing or reworking at the manufacturing site. The often large amount of monies tied up in returned products and their transportation mean that many managers have realised that their organisations would benefit from improving their reverse logistics processes.

It is however with the rise of concerns about environmental issues such as pollution and industrial waste that reverse logistics evolved into a more critical management challenge. The systematic disposal of goods through incineration and landfill has controversial environment impacts and several governments have actually passed legislation trying to reduce systematic disposal through better recycling schemes. In these cases, reverse logistics goes much further and now includes concerns about reclaimability and remanufacturability. Reclaimability is the ability of a manufacturer to reclaim its products at the end of their lifecycle (to recycle rather than dispose of the materials and components in those products). Remanufacturing is the ability to re-use and recondition the products into 'just like new' ones. Reclaimability is an important issue today in the automotive industry, with companies like BMW having committed themselves to producing completely reclaimable cars. Remanufacturing has been a longstanding practice in some industries, as for example the machine tools industry, where reconditioned machines are common market offerings.

Dowlatshahi (2000) conducted an exhaustive survey of the literature on reverse logistics, and he noted that the literature tended to be piecemeal and focused on isolated applications. This was explained by the fact that research on reverse logistics was rather new, and thus, had adopted exploratory rather than integrative research approaches. Dowlatshahi proposed a framework for a theory of reverse logistics by classifying extant research into strategic and operational factors.

Strategic factors were taken into account before operational ones as they framed and directed the application of reverse logistics in the broader competitive context in which firms operated. In stark contrast with the a-priori perception that reverse logistics would be an added cost for manufacturers, and therefore a drain on profitability, Dowlatshahi's (2000) review showed that many firms treated reverse logistics as an investment decision, as new markets, new products opportunities and new ways of generating revenues are expected. Other strategic factors were quality (the adoption of reverse logistics cannot result in a decrease in quality standards), environmental concerns (reducing pollution) and legislative issues (complying with current and future legislation on packaging, recycling, and reclaiming products).

Operational factors include:

- Cost/benefit analysis of the various reverse logistics options for organisations compared to the cost and impact of disposal, while taking into account the possible liabilities associated with non-environmentally friendly options.
- Improvement and analysis of transportation networks and systems.
- Improvement and analysis of warehousing systems.
- Integrating reverse logistics within supply chain management practices.
- Setting policies and processes facilitating recycling and remanufacturing.
- Optimising packaging so as to reduce negative environmental impacts.

Dowlatshahi's (2000) framework showed that there was more to reverse logistics than only transportation science issues. Reverse logistics could have a direct impact on many areas of operations management. For example, the once popular practice of design for assembly became counter-productive in a reverse logistics context: design methodology should focus instead on design for remanufacturing or disassembly instead. Manufacturing processes should be redesigned to allow for recycling and remanufacturing. Traditional operations management was based on the 'cradle to grave' product lifecycle. With reverse logistics, a paradigm shift in all operations management decisions is needed in order to move toward a permanently looping product lifecycle.

REFERENCE

Dowlatshahi, S. (2000) 'Developing a theory of reverse logistics', *Interfaces*, 30(3): 143–155.

Yield

> *Yield is the amount of valuable product that can be extracted from a process.*

HISTORICAL ORIGINS

The concept of *yield* comes from the food production industry. Yield is the amount of valuable product that can be extracted from a process. Consider a milk factory for example. Fresh milk is delivered by trucks, stored in tanks, sent through pipes to filtering and pasteurising machines, through more pipes to storage and then sent from there to final packaging. When 1000 litres enter the facility, less than 1000 litres of packaged milk will be available. There could be leaks, process interruptions where some product is lost, and finally, a certain amount of residual milk will be left in tanks and pipes. This residual milk is typically cleaned to avoid contamination. Cleaning also means that the first litres produced in the next batch will probably have to be discarded. Thus, there are potentially plenty of sources of *process loss*.

Yield management is about reducing process losses. How can we modify the processes, equipment and operating policies so that only a strictly minimum and unavoidable loss is incurred?

This definition of yield does not translate very well to other industrial contexts. For example, what is a process loss for an airline? In airlines the predominant concern is about unused or unsold capacity. When a plane takes off with empty seats, there is actually a process loss: a better organisation would have made sure that these seats were sold. In this context, yield management is the set of techniques used to make sure that capacity is fully utilised.

Note that this does not necessarily mean selling the service at a cheaper price. It is true that a simple solution to poor utilisation would be to decrease the price in order to increase demand and guarantee 100 per cent capacity utilisation. There may be customers, though, who would have been ready to pay more for the service. When we compare a service sold cheap, and a service sold cheap to 50 per cent of customers and sold at a premium to the other 50 per cent of customers, the question is which strategy will return more money? Clearly, the second strategy is a winner, and thus, failing to sell the service at a premium price to those customers willing to pay the price is another form of process loss. Yield management, therefore, is all about making sure that the maximum possible amount of yield (measured as revenues) is generated. Yield management is also referred to as *dynamic pricing* or *revenue management*.

YIELD MANAGEMENT TAXONOMY

There is a long history of research and practice of yield management in the service industry and Weatherford and Bodily (1992) developed a taxonomy of yield management practices based on 14 elements of the transactional context, a fact that illustrates the broad diversity of problems investigated in yield management. Their classification includes the following variables:

- Whether the problem is discrete (e.g. number of seats in an airplane) or continuous (e.g. electricity generation).
- Whether capacity is fixed or can be adjusted.
- Whether the prices are pre-determined or set jointly by buyer or seller.
- Whether there are varying degrees of willingness to pay by the customer – a buildup means that the service becomes desirable as the consumption time approaches whereas a drawdown means that the service becomes less desirable.

- Whether quantity discounts or group discounts are offered.
- Whether reservations are accepted.
- Whether cancellations of reservation are accepted.
- Whether the diversion of customers to other service providers is allowed.
- Whether 'bumping' customers by denying access to the service is allowed.
- Whether asset control mechanisms are used to regulate demand (e.g. only a fixed quota of low cost seats are available).
- Whether the rules used to improve yield are static or dynamic.

YIELD MANAGEMENT SOLUTION

A first category of yield management solution deals with the segmentation of capacity and two-part pricing. For example, first-class and second-class ticket systems take into account that the demand for first-class tickets is limited, and thus only a small portion of the capacity is set up as first class. This is widely used by trains, airlines, hotels, and entertainment venues. In many cases, the capacity can be divided into more than two classes, and multiple prices are then offered.

Marketing practices form the second solution to increase yield. A variety of discounts and promotional schemes can be used to increase demand off peak.

Beyond these static approaches to yield management, *price discrimination* means that the products are offered to different customers at different prices. Price discrimination is illegal in most countries, unless there is a clear justifiable basis to the discrimination. What matters is that some form of segmentation exists and can be justified for charging different amounts for the same service. Examples of 'fair' price discrimination are:

- *Geography*: For example, identical tyres and mattresses manufactured in France are sold for less in Morocco in North Africa. This is counter-intuitive as the cost of transportation makes the products more expensive in Morocco. The idea, though, is to recognise that the willingness to pay for the product is a function of personal income levels. From this perspective, it makes sense to charge more in a market willing to pay more and to attain 100 per cent utilisation by selling to markets where less is charged. This is only possible because customs restrictions prevent the re-import of the exported products.

- *Brand*: For many years, the French sport supermarket chain Decathlon sold its own brand of windsurf boards. These boards were actually manufactured by Alpha, a premium brand at the time. The only difference between the two products was the logo, but the Decathlon board sold at a third of the price of the Alpha board. Using a non-branded distribution channel and a branded distribution channel is another means of increased yield from a fixed capacity facility. In this case, it is important that customers cannot recognise the two products are the same. In the Decathlon's example, testers employed by the specialist press quickly recognised that Decathlon boards were in fact Alpha boards. This resulted in a sharp decrease in demand for the branded products, and eventually in the termination of the scheme.
- *Gender* is often used as basis for price discrimination: For example, it is common that a woman's haircut is priced much higher than a man's.
- *Other bases* for discrimination are age (student and senior citizen discounts) and professional affiliations (academic software licences).

Revenue Management (Talluri and Van Ryzin, 2005) is a more complex form of price discrimination, based on the recognition that a willingness to pay may build up as the date of provision of the service becomes closer. Assume that you need to travel tomorrow from London to New York. How much are you ready to pay for this service? Most customers would book the flight weeks, if not months or a year in advance! If you need the service tomorrow, it is usually because there is some degree of emergency to your need to travel. Passengers travelling for emergency purposes are ready to pay big money, and thus some airlines will reserve a few seats which will only be offered for sale at the very expensive 'last minute' fee.

The airline, though historical data analysis, may be able to decompose the demand for seats as (i) a last minute class (ready to pay the maximum fee); a week ahead class (ready to pay a premium fee); a month ahead (ready to pay an average fee); and a six months before class of customers (only willing to pay a low fee). The working principle of revenue management is to block the sales of seats corresponding to the forecasted demand of each class. Seats are first offered for sale at the six months before prices. When all these seats are booked, this price offer is withdrawn and a limited number of seats are now offered for sale at the month ahead price. The process is repeated until all the seats have been sold, the point at which the maximum possible amount of revenues has been obtained given the market conditions. Reliable and accurate forecasts of demand are key to the success of a revenue management initiative.

Finally, a last mechanism used to improve yield is over-booking. Service companies lose money every time a customer does not show up. A solution to the 'no-show' problems is to charge the customers regardless of whether or not the service was consumed. Another solution is, on the basis of historical cancellations and the no-show rate, to sell more than the capacity to serve. Take a 100 bedroom hotel with a historical no-show rate of 5 per cent. For every night, the hotel will sell 105 rooms, hoping that the five extra customers will occupy the five rooms sold to no-show customers. Over-booking can backfire though, as 105 customers could turn up on in one evening. One strategy is to divert the customers to another facility, for example to transfer them to a nearby hotel for the same cost. Another tactic is to 'bump' the customer, i.e. to ask some customers to quit the service system and then compensate them for accepting to do so.

REFERENCES

Talluri, K. T. and Van Ryzin, G. (2005) *The Theory and Practice of Revenue Management*. Berlin: Springer.

Weatherford, L. R. and Bodily, S. E. (1992) 'Taxonomy and research overview of perishable-asset revenue management: yield management, overbooking, and pricing', *Operations Research*, 40(5): 831–844.

Integrated
Management
Frameworks

Total Quality Management (TQM)

> *Total Quality Management, in its broadest meaning, denotes a strong organisational will to adopt quality management practices, to integrate them into the culture and systems of organisations, in order to attain a high level of quality performance.*

Total quality management, or TQM, is actually a difficult management framework to describe precisely. Deming (1994) captured this difficulty when he writes that: '*... the trouble with total quality management, the failure of TQM, you can call it, is that there is no such thing. It is a buzz-word. I have never used the term, as it carries no meaning*'.

Senapati (2004) reviewed a number of definitions of TQM and found a mixed bag. TQM is defined by some as a corporate focus on customer satisfaction, by others as spreading quality ideas company-wide, and by still others as a strategic focus on quality.

Definitions aside, companies that report having adopted TQM as a best practice have one point in common: they have adopted a philosophy, a unique quality-driven line of investigation about operations and organisational matters. Therefore, Total Quality Management can be defined as a quality-focused approach to improving operations. Although focused it remains flexible and managers can rely on the full portfolio of tools used in quality management for their interventions.

This means that a description of the different tools used in quality (e.g. SPC, cause and effect diagrams, quality circles) is not enough to appreciate what a TQM initiative is all about. Instead, the value of TQM is in the overall approach. Therefore, the next few sections concentrate on presenting the structuring and integrating features of TQM:

- The notion of a quality chain.
- Quality-based performance management frameworks.
- The concept of the cost of the quality.
- The importance of leadership, empowerment, and culture.

QUALITY CHAINS

One of the fundamental ideas behind TQM is the concept of quality chains. A quality chain is a linkage between a customer (who has expectations) and a supplier (aiming to fulfil those expectations). Note that customers and suppliers can be internal to a company. Overall performance can only be achieved in an organisation if all quality chains perform their transactions effectively. One broken link is enough to generate a system-level failure. Therefore all organisational processes should be understood as quality chains, and the tools of quality should be used to ensure that these chains conform to performance standards. One of the key features of this approach is to challenge the view that customers and suppliers are remote parties which are buffered away. With the quality chain view, any individual within an organisation – regardless of their role, authority and seniority – plays a key role in a quality chain. This means that issues surrounding customer satisfaction are everybody's concern and this is why TQM is often presented as a management framework based on customer satisfaction as a core value.

QUALITY PERFORMANCE MODELS

The adoption of total quality management is based on the premise that adopting quality management company-wide will result in enhanced corporate performance. Whether or not a TQM initiative results in higher performance levels has always been debatable in industry and academia, and the cost of a quality approach is one of the ways by which 'wasteful' quality initiatives can be avoided. Another approach is to implement a TQM initiative within a known and tested performance management framework in order to guarantee that improvements will result in tangible business benefits. The Baldridge TQM framework, which is used in the United States to award quality prizes to the most committed organisations, is one example of such a framework. The European Foundation for Quality Management (EFQM) framework is more commonly used in Europe. This is shown in Figure 50.

When conducting an audit of a company, EFQM consultants will begin by surveying an organisation and assessing a score on the first 500 'enablers' points. If the company scores too low the audit stops, as achieving results without the enablers would be impossible. If a minimum threshold score is achieved, the assessment can move onto round two,

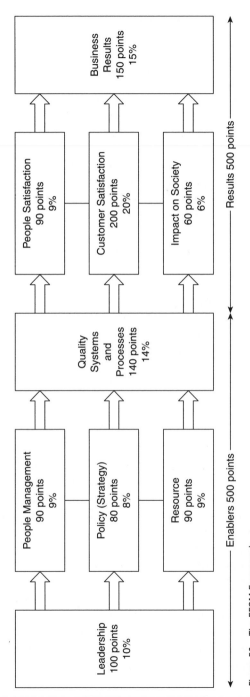

Figure 50 The EFQM Framework

where auditors can verify that quality systems and processes can lead to demonstrated impacts on satisfaction and profitability.

COST OF QUALITY

Adopting TQM is not a cheap initiative. Furthermore, in the modern business environment where many 'best practices' have been historically associated with failed and onerous projects, it is not surprising that many companies will try to avoid the expense of embarking on a TQM 'journey', as it is often described by consultants. In the 1980s, the controversy around the cost of a quality management initiative also existed. A key issue, for example, has always been to avoid over-quality, i.e. to improve the performance of products and processes to levels that the customer has not paid for.

Faced with such controversy regarding the business worthiness of quality, quality consultants devised an accounting tool called *the cost of quality report*. The cost of quality label is actually quite misleading, and should be interpreted as a reporting tool used to guide managers toward an optimal corporate investment in quality.

The starting point for this is to put in place an information reporting system which captures and compiles on a monthly basis:

- *Prevention costs*: These are the costs incurred in preventing poor quality events from taking place. The cost of quality planning, monies invested in design and process capabilities improvements and training costs are some examples of items which would be included in this category.
- *Appraisal costs*: These are the costs incurred in assessing conformance. The salaries of quality inspectors and the cost of maintaining test equipments are examples of such costs. Remember that with the advent of statistical process control, inspection costs were almost totally eliminated. Thus while appraisal costs cannot be totally eliminated, in a 'right first time' total quality culture such costs should be significantly lower than in traditional work environments.
- *Internal failure costs*: This category includes all the costs associated with a quality failure discovered whilst the product is still in the factory. This can include the cost of reworking or scrapping the product if a reworking is not possible or not economical.
- *External failure costs*: The costs of fixing or replacing a product which failed at the customer's site are aggregated in this category. These can

include warranty claims, after sales service salaries and the cost of parts and labour for technicians repairing the product. Needless to say, costs will rise quickly in the case of an external failure.

There are two ideas behind the cost of quality of reports. The first is to document the 'leverage' effect of investing in prevention. A common rule of thumb is that if a company invests £1 in additional prevention activities, it could save up to £10 in inspection and £100 in avoiding the cost of a quality failures! The second idea is to help managers to estimate what the optimal level of spending on quality is. If a company spends little on prevention and has an important 'cost of poor quality' bill, then it should increase its prevention spending. When the company gets to the point where more investment in prevention does not decrease the total cost of quality, this means that it has reached its optimal level of investment.

LEADERSHIP, EMPOWERMENT, AND CULTURE

Whereas many quality management approaches are driven by technical tools and skills, TQM has always put a strong emphasis on work culture and the role of leaders as quality 'role models'. Deming's 14 points about adopting a quality management initiative are an excellent summary of the softer human side of the cultural changes required for adopting a total quality approach:

1 Create a constancy of purpose.
2 Adopt the new philosophy.
3 Cease a dependence on inspection.
4 Do not award business based on the price tag alone.
5 Improve constantly the system of production and service.
6 Institute training.
7 Adopt and institute leadership.
8 Drive out fear.
9 Break down barriers among staff areas.
10 Eliminate slogans, exhortations, and targets.
11 Eliminate numerical quotas.
12 Remove barriers.
13 Institute a programme of education and self-improvement.
14 Take action to accomplish the transformation.

In their survey of TQM adoption by Australian manufacturers, Sohal and Terziovski (2000) confirmed that human factors played an important part as their conclusion was that the key success factors for TQM adoption were:

- A positive attitude toward quality (cultural differences are reported to be the biggest obstacle to TQM adoption).
- Leadership education and training.
- Integrating the voice of the customer and supplier.
- Developing appropriate performance indicators and rewards.

REFERENCES

Deming, W.E. (1994) 'Report card on TQM', *Management Review*, October: 26–27.

Senapati, N. (2004) 'Six sigma: myths and realities', *International Journal of Quality and Reliability Management*, 21(6): 683–690.

Sohal, A. and Terziovski, M. (2000) 'TQM in Australian manufacturing: factors critical to success', *International Journal of Quality and Reliability Management*, 17 (2): 158–167.

Throughput

> **Throughput is the maximum possible rate of use of an operations system when taking into account all the factors constraining production.**

HISTORICAL ORIGINS

In the 1970s, many manufacturing researchers started to work on *optimised production technology* (OPT). The idea behind OPT was to apply optimisation techniques to maximise productivity and flow. Although the OPT label is still used today, it has to a large extent been replaced by the work of Goldratt. In 1984, Goldratt and Cox published a business novel which suggested a new approach to improving performance in a manufacturing organisation. This book was extremely successful and

Goldratt went on to publish several other books which either expanded the underlying 'theory of constraints' or discussed its application in a non-manufacturing environment, such as marketing, strategy, and project management.

The *theory of constraints* (TOC) quickly diffused into academic circles. In operations management, it replaced and unified research on OPT. The theory of constraints also had a key impact in the accounting field, as TOC challenges traditional cost-based approaches to management. In accounting, the application of TOC is usually referred to as *throughput accounting*. Gupta and Boyd (2008) concluded after a review of the literature that as TOC addressed all aspects of operations management decisions, it could serve as a unifying theory for the discipline.

THEORY OF CONSTRAINTS: THE CONTENT

The central tenet of the theory of constraints is that all organisations have a goal. They use resources to achieve this goal but unfortunately resources can be, and often are, scarce. The lack of availability of a resource is basically a constraint which is restricting the organisation on its quest for performance. In order to achieve a higher level of performance, it is therefore necessary to understand what the constraints on production are, and – where possible – to remove them partially ('elevating a constraint') or completely. It is because of this focus on constraints that a number of authors refer to the theory of constraints as the field of *constraints management*. Boyd and Gupta (2004) describe TOC as being based on three dimensions: an organisational mindset, measurement systems, and the decision-making dimension.

In the traditional operations management mindset, an analyst adopts the top-level view of a system designer. The idea is to design a system which is optimal given some specifications. Optimality is usually defined as minimising the unit production costs. The flaw here is that only a minority of facilities will experience stable specifications in terms of product specifications and volumes of demand. A system designed to be optimal under certain demand conditions will, in a few years, probably become sub-optimal: as demand evolves or becomes more complex, the system will be used increasingly to produce configurations that it was never designed to produce. Adopting the theory of constraints requires managers to abandon their traditional costing approach and to concentrate on a different variable: *throughput*. Throughput is the rate at which products are processed through a facility. The new mindset, thus, is to stop looking at reducing costs and instead to try – by all means

throughput

271

possible – to increase throughput, as this generates revenues which will ultimately lead to the achievement of the goal (namely, making a profit).

This change of mindset is so radical that it requires a change in performance measurement systems. Instead of using the traditional cost structure of product costing, the theory of constraints is based on its own accounting framework. The three measures in this system are throughput, inventory (contrary to the traditional accounting definition, this means all assets used in the process), and operating expenses (non-asset expenses spent on operating the process). The priority is to increase throughput, then to reduce inventory (without affecting throughput), and finally to reduce the operating expenses.

Mindset and performance measurement systems define the decisional context in which TOC can be applied. Siha (1999) distinguished two different types of applications: decisions relative to the daily running of operations and decisions dealing with improving the process.

Running operations using the theory of constraints

A first issue here is to recognise that different process layouts will lead to different types of constraints issues. This is addressed through *V-A-T analysis*, where different processes are classified according to their nature. A 'V' process flow, for example, is an 'explosive' flow starting with a few materials which are processed down separate lines leading to several different final products. An 'A' process is the opposite: many raw materials ending in a unique product. The 'T' factory is one where a limited number of components are used to produce – at a final stage only – a wide variety of products. There are a number of research papers that have expanded on this basic classification to include more types, however the purpose remains the same, i.e. to document the different types of problems that can occur in different flow line configurations.

The theory of constraints requires a different form of production scheduling. The traditional MRP-based and inventory-supported production processes are replaced with the *Drum-Buffer-Rope* (DBR) scheduling approach. Using the DBR approach requires having identified the most limiting capacity constraint, called a *bottleneck*. This bottleneck is the weakest link in the flow line and is what is currently restricting the overall output of the facility. The bottleneck becomes the drum, i.e. the pace setting point of reference in the flow line. There is no point in having another process centre working faster than the drum, as the effort and money spent will not result in an increase in output.

The drum is actually a sensitive process centre. Let us imagine that an upstream process centre breaks down. If the stoppage is shortlived, the extra capacity of a non-bottleneck centre may be enough to catch up and keep the bottleneck fed. If the stoppage lasts too long, however, the bottleneck centre stops being fed and output will drop to zero. To prevent such a scenario from happening, a buffer will be used. A buffer is a small stock of bottleneck inputs used to isolate the bottleneck from any problems occurring elsewhere in the flow line. If a problem occurs the bottleneck process continues uninterrupted, fed by the buffer.

Finally, the rope means that the release of materials at the beginning of the line is directly triggered by the bottleneck. If the pace increases releases of materials increase, and vice versa.

Improving operations through the theory of constraints

The second decisional dimension of the TOC approach is to seek the improvement of the throughput of a flow line. A number of diagrams or operations management tools can be used to document a problem and to initiate the five-step improvement procedure:

1 *Identifying the constraint(s)*: This is the starting point as only improvement of the constraint will result in an overall system improvement. In a single product, single line facility, this is simple: the constraint is the machine with the longest inward queue of goods. In a non-linear flow line processing multiple products, finding the constraint is a different ball game: there may be more than one the bottleneck, or the bottlenecks may be dynamic, i.e. will switch under different production demands.
2 *Exploiting the constraint(s)*: Because the constraint is a limiting factor, decisions should be made to exploit it as much as possible. For example, products which are barely profitable should be routed away from the constraint.
3 *Subordinateing the non-constraints*: The decisions made about the constraint have an absolute priority over decisions regarding non-constraint areas.
4 *Elevating the constraint(s)*: Are there any ways, using improved work methods and an investment in technology, through which the constraint's capacity can be increased? In the low cost airline industry, the faster turnaround of planes was one example of removing a constraint that was keeping planes on the ground, where they were not

earning money. Reducing turnaround time to its minimum permits maximum utilisation of an expensive asset.

5   As the constraint is elevated, another process centre in the flow line will become the new constraint. When this happens, managers should *return to step 1* and tackle the new limit on output.

THEORY OF CONSTRAINTS IN SERVICE ORGANISATIONS

The theory of constraints was developed in manufacturing settings, and more precisely in the context of manufacturing facilities based on a flow line layout. All the principles behind the theory of constraints, however, can be applied to many other areas, and Goldratt himself has published a number of books documenting the extrapolations of the method to different contexts.

Applying the theory of constraints requires some adjustments. Siha (1999), for example, explains that the inventory is an unused service, e.g. an unoccupied seat in an airplane. Throughput is the money generated from selling the service. These minor adjustments made, there are many contexts in which service organisations can implement and derive benefits from the theory of constraints. Siha (1999) reviewed the literature and included scheduling the operations of the Red Cross in the aftermath of a hurricane, improving productivity in engineering services, reducing the lead time for mortgage applications and various applications in hospital settings, commercial banks, security firms and airlines. Siha also used Schmenner's service-process matrix to discuss how the theory of constraints could be customised for use in service factories, service shops, mass services, and professional services.

REFERENCES

Boyd, L. and Gupta, M. (2004) 'Constraints management: what is the theory?', *International Journal of Operations Management*, 24(4): 350–371.

Goldratt, E.M. and Cox, J. (1984) *The Goal: A Process of Ongoing Improvement*. Great Barrington, MA: North River Press.

Gupta, M.C. and Boyd, L.H. (2008) 'Theory of constraints: a theory for operations management', *International Journal of Operations and Production Management*, 28(10): 991–1012.

Siha, S. (1999) 'A classified model for applying the theory of constraints to service organisations', *Managing Service Quality*, 9(4): 255–264.

> **Responsiveness is the ability of an operations system to respond almost instantly to changes in market conditions.**

QUICK RESPONSE MANUFACTURING

Quick Response Manufacturing (QRM) is a basic extension of the concepts of **Time-based Competition.** Suri (1998) described QRM as a company-wide approach to reducing lead time. QRM is based on substituting cost-based management decisions with time-based management decisions. A particular point of managerial focus is to distinguish the contact time when a product is being worked on from elapsed time, and to recognise that elapsed time incurs non-value adding costs. Contrary to the common perception that faster 'rush' orders are more expensive, QRM recognises that a shortening of this lead time can actually lead to a decrease in production costs. Another common belief challenged by QRM is that to keep production costs low, machine utilisation should be maximised. A system dynamics analysis shows that high machine utilisation is associated with long queues, i.e. non value-adding elapsed time. QRM therefore suggests that in order to compete on shorter lead times a full utilisation should be avoided. Factories should be run at 75–85 per cent so that queues and delays never occur. This is often viewed as a controversial standpoint, especially from the viewpoint of the theory of constraints (see **Throughput**).

QUICK RESPONSE IN MANUFACTURER–RETAILER CHANNELS

It is at a supply chain level that the quick response (QR) approach has had the biggest impact. Some industries have adopted QR as their default mode of operations, as for example the apparel retail industry. Historically, this industry has been characterised by long lead times. Apparel retailers typically used to have to place large orders about six to eight months before the start of a sales season. For example, winter seasons clothes would be ordered and manufactured during the summer, and the following summer season would be ordered and manufactured during the winter. As the apparel industry is sensitive to fashion trends, it means that very little information about demand is available at the time of placing orders. This results in sub-optimal ordering practices, such as not ordering enough of certain items and too much of others. This is also why the apparel industry is famous for its discount campaigns, which are used to get rid of those items which were over-stocked.

Quick response manufacturing was clearly appealing for this industry: if manufacturers were able to respond faster to retailer demand, retailers could place orders later on – closer to the season's start, or even during a season – when much more accurate information about demand would have become available. Iyer and Bergen (1997) studied this fact by simulating inventory models in an apparel retail shop. Their modelling was based on the fact that retailers faced two forms of demand uncertainty. First, there is uncertainty about the daily demand for each product. For example, different numbers of people could enter a shop to purchase the product on different days. Second, retailers have to deal with aggregate uncertainty about demand before the start of the season, i.e. when the order for the product is placed.

The purpose of QR is to reduce as much as possible the second form of uncertainty by reducing the lead time for producing retail items. Typically, the adoption of QR has resulted in lowering lead times by one to four months, and in some cases, has allowed retailers to place 'top-up' orders during the season.

Through a simulation of the inventory systems of both retailer and manufacturer, Iyer and Bergen (1997) found that QR did not necessarily result in manufacturers being better off, unless both parties collectively engaged in actions so that the QR initiative would result in a win/win scenario. It is interesting to note that price incentives were not found to be part of such actions by Iyer and Bergen (1997); instead QR initiatives benefited from *service level commitments* and *volume commitments*.

One of the means for making QR optimal for both parties is to commit to higher service levels. A service level refers to the portion of demand that a seller will honour. In the apparel retail industry, shops will often only stock 70 per cent of the expected demand in order to avoid potential excess inventory costs (more details about why service levels are often low can be found in the newsvendor model; see **Inventory Systems**). Low service levels are against the interests of the manufacturer, as less than needed is ordered. In QR, both parties commit to much higher service levels such as satisfying 80–95 per cent of demand, and service levels of 100 per cent are not unusual. These higher service levels can be linked to contracts or sometimes implemented by cooperative advertisements. For example, a retailer could advertise that it will provide a replacement product for free if a jointly advertised product is not in stock. Another form of commitment is the practice whereby manufacturers will often agree to participate in a quick response initiative provided that the retailer agrees to display the products in a prominent location in the store.

Volume commitments are commonly used within QR environments. These basically mean that the retailer places an order for Q units at time 0, but without specifying which items, colours and versions are included in the Q units. This, in effect, is a capacity reservation process. At a later time closer to the season, and when vital information about demand has become available, the retailer will provide a detailed breakdown of the Q units to be manufactured. The benefit to the manufacturer is knowing that their capacity will be used.

Barnes-Schuster et al. (2002) proposed a general model based on real options in order to study different types of practices common in a QR environment, and they showed that **real options** are an effective means of co-ordinating manufacturer–retailer channels. In particular, they looked at:

- *Back-up agreements*: A retailer places an initial firm pre-season order, but simultaneously purchases the option to place an in-season 'top-up' order.
- *Quantity-flexibility contracts*: The retailer sends an initial forecast of demand to the manufacturer and a price is agreed upon. The retailer places a succession of orders up to the initial forecast as the season progresses. In some cases, the retailer may also have the right to update their forecast.
- *Pay to delay contracts*: This is a basic capacity reservation option, where an upfront premium is paid to book capacity. A further fee (the exercise price) is paid if the capacity is utilised.

The Spanish company Zara is a key case study for anyone interested in the quick response approach. Based in Galicia in the north-west of Spain, Zara is recognised as a leader in the management of a global supply, manufacturing, distribution and retail network. In a worth-reading and instructive case study, Ferdows et al. (2003) stated that in 2003 Zara was the only retailer that could deliver garments to its stores worldwide (507 in 33 countries) in just 15 days after they were designed.

Barnes-Schuster, D., Bassok, Y. and Anupindi, R. (2002) 'Supply contracts with options: flexibility, information, and coordination', *Manufacturing & Service Operations Management*, 4(3): 171–207.

Ferdows, K., Lewis, M. and Machuca, J. (2003) 'Zara: case study', *Supply Chain Forum*, 4(2): 62–67.

Iyer, A. and Bergen, M. (1997) 'Quick response in manufacturer–retailer channels', *Management Science*, 43(4): 559–570.

Suri, R. (1998) *Quick Response Manufacturing: A Companywide Approach to Reducing Lead Times*. Portland, OR: Productivity.

Time-based Competition

key concepts in operations management

> *Time-based competition is about deriving a competitive advantage from a system's ability to deliver products or services faster than the competition whilst guaranteeing punctuality of delivery.*

TIME AS A COMPETITIVE DIMENSION

The importance of the time to market concept was pioneered by Stalk and Hout (1990). Their idea was simple: mature industries fall into a routine of competing on the basis of cost, or on the basis of cost and quality. As a result, all employees develop the belief that only cost, or only cost and quality, matters. Sales people, production managers and top managers fail to appreciate that customers may also value the possibility of receiving a product faster. In the mid 1990s business managers discovered, much to their surprise, that customers were even ready to pay a premium for faster deliveries: in other words, leadtime – once considered a secondary variable, or at best an order qualifier – emerged as an order winner.

278

THE OPERATIONS SIDE

How easy is it, though, to accelerate production rate and guarantee faster deliveries? Stalk and Hout (1990) documented that logistical processes within firms were surprisingly poor. In the case of manufacturing, it was not unusual that a product would be processed during only 2 or 3 per cent of the time that it spent in a factory. What about the 97 per cent of the remaining time? There the product just sits in inventory, waiting for a form, a part, or an available machine to be processed on.

Stalk and Hout also discovered that in addition to the competitive advantage resulting from a shorter leadtime the resulting process of improving the logistics of operations actually reduces manufacturing costs, a fact that Japanese manufacturers were familiar with thanks to their **Just-in-Time Inventory** production systems Stalk and Hout's management framework, Time-based Competition (TBC), was broadly adopted and applied to many areas of manufacturing and services.

TIME TO MARKET

Possibly the highest impact of TBC was, however, in the area of new product development. Prior to the formulation of the principles of TBC, US and European businesses, market share was being seriously eroded by Japanese competitors, who had introduced new products at a much faster rate. This explains why 'Time to Market' became such a prevalent measure of performance in modern business life. Chrysler, for example, reported that by using the principles of TBC to improve its new product development process its development cycle was cut from five years to three and a half and that the overall cost of development was reduced by 30 per cent. There are many theories and empirical data that support the idea that being first to market is a key competitive dimension. The economic theory of *First Mover Advantage* stipulates that the firm which releases a new product first will always dominate the market share in the industry.

In general, it is agreed that time to market performance is important but not without risks. Real option theory, for example, has been used to develop the theories of second mover advantage and of follower advantage. Whereas a first mover may have a market lead in the first generation of a product, second movers are often the first to release better

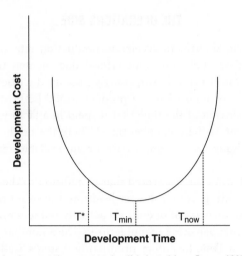

Figure 51   The development time–cost trade-off (adapted from Bayus, 1997)

second generation products, and therefore will often gain leading market shares in the long run.

Bayus (1997) has shown that there is a trade-off between time-to-market and product performance. This trade-off is better explained with the example shown in Figure 51.

Firms operating at T_{now} can increase their profitability by improving their development processes to T_{min}: they can derive a competitive advantage as they introduce products more often whilst also benefiting from a reduction in development costs. The move from T_{now} to T_{min} is a straight application of the time-based competition principles.

Firms operating at T^* are the pioneering firms which will exhibit the highest all around performance in the industry. They are first to market which means that they can capture first mover advantages. Their development costs T^* are higher than T_{min}, and the performance of their product may be marginally less attractive than a product developed in T_{min}, but these disadvantages are offset by the advantages of being first to market.

A firm operating on the left-hand side of T^* would indeed always be first to market, but its product is likely to be of a lesser quality than a product introduced later by a competitor. Thus, on the left-hand side of T^*, the disadvantages of speedy development are not offset by its advantages.

TIME-BASED STRATEGIES

Daugherty and Pittman (1995) interviewed ten manufacturing and distribution executives of Fortune 500 companies in order to understand how time advantages could be derived. Their key conclusions were:

- *Time management*: The capability of the firm to keep tabs on manufacturing and distribution process is important.
- *Increase responsiveness*: Most of the respondents had restructured their organisation so that they had the capability to adapt to changes in market conditions. Not only does this require better systems and processes, but it also requires being more attentive to customer needs. Many of the firms in the survey mentioned the importance of 'one call response' strategies in terms of getting immediate answers to customer queries. Using a priority ranking system, which differentiates key accounts from marginal customers, allows for providing high level of responsiveness for the right customers.
- *Flexibility*: This can be an especial challenge at the distribution stage of product delivery and can be achieved by better planning and better contractual relationships with carriers.
- *Communication and information*: Information flows must be instantaneous. This is achieved by an electronic data interchange (EDI) between all parties.

TIME-BASED MANUFACTURING

Koufteros et al. (1998) considered that Time-based Competition is the result of the evolution of Just-in-Time (JIT) – which focused on internal inventory and cost reduction – to an external focus on time and customers. Thus, TBC and JIT are just two facets of the same pursuit: to be able to utilise capacity only when needed, and as needed.

Koufteros et al. demonstrated empirically that:

- Shop-floor employee involvement in problem solving and process improvement is the foundation of time-based manufacturing. This is consistent with the idea that a TBC strategy requires responsiveness, information, and flexibility.
- Employee involvement means that the following time management capabilities can be developed and lead to time performance:

- ○ Fast re-engineering setups.
- ○ The use of flexible and adaptable cellular manufacturing layouts.
- ○ The success of quality improvements efforts.
- ○ Effective preventive maintenance.
- ○ The establishment of relationships with dependable suppliers.

TBC IN THE SERVICE INDUSTRY

Blackburn (1992) was the first to highlight that the service industry could also benefit greatly from the adoption of time-based strategies. He provided the example of a life insurance company requiring 72 hours to process a new application. After a process analysis, it appeared that only seven minutes were actually spent on value adding activity: that's 0.16 per cent of the total lead time!

Blackburn's conclusion was that service processes were slow because they were based on the traditional method of batch manufacturing. His recommendations were to analyse and redesign processes; reduce batch sizes; eliminate waste and non value-adding activities; use time management capabilities such as JIT; and adopt a culture of doing things right the first time.

REFERENCES

Bayus, B. (1997) 'Speed-to-market and new product performance trade-offs', *Journal of Product Innovation Management*, 14: 485–497.

Blackburn, J. (1992) 'Time-based competition: white-collar activities', *Business Horizons*, July–August: 96–101.

Daugherty, P. and Pittman, P. (1995) 'Utilisation of time-based strategies', *International Journal of Operations and Production Management*, 15 (2): 54–60.

Koufteros, X., Vonderembse, M. and Doll, W. (1998) 'Developing measures of time-based manufacturing', *Journal of Operations Management*, 16: 21–41.

Stalk, G. and Hout, T. (1990) *Competing Against Time*. New York: Free.

Lean

In operations management, lean means the ability to produce a product or service with only the resources which are strictly required to do so.

LEAN MANUFACTURING

In other words, it means producing with no 'fat', with no organisational slack or buffers, or with no 'safety net'. The history of lean thinking is a relatively complex one, and therefore it is useful to see how the concept has evolved and been renamed and augmented over the years.

The pioneering industrial work that led to the formulation of lean thinking started at the Toyota Motor Company as early as after World War II, although it was really in the 1970s that Toyota finalised a productive system with a genuine competitive advantage, commonly known as the *Toyota Production System (TPS)*. The TPS was first documented by Japanese writers who had worked at Toyota when the approach was being developed: Monden (1983) was a cost accountant and Ohno (1988) was the chief engineer. At this stage the TPS consisted of a number of practices, which taken together formed a totally new way of managing production. These practices – centred on the management of factories – included:

- The elimination of unnecessary inventory, tools, and artefacts that hide, buffer, hamper, or reduce the visibility and the flow of products in the factory. This concern with order, visibility, cleanliness and 'leanness' was popularised by the '5S' framework.
- The communication through visual displays of production information to all parties.
- The adoption of the concept of autonomation, whereby each worker is autonomously responsible for quality control at his workstation and has the authority to stop the entire production line should a quality issue arise.
- The identification of long change-over times as a costly waste, and the redesign of equipment and fixtures in order to reduce change-over times (SMED – single minute exchange of dies).
- Change-over time reduction led to the adoption of *pull scheduling*, also known as *Just-in-Time* (JIT) production systems, facilitated at Toyota through the use of kanban cards (see **Just-in-Time Inventory**).
- Change-over time reduction also allowed for the development of *flexible manufacturing systems* (FMS) capability, and the possibility of smoothing production (see **Flexibility**).
- The use of manufacturing cells.
- The adoption of quality management practices at all levels of the factory.
- Reducing waste.

Toyota's approach to managing waste is based on a distinction between eliminating waste at the different planning stages and also on observing residual waste, called 'muda'. The job of managers is to observe this 'muda' and to redesign processes and work so that it can be eliminated. The seven 'muda' that managers should look for are:

- Transportation (the unnecessary carrying of products).
- Inventory (only keeping absolutely essential inventory).
- Motion (only performing motions which are essential and belong to the value stream).
- Waiting (as a non-value adding activity, identifying bottlenecks and removing them).
- Overproduction (not producing ahead of uncertain demand).
- Overprocessing (for example, spending too much time on a task because the tool used is inadequate).
- Defects (inspection as a non-value adding activity, prefer revising the design so that defects can be eliminated altogether).

LEAN THINKING

In 1990, Womack et al. wrote *The Machine That Changed the World*, which quickly became a bestseller. Based on the results of a multi-million dollar benchmarking study of the global automotive industry orchestrated by MIT, the book was a carefully documented account of the productivity gaps in the automotive industry between Japanese and Occidental manufacturers.

By the time the benchmarking study was done (in the late 1980s), Japanese production practices had already evolved. Particularly – in contrast with the original focus on production cells and factories – Japanese manufacturers had extended their practices to their supply chains and supply chain integration was a key element of their success. The authors of *The Machine That Changed the World* made the explicit decision that they should find a name for what they were describing. They rejected the idea of calling it the Toyota Production System, arguing that they were documenting a more general and more developed approach to management. It is then that the term 'lean' was born.

Hines et al. (2004) argued that most of the criticisms that have been formulated against lean thinking have actually been formulated against lean manufacturing, i.e. against the original formulation of the lean concept. These criticisms included a lack of contingency behind the approach, the exploitative character of the approach from a human resource point of view, and the lack of a strategic perspective. Garrahan and Stewart (1992) are well-known critics via their book about the commercially successful UK-based Nissan factory. Katayama and Bennett (1996) also provided a Japan-based multiple case study discussion of the limitations of the 1980 concept of lean production and identified an alternative form of production system, *adaptable production*, as a more suitable alternative to lean production in the economic context of Japan in the 1990s.

In 1996, Womack and Jones published *Lean Thinking*, a follow-up to *The Machine That Changed the World*. According to Hines et al. (2004) this second instalment addressed the previous limitations of lean and presented a more mature specification of the features of the lean management approach. Lean thinking can be described as taking place at both a strategic and at an operational level. At a strategic level, lean thinking requires a commitment to focusing on all managerial and design decisions around the value stream, i.e. the set of sequenced steps by which value is created for the end customer. This is captured by the five key principles of lean thinking:

1 Specify *value* from the viewpoint of the end customer.
2 Identify all steps in the *value stream*.
3 Improve and smooth the *flow* of value-adding activities in the value stream.
4 Let customers *pull* value.
5 *Pursue* perfection.

At the operational level, the strategy is implemented by adopting lean production principles (for example, the use of Just-in-Time technology) but also by adopting a battery of other complementary operation management tools. These include six-sigma and statistical process control; Total Productive Maintenance; production control techniques such as MRP and ERP systems; the theory of constraints; agility, responsiveness, and total quality management.

It is possible to conclude that the latest specification of lean thinking is now a value stream-centred collection of powerful 'best-in-class' operations management strategies and techniques. Thus, it is not surprising that lean thinking is at the time of writing this book one of the most lucrative operations management consulting lines of business. It is especially in the service sector and in the public administration sector that

lean

lean thinking is currently gaining ground and being used by organisations to streamline their service provision systems.

REFERENCES

Garrahan, G. and Stewart, P. (1992) *The Nissan Enigma – Flexibility at Work in a Local Economy.* London: Mansell

Hines, P., Holweg, M. and Rich, N. (2004) 'Learning to evolve: a review of contemporary lean thinking', *International Journal of Operations and Production Management,* 24 (10): 994–1011.

Katayama, H. and Bennett, D. (1996) 'Lean production in a changing competitive world: a Japanese perspective', *International Journal of Operations and Production Management,* 16 (2): 8–23.

Monden, Y. (1983) *The Toyota Production System.* Portland, OR: Productivity.

Ohno, T. (1988) *The Toyota Production System: Beyond Large-Scale Production. Portland,* OR: Productivity.

Womack, J. and Jones, D.T. (1996) *Lean Thinking: Banish Waste and Create Wealth for Your Corporation.* New York: Simon and Schuster.

Womack, J., Jones, D.T. and Roos, D. (1990) *The Machine That Changed the World.* New York: Rawson.

Agility

> *Production is agile if it efficiently changes operating states in response to the uncertain and changing demands placed upon it (Narasimhan et al., 2006).*

HISTORICAL ORIGINS AND DEFINITION

Agility, like other integrated management frameworks, is a system of practices surrounded by a specific cultural or philosophical orientation. Historically, the origin of agile manufacturing is a reaction to the intensification of mass production. In job or batch production systems, resources are naturally very adaptable as all orders have a degree of uniqueness to them. In order to succeed in large-scale production, the strategy has always been to seek economies of scale effects by using dedicated equipment.

The downside of dedicated equipment is that it becomes obsolete and useless as soon as the demand changes. Whereas lean manufacturing focuses on doing more with fewer resources, agility means the ability to quickly change over and convert existing resources in order to continue operating even if the demand specifications have changed significantly. In the late 1910s, Henry Ford's previously very successful Model T was losing its market share to General Motors' newly introduced line of cars. Ford responded to this competitive challenge by launching the Model A. It took two years for the Ford Motor Company to refurbish the Le Rouge industrial complex to switch from the production of the Model T to the Model A. This is one example of a total lack of agility. Very large-scale and dedicated production systems are only viable in environments where demand is stable or evolves very slowly.

Narasimhan et al. (2006) reviewed the operations management literature and showed that the concept of Just-in-Time, flexible manufacturing, lean and agile are often defined in very similar ways. Authors will often try to provide descriptions of these management frameworks that are as exhaustive as possible. This unfortunately results in potential confusion as all of these approaches end up being based on the use of the same practices. For example, it would be easy to confuse flexibility and agility, as agility evidently requires some form of 'flexibility'. The distinction between flexible manufacturing systems (FMS) and agility is that FMS are only designed to handle known and expected differences in demand, as for example low volumes of an item or two different versions of the same product. Agility, by contrast, is about responsiveness to unforeseen changes in demand and about the ability to shorten new product development, process changeover, and the ability to scale production up or down as needed.

AGILE CAPABILITIES

Aware of the potential confusion and overlap in the literature between the lean and agile production paradigms, Narasimhan et al. (2006) surveyed several hundred US manufacturers and used a classification method to discover the underlying patterns to production practices. Manufacturers were classified as belonging either to a low performer group, a lean production group, or an agile production group. Narasimhan et al. found that agile producers had 'superior abilities in terms of quality, delivery, and flexibility' which were derived from the use of 'advanced manufacturing technologies, supplier alliances, high skill employee training, and customer sensing mechanisms'.

Narasimhan et al. (2006) also used their data to revisit a long-standing debate in the literature regarding the relationship between lean production and agile production. They concluded that their data lent support to the idea that agility may require lean capabilities, but that lean capabilities do not require agile practices.

AGILITY AND THE SERVICE SECTOR

Agility has been an active research stream in manufacturing management, and research dealing with the adoption of agile thinking in service contexts is much more recent (from the new millennium onwards). When one considers labour intensive forms of services, such as hairdressing and traditional forms of retail banking (i.e. based on a personal advisor organisational structure), it is tempting to conclude that agility should be a natural strength in these systems as they have intensive customer contact modes, and many of the decisions should be naturally made through flexible adjustments.

The service sector, however, is not only composed of labour-intensive organisations. Moreover, many traditionally labour-intensive service sectors have evolved significantly through investments in technologies in order to increase efficiency. This has been the case with the retail banking sector where telephone and internet banking services have replaced the personal financial advisors. In any service sector dominated by strict, technology-based process models and where uncertainty is present, there is scope for benefiting from investing in agility. In the rest of this section, we shall look at examples in the fields of retail banking, port management, and information management.

Menor et al. (2001) used a classification technique to analyse the performance and practices of retail banks. They obtained four groups of banks labelled agile, traditional, niche, and straddlers. The agile group had higher levels of resource competencies, was based on higher levels of investment in infrastructure and technology, and exhibited a higher financial performance than the other groups.

Paixao and Marlow (2003) discussed the United Nations' description of the evolution of ports as going through 'generations'. Currently, the third generation of ports has extended the basic services of first generation ports (cargo loading and unloading) into a wide variety of logistics services and other port-related value-added activities. Paixao and Marlow argued that the environment in which ports operate today is so uncertain and unpredictable that this undermines the potential profitability of port infrastructures and services. Based on this diagnostic, they recommended agility as a strategy and proposed a stepwise process by which fourth generation ports – agile ports – can be developed.

Information management is the organisational support function dealing with the provision of information to decision makers. Modern firms have over time refined manual information systems into powerful computer-based information systems, as for example with *Enterprise Resource Planning* systems (see **Integration**). These computer systems have historically been based on centralised information architectures. For example, it was always considered bad practice to run duplicate databases in an enterprise network, as the update of a field in one database might not be carried out automatically in the other database. To avoid such issues, firms invested in data warehouse technologies: a data warehouse is a very large, unique and central repository of all the data of an organisation. Implementing or developing centralised information systems proved to be expensive as future needs were often uncertain and could result in the radical re-engineering of existing systems. The concept of agility was used to justify the need for a radically new form of information system architecture: the *Service Oriented Architecture* (SOA). The idea behind SOA is to build a map of all the applications and interfaces and relationships between applications. Instead of being a unique, central system, an organisational information system is conceptualised as a network of modules, each involved in a service supplier/customer relationship. The resulting architecture duplicates databases (but interfaces them so that automatic updates take place) and systems so that the whole system can evolve at the module rather than at the platform level. SOA is all about agility in the use and development of information systems.

REFERENCES

Menor, L.J., Roth, A.V. and Mason,C.H. (2001) 'Agility in retail banking: a numerical taxonomy of strategic service groups', *Manufacturing and Service Operations Management*, 3(4): 273–292.

Narasimhan, R., Swink, M. and Kim, S.W. (2006) 'Distentangling leanness and agility: an empirical investigation', *Journal of Operations Management*, 24: 440–457.

Paixao, A.C. and Marlow, P.B. (2003) 'Fourth generation ports – a question of agility?', *International Journal of Physical Distribution & Logistics Management*, 33(4): 355–376.

> *A supply chain is a set of inter-connected operators that play a role in the combined manufacture, distribution, and provision of a product or service to a final customer.*

SUPPLY CHAIN

The end customer typically knows little, or indeed nothing, about supply chain composition. Figure 52 shows one example of a supply chain where an end customer has a choice of shopping between two different retailers. By buying a product at retailer 1, the end customer conducts business with supply chain 1, indicated by the solid arrows. If the customer were to buy a product from retailer 2, business is won for supply chain 2, the one shown with dashed arrows. Each level within a supply chain is called a supply chain *echelon:* for example, the retailing echelon is composed of two members. Note that some members, namely the wholesaler and supplier 2, belong to both supply chains, and win business irrespective of the end customer choice.

Figure 52 is just one example of a possible supply chain network structure: there are in reality many types of network topologies, varying from a simple linear supply chain to more complex patterns. Dubois et al. (2004) argued that too often managers only concerned themselves with the 'transvection' view of supply chains. This perspective means that we only think of the sequential flow of products linked to the purchase of a finished good in a specific supply chain. Each member of the supply chain in Figure 52 has other suppliers – and potentially other customers. These are not shown only because they do not fit in with the direct 'transvection' logic. These other suppliers, though, can bring forth delays and quality issues within the supply chain.

Another common consequence of the transvection perspective is to develop a *competing supply chain* paradigm. For example, in Figure 52, the competition between retailer 1 and retailer 2 is a storefront for the competition between the two supply chains. There is empirical evidence that shows that top performing firms belong to top performing supply chains (Lowe et al., 1997). Dubois et al. (2004), however, expressed concern with this view and argued that supply chains should always been analysed in their context, rather than as isolated transvection chains. For example, although the notion of competition between supply chains is seductive, it becomes confusing when we consider the case of supplier 2 and of the wholesaler! Dubois et al. (2004) noted that most of the research on supply chain management had focused on transvection chains rather than on the patterns of interdependence between different supply chains.

SUPPLY CHAIN MANAGEMENT

Supply chain management is a set of approaches utilised to efficiently integrate suppliers, manufacturers, warehouses, and stores, so that merchandise is produced and distributed at the right quantities, to the right locations, and at the right time, in order to minimise system wide costs while satisfying service level requirements.

(Simchi-Levi et al., 2003)

Given the above definition of supply chain management, one could ask how different is supply chain management from operations management? Concerns surrounding service level, right time and right location issues are discussed many times in the context of the various concepts in this book. Many see within supply chain management a simple extension of purchasing management, i.e. the activity of managing the flow of incoming parts and components into a firm. Marketing specialists see in supply chain management an extension of distribution management, i.e. the management of the processes through which products are distributed to customers. Logisticians also see supply chain management as old wine rebottled with a new name: logistics, or logistical management, has always studied the inflows and outflows of products to and from organisations.

Dubois et al. (2004) bring a different perspective to the question of supply chain management by suggesting that managers should focus on managing *in* supply networks instead of attempting to manage the networks. This idea is illustrated in Figure 53 which shows that the techniques, tools, and concepts of operations management can be applied at three different levels. On the left-hand side, operations management is applied within an organisation: its scope is *intra-organisational*. In such a

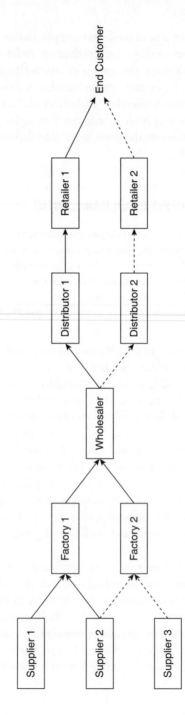

Figure 52   Example of a supply chain

configuration, a supply chain management department will exist: it is concerned with managing the relationship capital with suppliers and with distributors. Although useful, this approach has largely been abandoned today as the rise of supply chain management as a discipline is nothing else than the recognition that intra-level performance is affected by external supply chain members (Lowe et al., 1997). Therefore, managers have started to explore if the scope of supply chain management could be extended.

In the centre diagram in Figure 53, the supply chain management function has been pulled out from a central, 'pivot' firm. Note that in this centre diagram, the supply chain manager exerts a centralised control over all the supply chain members. The supply chain, in this perspective, is a *meta-organisational* system, i.e. the assemblage of different organisations who are joined by contracts and partnerships agreements. The purpose of the supply chain manager is to optimise the performance of the meta-organisation, although the definition of performance will be based on that imposed by the sponsoring firm. Why do other firms accept a centralised management control unit? This could be because the pivot firm is so powerful that it can impose terms and conditions on its suppliers and distributors. Note that in this configuration, only the supply chain manager has a global network visibility, as other members only negotiate from a buyer-seller perspective (a *dyadic* relationship).

The right-hand side illustrates what Dubois et al. (2004) saw in supply chain management. The focus should not be to manage a meta-organisational system, but to manage the firm as a part of a large inter-organisational system, in which all members have a stake. In order to improve network performance, some firms may chose to invest in inter-organisational systems, such as shared information systems, an e-business infrastructure, or joint ventures. Note, however, that there is no centralised control with the inter-organisational network view. The internet as a distributed system is a good example of an inter-organisational network. Applying operations management to this inter-organisational context is what makes supply chain management a new discipline.

SUPPLY CHAIN INTEGRATION

Supply chain integration is the prime activity of supply chain management. It is about linking systems, practices and objectives together

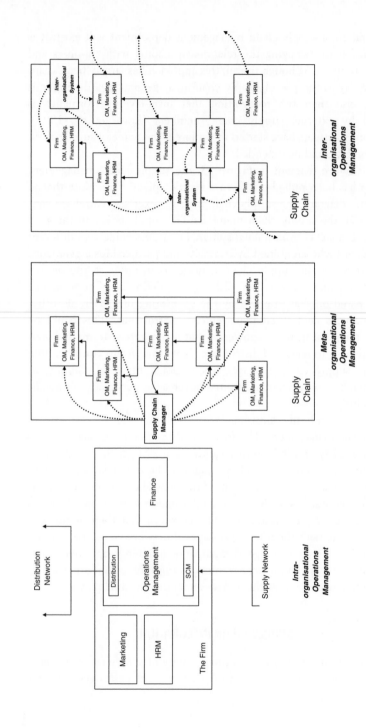

Figure 53   Contrasting different levels of application of operations management

within the supply chain networks that a company belongs to. An example of supply chain integration is a supplier accepting to offer more frequent deliveries to a customer. The customer benefits from the practice as their work in process inventory is reduced and the supplier benefits from the fact that it may offer opportunities for production smoothing and reducing its investment in finished goods inventory. One of the downsides is a potential increase in transportation costs: the two firms may decide to invest jointly in a fleet of smaller lorries, or may be able to sign a long-term contract with a trucking firm.

KEY ISSUES IN SUPPLY CHAIN MANAGEMENT

Supply chain management can be described as the management of the same resources as those managed in operations management, but at an inter-organisational level. Key issues in supply chain management are:

- *Inventory*: How inventory should be distributed along a supply chain remains one of the fundamental questions in supply chain research. Excess inventories and inventory shortages can have negative consequences on firms. Whereas it is easy to optimise inventory rules at the firm's level, extending the reflection to a supply chain makes the problem much more complex. The 'bullwhip effect' is an empirically proven phenomenon whereby information about demand variability gets distorted as it travels upstream in the supply chain. The field of *supply chain dynamics* is exclusively concerned with the management of supply chain inventory and with avoiding the bullwhip effect, as it can often result in dramatic inventory shortages and build-ups in a supply chain.
- *Plant and equipment*: A first key question is the design of supply networks. A well established specialist research area in operational research, *supply chain design* investigates the best possible network topologies. This is also a key issue in international operations management, where managers have to design *global production networks* (GPNs) whilst taking into account changing demand conditions, foreign currency volatility, etc. Finally, a second key issue is how and when firms should invest in *inter-organisational systems* in order to improve simultaneously their performance and that of the network.
- *Human capital*: Key issues includes the management of joint venture workers, the exchange of workers between supply chain members,

and the training of workers and managers in order to prepare them for working in a collaborative networked environment.

- *Organisational capital*: Supply chain design is concerned with the design of physical facilities within a supply chain. How are these facilities co-ordinated and which organisational structures should be used in conjunction with supply chains are important questions. Giannakis and Croom (2004) refer to this research stream as the school of *synthesis*, and describe it as being based on industrial organisation economics and relying on theories such as social network analysis, the theory of the firm, and Williamson's concept of transaction cost economics. An increasingly important issue, for example, is *supply chain learning*. The objective of supply chain learning is to make sure that the different firms in a supply chain are organised so that they can learn together and from one another in order to increase their performance.

- *Innovation capital*: Traditionally, innovation has been a commercially-sensitive fortress within corporations. Increasingly, innovation now takes place in collaborative networks. A lot of research has documented how a firm's innovation capabilities can be leveraged by including suppliers in innovation processes.

- *Process capital*: Inventory mistakes, quality issues, delays and customer dissatisfaction usually stem from a lack of integration between processes. Giannakis and Croom (2004) refer to this stream of research as *synchronisation*. A variety of tools have emerged to model processes from the perspective of the customer rather than from the perspective of the firm. This is especially useful in the service sector where a service failure often occurs because of a lack of integration along the service supply chain. End to end process modelling, operations cycles and customer journeys are examples of cross-boundaries methods of process analysis.

- *Relationship capital*: This is one of the most fertile areas of research in the field of supply chain management and is called the *synergy* research stream by Giannakis and Croom (2004). Traditionally, relationships between customers and suppliers were quite adversarial. Many national construction industries still have the reputation of being based on tense supply relations. Transaction cost theory stipulates that firms can control their suppliers by using three methods: by taking them over, through the use of contracts, or through collaborative partnering agreements. Supply chain management research is especially concerned with the efficiency of contracts, with the nature and effectiveness of collaborations, and with comparing these two alternatives.

DEMAND CHAIN

Supply chain managers have always concerned themselves with the management of the flow of products from suppliers to the end customers. In their investigation of disruptions to this flow, they discovered that a key issue was the management of demand information.

Consider the following example: a supermarket decides to attract customers via an aggressive advertisement programme where many 'two for the price of one' promotional offers are made. As a consequence, the supermarket chain is going to place larger orders than usual with its wholesaler, which will in turn place larger orders with the manufacturer. The manufacturer, unaware of the exceptional nature of these orders, may mistakenly read them as a sign that demand is peaking up. As a result, it may approve outstanding plans for expansion, rejected so far due to a lack of evidence of growing demand. What happens next? As customers have stocked up on the promoted goods, the manufacturer is more than likely to experience a sudden drop in demand when it is in the midst of its expansion: this may be enough to precipitate a profitability crisis for said manufacturer.

Promotional campaigns are one of the many factors that lead to the 'bullwhip' effect, the distortion of demand information as it travels upstream along a supply chain. Products travel downstream, from supplier to retailer, whereas demand information travels upstream, from retailer to supplier. A *demand chain* – the chain of firms through which demand information flows – is therefore the mirror image of the supply chain.

DEMAND CHAIN MANAGEMENT

Demand chain management is the set of managerial activities by which managers exchange information about demand for the sake of improving the supply chain performance. Demand chain management is especially concerned with eliminating supply chain problems stemming from poor information management, such as the bullwhip effect. Frohlich and Westbrook (2002) pointed out that demand chain management is a relatively modern practice as it is only with the development of modern internet technologies that a real-time interactive information exchange between echelons became possible.

In contrast to supply chain management which is concerned with supply chain integration, demand chain management targets *demand integration*. Examples of demand chain integration are:

- *Improving the demand visibility*: all echelons within a supply chain have access to real-time demand and inventory data across the supply chain.
- *Joint planning*: a promotional campaign, for example, is planned as a joint effort, so that all parties understand the real nature of demand volatility.

Frohlich and Westbrook (2002) also pointed out that internet technologies can be used both for supply integration and for demand integration. It is only when these are combined, however, that true demand chain management capabilities have been fully deployed.

Juttner et al. (2007) expanded this definition and proposed that demand chain management involved:

- Integration between demand and supply processes.
- An organisational perspective whereby a structure is designed to align the integrated processes with different customer segments.
- A relational perspective, which requires improved work relationships between the marketing and supply chain management departments, along with a redefinition of the role of marketing in the demand chain management process.

Through a case of study of Nokia Networks, Heikkila (2002) showed that demand chain management is essential in dynamic and fast changing environments where suppliers need to be able to quickly adapt their offerings to a variety of evolving customer needs.

REFERENCES

Dubois, A., Hulten, K. and Pedersen, A.C. (2004) 'Supply chains and interdependence: a theoretical analysis', *Journal of Purchasing and Supply Management*, 10: 3–9.

Frohlich, M. and Westbrook, R. (2002) 'Demand chain management in manufacturing and services: web-based integration, drivers, and performance', *Journal of Operations Management*, 20: 729–745.

Giannakis, M. and Croom, S. (2004) 'Toward the development of a supply chain management paradigm: a conceptual framework', *Journal of Supply Chain Management*, 40(2): 27–37.

Heikkila, J. (2002) 'From supply to demand chain management: efficiency and customer satisfaction', *Journal of Operations Management*, 20: 747–767.

Juttner, U., Christopher, M. and Baker S. (2007) 'Demand chain management – integrating marketing and supply chain management', *Journal of Operations Management*, 36: 377–392.

Lowe, J., Delbridge, R. and Oliver, N. (1997) 'High performance manufacturing: evidence from the automotive components industry', *Organization Studies*, 18(5): 783–798.

Simchi-Levi, D., Kaminsky, P. and Simchi-Levi, E. (2003) *Designing and Managing the Supply Chain* (2nd edition). New York: McGraw-Hill.

supply chain

index

index